Strange Fruit

Strange Fruit

Racism and Community Life
in the Chesapeake—
1850 to the Present

John R. Wennersten

Washington, DC

Copyright © 2020 by John R. Wennersten
New Academia Publishing, 2021

All rights reserved. No part of this book may be reproduced or transmitted in any form or by any means, electronic or mechanical, including photocopying, recording, or by any information storage and retrieval system.

Printed in the United States of America

Library of Congress Control Number: 2021913456
ISBN 978-1-7359378-4-7 paperback (alk. paper)

New Academia Publishing, 4401-A Connecticut Ave. NW, #236,
Washington, DC 20008
info@newacademia.com - www.newacademia.com

Every illustration or photo comes from the Prints and Photographic Division of the Library of Congress, if not otherwise noted.

To Ruth Ellen and our history-loving family

Contents

Preface ix
Acknowledgements xiii

Introduction: A Place in Time 1
Chapter One: Antebellum Somerset: Slavery and "Free Negroism" 11
Chapter Two: War and Emancipation 45
Chapter Three: The Freedmen's World 71
Chapter Four: Part Arcadia, Part Wolf 97
Chapter Five: Strange Fruit 113
Chapter Six: These Low Grounds 145
Chapter Seven: Riots, Fire Hoses and Dogs 163
Chapter Eight: The Black College Down the Road 185
Chapter Nine: *Semper Eadem* 203
Chapter Ten: Afterword 219

Index 223

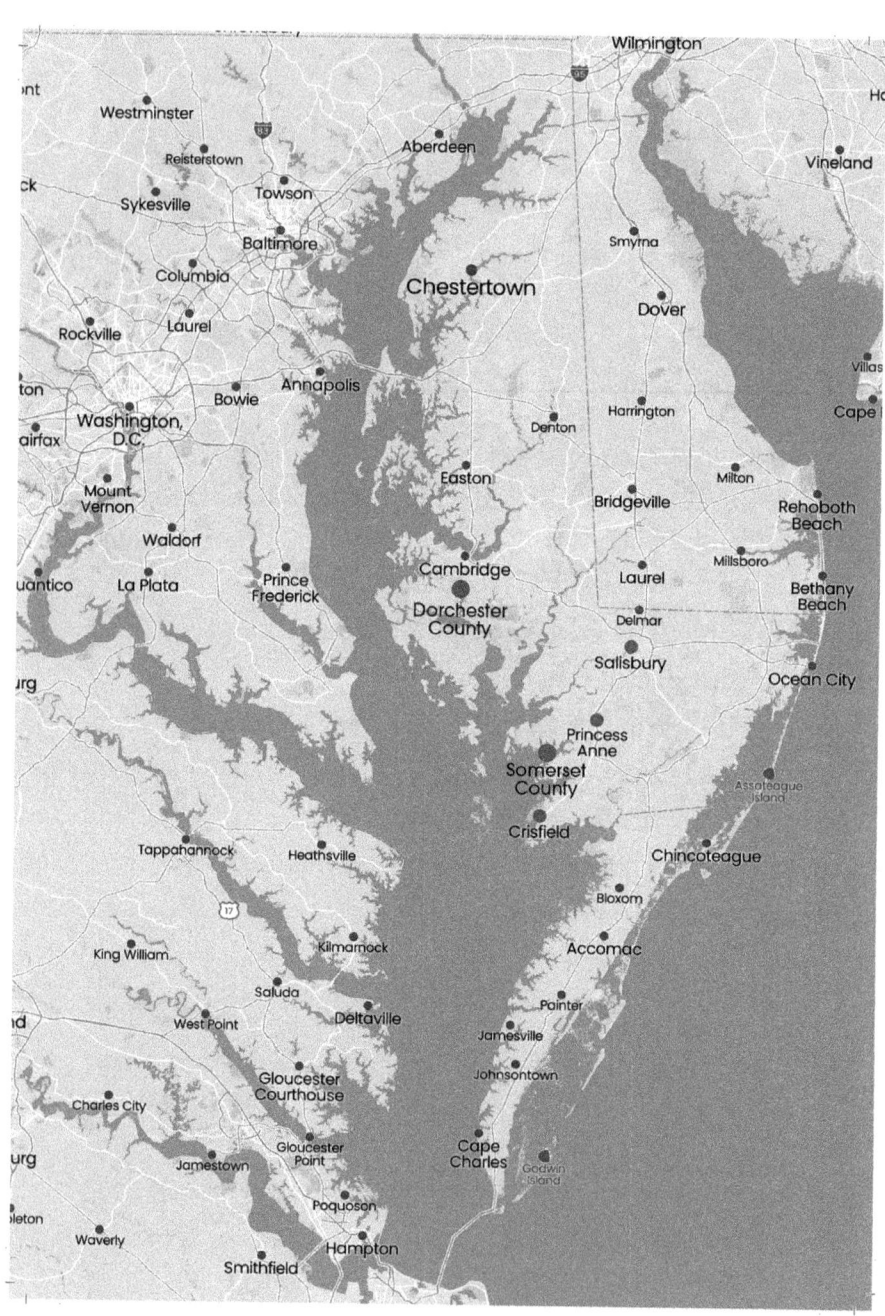

The Eastern Shore of Maryland.

Preface

I have written this book about Somerset County and the surrounding region with a specific purpose in mind – to trace the course of racism and society in a tidewater county in Maryland's Chesapeake Bay country from 1850 to the present. Tidewater Somerset provides us with a palette for understanding racism and the evolution of racial ideas often overlooked by scholars. I have sought to ascertain what specific influences and trends, as well as political and cultural developments have played out at the micro-level in Maryland over time that might test or call into question assumptions about the nature of race relations that we have on the national level. My remarks, both scholarly and personal, will help us find our way in the story of race in the Chesapeake Bay country. Race provides the scaffolding, the frame that forms the underside of our national story. And in this story we will see Black actors in the human drama of oppression and freedom living lives that are both critical and self-aware.

Tidewater Somerset is important. To ignore the rich three and one half century history of this county on Maryland's Eastern Shore is to turn a blind eye to the important forces that have shaped the history of the state and helped to condition what attitudes we currently have about race and community in our nation. In local history we can see patterns of culture and behavior that often condition and undergird our assumptions about the national past.

Somerset helps us to define how we think about the world with attitudes that range from the heroic to the demonic. It is easy to dismiss local rural culture as mere "flyover country" or what HL. Mencken once derided as "an Alsatia of morons." Somerset's rich history has also had more that its share of men and women of courage and integrity.

Today there is considerable discussion among scholars and citizens about our national purpose and the role of diversity. Unfortunately as these discussions continue, there is little investigation of local history that underpins and defines our notions of race and national culture. Local history at the community and county level can offer important building blocks to rebuild our somewhat shattered national historical consensus. If we are to have a comprehensive view of the national historical experience we have to go back to the roots; for in the end all history is local, argue David Kyvig and Myron Marty in their excellent book, **Nearby History**. The study of local history unlocks a range of possibilities to learn and profit from areas of historical investigation that too often have been the solitary realm of genealogists, antiquarians and amateur history buffs. We all need to know who we are and how we have become that person. To ignore the local past is to force us to start afresh without memory, Kyvig and Marty write. "The ability to observe and record what has taken place in the nearby world constitutes an essential aspect of human intelligence and well-being."[1]

Unfortunately, emphasis in the historical community today is on new technology, which analyzes "big data" in studies of those who were historically inarticulate, leaving no record such as diaries, speeches, and judicial proceedings. In many aspects, complain Philip Foner and a few others, history has become a subset of gender studies, queer studies and ethnic and racial analysis. This new way of looking at the past has high standing in the historical community and has led many historians to be disdainful of what they call "traditional sources."

I am very well aware that this new kind of history offers dimensions of historical perspective that we need in understanding our past. But we still have to start at the roots of things as we seek enlightenment if we are to have a coherent view of every level of the experience. Local history cuts across the personal and the public realms of experience. It gives us a chance to engage the historical consciousness of ordinary citizens. Of course, I am aware that the practice of local history may encounter narrow-minded community pressure to censure work that challenges prejudiced or mythic assumptions about local authority or cultural development.

Despite recent developments in the field of women's studies and ethnic and racial history, there is still a yawning gap between professional historians and keen amateurs using history to unlock the story of local heritage. Joseph Amato in his book, **Rethinking Home**, has written that local history offers a platform for investigating the most intimate of historical matters. Amato argues that local historians are willing and enthusiastic about engaging a wide public. Most historians are not.[2]

Many years ago I had the privilege of attending Peter Laslett's seminar at Trinity College, Cambridge, on History of Population and Social Structure. Out of his early research on population in two counties prior to the Industrial Revolution came his seminal work, *The World We Have Lost.* His book was path breaking and highly successful and helped historians in England and elsewhere focus on local demography.[3] Laslett later founded the journal, ***Local Population Studies***. In similar fashion, Oxford historian Mary Beard in her recent work ***SPQR***, delves deeply into the local life of the Roman Empire through the examination of the writings of Livy, Sallust, and Cicero.[4]

Closer to home, Ira Berlin in his classic study of the first two centuries of slavery in North America suggests that by examining the local we can see a contested social terrain in which men and women struggle to control their destinies. When we look at local lives of African Americans we see not only a story of changing social relationships but also we can, in Berlin's words, "capture the messy inchoate reality of every day life in the community of southern slaveholders" and emancipation's aftermath.[5]

The study of local history unlocks a range of possibilities to learn and profit from areas of historical investigation that too often have been the solitary realm of antiquarians, genealogists, and amateur history buffs. We all need to know who we are and how we became that person. If we seek enlightenment, clarification and understanding we can find it in the heritage of the tidewater regions where "A hundred years ain't a very long time on Maryland's Eastern Shore." We would do ourselves a disservice not to take Somerset seriously because the drama of human life as we know it in this country is found in Somerset's past.

To paraphrase Shakespeare, let us hear the brief and abstract chronicles of their time. Hopefully we shall construct a story of action and comport worthy of their visions, violence, petty schemes, and daily struggles. Let their voices come to us across dark Chesapeake waters and through the fog of memory of long ago.

Notes

1 David Kyvig and Myron Marty, ***Nearby History***, 3rd edition, Rowan and Littlefield, 2010.
2 Joseph Amato, ***Rethinking Home, A Case for Writing Local History***, University of California Press, 2002.
3 Peter Laslett, ***The World We Have Lost, England Before the Industrial Revolution***, 4th edition, Routledge, 2004.
4 Mary Beard, ***SPQR, A History of the Roman Empire***, Liveright Press, 2015.
5 Ira Berlin, ***Many Thousands Gone, The First Two Centuries of Slavery in North America***, Harvard University Press, 1998.

Acknowledgements

This book would not have been possible without the enthusiastic support of Jim Johnston and Ray Smock, scholars extraordinaire of state and national history. They are always willing to read my book proposals and manuscripts even when they are little better than discordant note collections.

At a time of the Covid pandemic, when most public libraries in my region were closed, Thad Garrett, Librarian of the Cosmos Club in Washington, D.C. rendered valuable assistance in helping me track down hard to reach books and articles. Thad's work helped me to write a better book.

During the twenty-four years that I taught history at the University of Maryland, Eastern Shore I encountered numerous people whose memories and experiences helped me to frame an angle of vision for understanding the racial dynamics and social infrastructure of the Chesapeake. Sadly, many have passed on.

The warmth and insights of Dr. William P. Hytche, Professor Dick Thomas, Omega Frazier, Mary Fair Burks, Tony Bruce, John Dennis, and L. Q. Powell, will always be remembered.

Lastly, my wife, Ruth Ellen, has sustained me through numerous book projects. She has always been my editor and realist in residence.

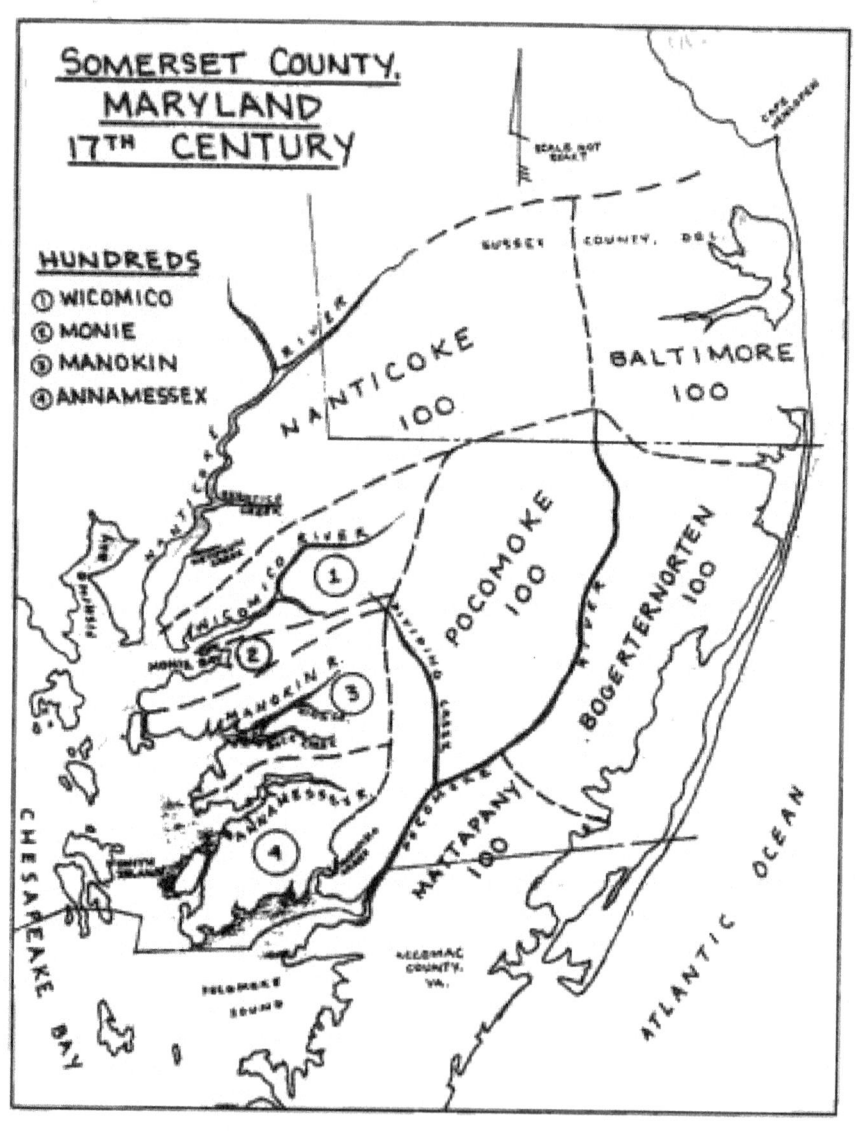

Map of the Hundreds of Somerset County, Maryland as of 1668, Somerset County, Maryland Hall of Records.

Introduction:

A Place in Time

I
Soil and Sea

Away down on Maryland's Eastern Shore there is a place called Somerset County. For over three centuries the people of this tidewater community have earned their living from farming and the wildlife of Chesapeake Bay. The county, part of the Delmarva Peninsula (Delaware, Maryland, and Virginia) has a gentle marine climate. The growing season averages two hundred days with an annual rainfall of forty-two inches; and many farmers can harvest two crops a year on their land. The sandy soil is good for vegetable crops and the low lands of the county provide good pasturage. Apple and peach orchards and rich fields of strawberries have conditioned Somerset's agricultural story. Somerset is rich in timber and ample reserves of pine, oak, and maple have historically fostered a vibrant local shipbuilding industry. Until recently, a boatyard could be found on every river and navigable stream in the region.

The Eastern Shore has often been referred to as the land that time forgot. Stretching from Cecil County in the north, the region follows Chesapeake Bay southward to form a diamond of tidewater counties shaped over the millennia by the sand deposits of the Susquehanna River. Most residents identify more with the region as a social entity than as its being part of the state of Maryland. Settled in the seventeenth century, the Eastern Shore is the oldest or "most American" of populations. Most of the people on the Eastern Shore can trace their roots to the colonial migrations from England and Ireland in the seventeenth and eighteenth centuries or to the African slave trade. The Eastern Shore of Maryland has always loomed large in the popular imagination of the Atlantic seaboard. In the 1870s big city writers like John Williamson of *Century Magazine* wrote romantic tributes to the Eastern Shore. It was for them an enchanted region of beautiful sea-kissed ports, colorful manor houses, genteel traditions, and pleasant living. Today, publications like the *National Geographic* and the *Washington Post* continue to describe the region in Edenic terms. It is a region of small towns and villages like Princess Anne, Salisbury, Cambridge, and Chestertown. Until recently, the Eastern Shore was one of the most geographically isolated regions of the United States. The building of bridges across the Bay since 1952 have connected the region somewhat to metropolitan centers. But the Eastern Shore is still a feisty, politically conservative, provincial, and self-absorbed region. Over the centuries, the Eastern Shore has retained its great natural beauty; but this beauty has often masked the darker currents of racism and violence that are also part of the region's culture.

Throughout history Somerset County's environment has been harsh. Hurricanes and floods lash the region. The county's swamps and marshlands have provided fertile breeding grounds for mosquitoes bearing yellow fever and malaria. Fierce summers sap human vitality. As the community has long been isolated from other areas of the state, Somerset remains suspicious of outsiders.

II
Origins

Somerset's origins are the fabric of Maryland history. As early as 1634, when the first Englishmen on board the *Ark* and the *Dove* arrived to settle Lord Baltimore's proprietary grant, fur traders doing business in beaver pelts with the local Manokin Indians already traveled Somerset's marshes and forests. In the seventeenth century Somerset was contested territory. Lord Baltimore and a Virginia adventurer named William Claibourne struggled for mastery of this region. Operating from a base on Kent Island up the Bay, Claibourne was eager to protect his trading relationships with the Indians and to merge Somerset into the growing Virginia colony.

In 1635 the first naval battle in American history took place in the Pocomoke Sound between the vessels *St. Helena* and *St. Margaret* owned by the Calvert family, and William Claibourne's sloop, *Cockatrice*. The battle was a victory for Maryland but was inconclusive in terms of the territorial feud. Claiborne was one of many schemers and opportunists who contested Lord Baltimore's authority in the New World. By 1660 political conditions in England permitted the Calverts to pursue their rights to Somerset and Cecil Calvert, the proprietor, encouraged local settlers to emigrate to the colony to protect his Eastern Shore border from further encroachment by the Virginia colony.

III
Settlers

Lord Baltimore was able to attract settlers to this region after Virginia passed a drastic law against Quakers that forced them to pay for an established Anglican Church. Although the Calverts were Catholic, they pursued a policy of religious toleration. And Quakers, because of their religious views and clannishness, were unpopular. According to Virginia authorities at that time, Quakers were an "unreasonable and turbulent sort of people . . . Teaching lies, miracles, false visions, prophesies, and doctrines tending to disturb the peace, disorganize society and destroy all law and government and religion." While mostly concocting politically erroneous views, Virginia was annoyed by Quaker disapproval of slavery and forced servitude and eager to have the dissenters leave.

Among the first Virginia emigrants to settle in Somerset were Virginia dissenters like Randall Revell who quickly amassed land warrants from the Calverts for 2,325 acres of land on the Annemessex River. By 1666 the population of this area had grown considerably and Cecil Calvert added a new county to his proprietorship named Somerset in honor of his sister, Lady Mary Somerset.[1]

Those who came to the Somerset wilderness in the late seventeenth century left names of the land indicative of their aspirations and experiences. Men with faith in the new land entitled their plantations "Make Peace," "Rest," "What You Please," and

"Chance." Others more realistic about life in a harsh frontier environment named their tracts accordingly "Purgatory" "Self Preservation" and "Damned Quarter." The introduction of the Presbyterian faith in the county by Reverend Francis Makemie with its doctrines of individual salvation underscored a rough-hewn democracy that would take little direction from British authorities. Also free men and women of color, attracted by reasonable land prices for farming and mindful of Virginia's changing conservative and racial political climate moved to Somerset. That the first African Americans in Somerset were free men has been ably documented in the book, **Myne Owne Ground** and the research of others.[2] In the late seventeenth century there were many free Blacks living in the county.[3]

From whence came these free Blacks? Anthony Johnson, originally named "Antonio, a Negro" and his wife Mary, were probably part of the "twenty negars" recorded by John Rolfe in Jamestown in 1619. Some like the Johnson, Driggus and Cane families had been transported as slaves probably from the African Portuguese colony of Angola. They worked themselves out of slavery and purchased their wives' freedom as well in the 1619-1624 period. By 1650 the Johnsons owned 250 acres of land in Northampton County and at least one slave. Also by that time they had two grown sons, John and Richard.

John Johnson was in the Accomac County Court in Virginia courts on a charge of bastardy by siring a child from a white woman whom he had to support. As he had attained the status of planter with an estate of several hundred acres and cattle and was recognized as an Englishman and a Christian, he was treated no differently than the White men with whom he did business. John Johnson was a "freeman," an important designation. In 1666 free Blacks Anthony and Mary Johnson migrated from Virginia and settled a tract of three hundred acres called "Tonies Vineyard" on the south side of Wicomico Creek. Like most free Blacks, the Johnsons entered Somerset from Northhampton County, Virginia. During this period free Blacks of either gender were not treated much differently than their fellow Whites. For example Mary Puckham at this time acquired a plantation and the Puckham brothers established successful carpentry businesses. Anthony Johnson and his family members handled their own legal matters and sued in court. As late as 1685 there appeared to be little proscription of the rights and privileges of free Blacks. They held land, paid taxes, had access to the courts and transacted freely with White planters. Like the contentious group of White men who settled in early Somerset, the Johnsons regularly appeared in criminal suits. John Johnson sued Randall Revell, his creditor and planter mentor and was regularly called upon to swear oaths in court, something even few White men were able to do.[4]

Manuel Rodriggus anglicized his name to Emanuel Driggus. His wife became Mary Driggus. Over time the Driggus clan established a kinship network in Somerset County that sold sweet potatoes, pork and chickens in the Somerset community. Free in status, some were former indentured servants probably brought up from the British Caribbean to work their time in Virginia's fields. The term "cowboy" so redolent of the culture of the Wild West originated on the Eastern Shore when free Blacks served as "cow boy" herders of cattle in local forests and pastures. Others came under the auspices of Spain and Portugal whose possessions in the western hemisphere encouraged emigration and settlement. Most were Black and tan in color and identified with European culture– a far cry from African slaves transported by force as the eighteenth century dawned. Miscegenation in seventeenth century Virginia was not uncommon and free Blacks mixed with both Whites and local Indians. A small number of people at this time constituted an interesting racial mosaic – Black men with Indian wives, White indentured women with slave husbands, others of undetermined racial origin like members of the Driggus family who could and did pass for White. (A persistent belief in both the tidewater and Appalachia is that some people are "Melungen," part of a historic tribe of Turkish, and European gypsies who intermarried with Indians. The term "Melungen," however, is mostly mythic. Recent DNA studies have shown that Melungens are descendants of free Blacks, slaves, Indians and poor Whites. These people were known for their tan skin and straight hair.)

During the eighteenth century, however, the status of free Blacks deteriorated markedly as local planters began to use slaves to harvest the economically lucrative cash crop of tobacco. Tobacco as a plant required constant work and attention; and several hundred White indentured servants were in the county by 1670. Randall Revell, like many of the large landowners in the county at this time, built his tobacco empire on the backs of White indentured servants. Between 1690 and 1700 a majority of these servants came from Ireland and Newgate Prison in London. Most servants had to serve at labor for five years and were treated harshly. By 1690, indentured servants constituted ten percent of the county's population.

Slavery was introduced in Somerset in the eighteenth century when the supply of White indentured servants began to diminish because of improved economic and social conditions in England. Slave ship captains touted a captive labor force inured to climate and easily controlled in a White society where the militia and the courts and growing anti-Black public prejudice kept Africans in a tight political and cultural grip. By 1750 African slaves with their strange customs and transmogrified English were part of Somerset's thriving commerce with the Caribbean.[5] Slave labor produced tobacco, barrel staves, shingles, planks and ship timbers. Scotch-Irish settlers who came to the county at this time had little access to Somerset's engrossed farmlands. Instead, they found profit in lumbering and acquired slaves as their fortunes grew. Further, slaves came to Somerset as imports from the West Indies, particularly Barbados. While it's difficult to ascertain with precision, some scholars estimate that by 1776, slaves comprised forty-five percent of Somerset's population. By the mid-eighteenth century tobacco had ceased to be the main cash crop of the county. The soil on the lower Eastern Shore, especially in Somerset was not as well suited for tobacco growth as it was for corn or wheat. Writes historian Lois Green Carr, "only a fifth of present Somerset could ever produce high yields of tobacco and that quality was generally low."[6]

Tobacco growing in this area simply did not make sense when corn and wheat could be grown more efficiently. Corn especially would make Somerset a "feeder" to slave –oriented communities that were evolving in the far South and in the Caribbean where tobacco, sugar, and rice monocultures were firmly established. And how did the transition from tobacco to grain affect slavery in Somerset? After 1750 local planters used their captive labor force for a variety of purposes in the lumber, farming and shipbuilding economies. Lumber planks and shingles and corn produced by slave labor showed that the slave system was as adaptable to economic change as free labor and was far cheaper.

Agricultural diversification in the early years of the county freed the community from a dangerous reliance on one crop and a network of trade between Somerset, southern plantations and the Caribbean sugar islands evolved to give Somerset a modicum of prosperity. Schooners and sailing rams manned by coasting captains with Black crews sailed the Atlantic coast to Jamaica and other sugar islands carrying produce, grain and lumber and returned with cargoes laden with molasses for rum distilleries. In order for this diversified market to really take shape, much labor was required. Racial slavery in a region starved for White farm labor fit the bill.[7]

III
Politics, Methodism and Slavery

In the years leading up to the American Revolution, Somerset became a religious battleground between Presbyterians and Methodists fighting for converts and taking hard positions on subjects like political independence of the American colonies and slavery. The most influential minister in the community was Francis Makemie, the founder of the Presbyterian Church in America (1658-1708). Makemie's faith was a fiery distillation of predestination and hatred of Quakers and abolitionists. Makemie was an early protester against imperial authority. To those restive under British rule Makemie's message was clear: freedom from British taxes and restrictions. Mackemie was briefly arrested by British authorities for preaching without a license, a fact that endeared him to his parishioners. Somerset Presbyterians gathered around the Maddox plantation to hear Makemie's particularly unique blend of championing freedom and independence for Whites and perpetual servitude for Blacks. Makemie was also a travelling merchant who sold housewares to local farmers along with Presbyterian doctrine. When Manokin Presbyterian Church was constructed in Princess Anne, it contained a "slave loft" where Blacks could listen to versions of an on-going sermon usually referenced to the Biblical injunctions of St. Paul and St. Peter – "slaves obey your masters." Meanwhile bewildered Anglican parsons of the British established church who assumed that they would be kept in a manner benefiting their office received a rude awakening by Somerset's angry non-conformists. The large number of transported English convicts in the county at this time also tended to add law and order to a community that also had a worrisome slave population. Further, it was a community experiencing economic difficulties because of high British duties on Maryland wheat. Late in 1775 Somerset's angry farmers led by Peter Chaille, Selby Webster, Joseph Dashiell and Zadoc Hinman would issue the Declaration of the Association of Free Men of Somerset, which would be a harbinger of the Declaration of Independence.

In Somerset, however, revolutionary talk was cheap. Few men in Somerset were willing to enlist in the continental army. Most of the Methodist preachers in the area were Tories and the revolutionary Maryland government in February 1777 dispatched General Henry Hooper and an armed force to quash a Tory insurrection in the county and restore order. To add to Somerset's problems, many slaves deserted the plantations in droves and joined the British army. Lord Dunmore promised freedom to all slaves who joined the Loyalist cause. Historian Ira Berlin writes that "between 1755 and 1790, the state's free Black population grew 300 percent to about 8,000. And in the following ten years it more than doubled."[8]   While slaves and their allies hammered away in their struggle for freedom during the Revolution, slavery and freedom seemed to evolve along a parallel course. After the Revolution, Somerset's economy would stagnate as county merchants were denied access to markets in the British Caribbean. By 1807 distressed farmers were willing to believe in miracles and flocked to the anti-slavery evangelistic crusades of a thirty-year-old waterman named Joshua Thomas, nicknamed "Parson of the Islands." Methodism with its concern for human freedom and toleration would leave its mark on the county. Over a century of tobacco cultivation had exhausted the soil. Yet during hard times in the 1840s many small Methodist farmers were forced to sell their lands and leave the county for the western part of Maryland. Quakers found their barns aflame at night and received threats of bodily harm. They, too, left the county by the time the Anglicans and Presbyterians had formed alliances with the planter class to tighten their grip on the community. A resurgence of demand in the Caribbean for flour and barrel staves bolstered the maritime and agricultural economy as ship captains like Littleton Long bought farm produce and lumber in Somerset. Blacks, after the long tobacco recession, were worth something on the market and the churches almost in chorus intoned, "Slaves Obey Your Masters." The region's early history suggests that Methodism, antislavery and a free Black community had been subdued by an economically powerful planter class dependent upon slavery and racial control for its prosperity. In the Chesapeake a two-caste system with rigid divisions between Black and White came to exemplify the region. In an age of revolution and social change, unlike the North, slavery on the Eastern Shore did not crack. Slavery in Somerset County and on the Eastern Shore would remain firmly entrenched.

The primary purpose of this book is to follow and interpret the currents of racial domination of Blacks in the region from this time onwards. As we shall see in this investigation the historical transit from slavery to freedom was neither direct nor linear. In terms of race relations on the Eastern Shore of Maryland, there were progressions and retrogressions. By looking at racism at a local and regional level we can see those forces that helped to give the American South its social and cultural identity.

Notes

1 For an excellent history of Somerset during its early formative period consult Clayton Torrance's classic work, *Old Somerset on the Eastern Shore*, Richmond, 1935. While an Episcopal minister in Princess Anne in 1930s, Torrance discovered a treasure trove of local documents pertaining to Somerset history. Prior to his ordination, Torrance was a bibliographer and editor of *The William and Mary Quarterly*.
2 T.H.Breen and Stephen Innes, *Mine Owne Ground, Race and Freedom on Virginia's Eastern Shore, 1640-1676*, Oxford University Press, 2004.
3 Ross M. Kimmel, "Free Blacks in Seventeenth Century Maryland," *Maryland Historical Magazine*, Vol. 71, No. 1 Spring, 1976. See also Mary Olive Klein, "Rediscovering Free Blacks in Somerset County, Maryland, 1663-1763," Unpublished Master's Thesis, Salisbury State University, 1993, National Park Service Ethnography Program, *Africans in the Chesapeake*. Pamphlet, n.d.

4 *Ibid.*
5 Lois Green Carr, "Diversification in the Colonial Chesapeake: Somerset County in Comparative Perspective," in Lois Green Carr ed., *Colonial Chesapeake Society*, University of North Carolina Press, 1988.
7 Ira Berlin, *Many Thousands Gone, The First Two Centuries of Slavery in North America*, Cambridge, 1998, p.281.

Chapter One

Antebellum Somerset: Slavery and "Free Negroism"

"Slavery is the Next Thing to Hell."
Harriet Tubman

National Overview

The decade of the 1850s in the United States witnessed fierce debate and armed conflict over the future of racial slavery in this country. The publication of Uncle Tom's Cabin in 1852 and John Brown's historic insurrection at Harpers Ferry, Virginia, in 1859, helped to galvanize the abolitionist movement. While most of the debates over slavery and its extension into the western territories were about constitutionality and the powers of Congress, many northern citizens, and not just abolitionists, saw the South as an undemocratic region controlled by a "slave power conspiracy." In the north a growing free Black population in urban centers was a defiant counterpoint to racial subjugation.

At the local level in the South, slavery's preservation was an intense emotional issue about the survival of a way of life that had given identity and social justification to a political economy that had lasted nearly two centuries. Meanwhile the South justified slavery in a number of ways. It was not simply a necessary evil but a positive good whose blessings gave "Negro savages" lifelong prosperity and protection from the evils that southerners observed in the northern industrial system. The north, in southern opinion, was dangerous, fast-paced and greedy. On the other hand, the South was civilized, stable, orderly and moved at "human pace." According to the Census of 1860, only around 385,000 individuals or 4.8 percent of southern Whites owned slaves. Most southerners, however, remained intensely committed to the maintenance of a racial caste system in their region. *The North underestimated the southern power of fear and hate below the Mason-Dixon line towards those who would overthrow its way of life.*

Somerset County on Maryland's Chesapeake Shore, like other jurisdictions in the region, endeavored to cling fast to its plantation economy and racial slavery. Maryland's proximity to the free states of the North encouraged slaves to flee their masters. The Nat Turner uprising of 1831 terrified Whites throughout the south. The presence of a large free Black population in Somerset and on the Eastern Shore was a constant challenge to White hegemony.

I
Planter Life

In late October 1850, the streets of Princess Anne were thronged with farmers and villagers enjoying the social and business life of county court in session. Excited children, droning auctioneers, slaves peddling candy on the courthouse steps, braying mules, and barking dogs contributed to the noise and festivity and offered a pleasant alternative to the humdrum of rural life in tidewater Maryland. Farm wagons rolled into town bearing potatoes, eggs, flour, and smoked hams for sale to local commission merchants; and in the crowded blacksmith shop on Back Alley, James Humphreys toiled at his forge as farmers waited to have their implements mended and their horses shod.

Somerset County was a stable agricultural community of 22,556 that identified strongly with the provincial society of the tidewater South. (In 1747 tobacco was 90 percent of the colony's agricultural production. By 1859 tobacco consisted of only 14 percent of the state's agricultural production.) Somerset's old tobacco economy had been gradually replaced by 1830 with cereal growing; and planters shipped their wheat and corn up the Bay to Baltimore flour mills.

Local life was marked by a self-consciousness and reserve molded by two centuries of slavery, farming and oystering on the Chesapeake. By 1850 slaves were used at harvest time and at other times relegated to work in timbering, construction or in the several boat yards of the county. Slaves were also "rented out" to small farmers and craftsmen who needed short term labor. By the rural standards of the Eastern Shore, the county had a fairly large population of 15,332 Whites, 5,089 slaves, and 4,571 free Blacks.[1] (The total population of Somerset in 1850 was roughly the same as it was in 2020).

Tradition and family determined one's place in the county and strangers found it difficult to make headway in local business. Prideful residents maintained a suspicious attitude towards reformers who sought to tamper with local institutions. Newspaper accounts of the tarring and feathering of abolitionists were read with particular approval. The local population enjoyed a leisurely pace of life and looked askance at the less polite, ethnically diverse, and expansive communities of Baltimore and western Maryland.[2]

At the Court House men gathered to gossip, talk politics and haggle with lawyers. Somerset residents were occasionally as mean as a pack of greenhead flies; and more often than not, contentious and given to legal feuds. The local chancery and general court records reveal the 1850s as an interminable series of squabbles over land titles, property rights, boundaries, and bad debts.[3] County lawyers, ranging from homespun to genteel, thrived on the litigation. Legal suits were petty, involving personal grudges more than money. At other times law suits against debtors who fled the county and husbands who had abandoned their wives filled the docket. Often the court had to stop vendettas in the community. John Warwick, a hot-tempered farmer, was jailed when the court became convinced that there would be no peaceable end to Warwick's financial and personal quarrel with the Dryden family. The court did not order his release until he had posted his home as security for a peace bond.[4]

Saturday nights in Princess Anne were full of bustle and life. On the outskirts of town free Negroes would gather and set up booths to buy and trade fruit and pastries. By firelight Blacks would play pattywack, a kind of spontaneous rhyming. Pattywack began with a refrain of "juber up, juber down, juber all around de town" and continued for hours. The Somerset Hotel on Main Street run by Captain Theodore Dashiell offered a well-stocked table and bar to planters and their families. A short distance north on Main, the Washington Hotel hosted public dances widely enjoyed by county residents. In the merriment songsters would call out a familiar reel:

"HERE WE GO TO BALTIMORE,
TWO BEHIND AND TWO BEFORE,
ROUND AND ROUND WE GO,
WHERE OATS AND PEAS AND BARLEY GROW!"[5]

A hardy and ambitious elite of slaveholding planters and lawyers tightly controlled the economic and political life of Somerset County. Local residents referred to the Crisfields, Dashiells, Johnsons, Handys, Polks, Dennises, Woolfords, Curtises, Sudlers, Longs and Joneses as "people of quality," the local phrase for describing members of the gentry. Somerset's leadership was heavily inbred – an elite of affluent cousins playing marital ring around the rosy and accustomed to having their own way. A brief glance at several Somerset families sheds light on the affairs of the gentry at this time.

The son of a wealthy planter, John Washington Dashiell was a prominent physician in Princess Anne who lived in the town's most opulent residence, Teackle Mansion. Medicine, however, was more an avocation than a profession as he often entered commercial ventures in shipping and real estate ventures with other members of the Dashiell clan. James F. Dashiell, an attorney and member of the Maryland legislature, was connected by marriage to the powerful Jones Family. His cousin, Hampden Dashiell, a wealthy dry goods merchant, used courthouse and family connections to amass sizeable holdings in real estate.[6] Related by marriage and kinship to the Dashiells, the Dennises were good breeders and shrewd politicians. Close relatives of the prominent Upshur family of Virginia, the Dennises were widely known in tidewater society as being well-mannered, wealthy and cosmopolitan in outlook. The family traced its lineage in Somerset back to the early seventeenth century and of all families it came closest to being aristocracy in the county. The Dennis sons were educated in the north at Princeton and the University of Pennsylvania. At his plantation, Beverly, George R. Dennis was an avid farmer, business promoter, politician and a well-trained physician. His brother, James, represented family and county interests in the Maryland House of Delegates.[7] Families such as the Dashiells and Dennises were not only skilled at grasping opportunities but were clever enough to create them as well.

The most flamboyant and enterprising of the local gentry was John W. Crisfield. Born in 1808 and reared in Kent County, Maryland, Crisfield opened a law office in Princess Anne in 1832 after graduating from Washington College and reading law under his brother-in-law in Chestertown. Crisfield rose quickly in Somerset society. By 1840 he was a prosperous barrister, editor and owner of the *Somerset Herald,* moneylender, courthouse sage and pillar of the local Manokin Presbyterian Church. When most local lawyers asked $2.60 a day for their services, Crisfield commanded over $26.00.[8] With his business and law partner William R. Byrd, Crisfield established a large and prosperous flourmill at Rockawalkin in the northern part of the county. A fortuitous marriage into the prominent Handy family increased his power and influence. By 1849, Crisfield had already served a term in Congress and opposed the Mexican War. When court was in session, Crisfield could usually be found at the poker table at the Washington Hotel, a favorite local haunt.

Like Crisfield, Thomas Sudler grew rich by money lending and land speculation. Active in local politics and subsequently sheriff of the county, Sudler lived comfortably on his plantation, Sudler's Conclusion. Sudler enjoyed hunting possum and maintained a revolving account with Ruhl and Craif, Baltimore liquor merchants, for entertaining his thirsty fellow hunters. He also imported sweet and dry wines from Philadelphia.[9] Of the local gentry, Theodore Dashiell was both ambitious and secretive. In addition to his prosperous hotel, Dashiell had the stagecoach franchise for transportation to all points between Princess Anne and Salisbury. His relatives, the Covingtons, also had an eye for profit. Philip Covington turned a tidy sum of $7,791.70 by hiring out his slaves to less prosperous farmers who needed temporary labor at harvest time.[10]

The Carroll family of Kingston Hall on the Annemessex River was slave-poor and proud. Thomas King Carroll had been governor of Maryland and was a likeable, dignified man. Unfortunately, his mismanagement of his plantation precipitated a financial ruin that ultimately forced him to sell Kingston Hall and leave the county. His daughter Anna Ella Carroll, a plain but high-minded woman, taught school to improve the family's financial status. Governor Carroll refused to sell his slaves and after his death Anna Carroll nearly bankrupted herself by freeing her father's slaves.[11]

During the 1850's land engrossment by the wealthy gentry proceeded rapidly. The tidewater elite each year claimed more land and evidence indicates that by the eve of the Civil War, Somerset contained in addition to slaves and impoverished free Negroes, a large class of landless Whites. Thus did Somerset at this time resemble more a feudal society than a democratic community. Planters like William T. Polk, the Clerk of the County Court who knew the precise value of every acre of land and net worth of practically every family in the county, bought large parcels of land at auctions and tax sales often at a fraction of their worth. From 1850 to 1860 the value of Polk's land holdings rose from $3,000 to $18,500. Most Whites in the county had total assets in real estate and personal property under $1,000 and could not compete against the gentry. By 1860 the best productive arable lands were already in their hands. In Brinkley's District, for example, the number of White land-owning farmers over eighteen years of age shrank from 170 in 1850 to 90 in 1860. Even allowing for a considerable margin of error in the census date, the pattern of land engrossment is nonetheless striking. The census schedules reveal similar developments in the districts of Dames Quarter, Hungry Neck and Salisbury. In the census of 1860 large numbers of White men are identified simply as "farm hands." In this period many young White men turned to the sea for their livelihood.[12] In Somerset, watermen, sailors, tradesmen and small farmers comprised the largest group. Although weak politically, the watermen of Somers Cove [it became the port of Crisfield] were a stubborn lot who upheld a strong but effective code of justice with cargo hook and pistol. Their leader, Southey Miles, dealt with the gentry as the watermen's acknowledged leader. Miles bought the oysters they harvested and sold them to seafood merchants locally and in Baltimore. Sea captains like Levin Colbert took shares of cargo profits from long voyages to the Caribbean and invested in farmland. Several local wives of watermen and blacksmiths like Susan Insley worked as midwives delivering babies of poor White women and slaves.[13]

Table 1

	Table One: Value of Somerset Real Estate Holdings		
	Year		
Name	1850	1860	Profession
George W, Bauchamp	$4,000	$16,000	Planter
John W. Crisfield	$17,000	$55,000	Lawyer
John Curtis	$5,000	$20,000	Planter
Theodore Dashiell	$3,500	$12,000	Hotel owner
George R. Dennis	$11,000	$25,000	Physician
William Johnson	$5,000	$26,000	Merchant
Edward Long	$10,000	$45,000	Lawyer
Southey Miles	$2,000	$12,000	Ship captain/Land speculator
William Polk	$3,000	$18,500	Clerk of the County Court
George Riall	$12,000	$25,000	Planter
Levin Woolford	$11,000	$15,000	Clerk of the General Court

Source: Property Schedules, Somerset County Maryland, U.S. Census of 1850 and US Census of 1860

Despite differences in social position and wealth, the gentry and plain people were nonetheless united in support of Somerset's racial system. For all their difficulties Whites found their situation much better than that experienced by a hapless mass of slaves and free Negroes in the county.[14] For residents of the county, the concept of "freedom" was defined by the slavery system; and slaveholders identified with the Deep South. Thus Somerset was molded in the context of circumstances involving racial control; and county authorities sought to have the 4,571 free Blacks in their midst as close to a condition of servitude as possible.

As early as 1822 Maryland slaveholders had begun to worry about the viability of the peculiar institution when so many free Negroes existed in their midst. Forming the Maryland Colonization Society, in 1822, Maryland planters began to resettle native-born free Blacks on the island of Fernando Po near Cape Palmas on the Southeast Coast of Africa. Later in 1831 the state legislature appropriated $10,000 to transport manumitted slaves and free Blacks as a "remedy for slavery." Planters in Somerset supported Charles Carroll, the wealthy planter from Prince George's County on the Western Shore of the state. "The colored man, "Carroll said, "must look to Africa as his only hope of preservation and happiness." Carroll owned three hundred slaves and was duly concerned about the free Negro situation. County families like the Dennises, Lankfords, Ballards and Cottmans were staunch supporters of the Maryland Colonization Society and worked to colonize emancipated Blacks in the region known as "Maryland In Africa," (now a county in the Republic of Liberia).[15] Thomas King Carroll was a leader in the management of the society. Also, local Methodists looked upon slaveholding as wickedness in the eyes of the Lord and labored to keep Somerset's conscience attuned to the subject of Black freedom.[16] Methodists always focused on how slaves were denied the simple pleasures of being human. It was hard, however, for anti-slavery dissenters to remain on the Eastern Shore. Slave society demanded order that eventually stifled mavericks.

Ultimately the Maryland legislature appropriated $260,000 for free passages for Blacks to settle at Fernando Po and five acres of land. The settlement struggled until 1853 before being incorporated into Liberia, the American Colonization Society's repatriation experiment led by the talented mixed race governor and abolitionist, John Russworm.[17] The experiment was not much of a success, however, because Blacks wanted to remain in what they considered the land of their birth and their true and appropriate home.

Ironically these former slaves and freedmen and their descendants in Maryland in Liberia became slave traders themselves and raided the interior for captives to be sold to Spanish palm oil plantations on the African Coast. This practice lasted into the 1930s.[18]

During the Civil War Somerset found itself playing for the same stakes as the Confederacy – defending a system and way of life that could easily spin out of their control. In Somerset County there was no room for "moderation" or "gradualism" in matters of racial reform. A significant number of mixed race or mulatto free Blacks bearing the same name as Whites in the county testified, however, to the fact that some type of "reform" was taking place in the barns of the county.

II
Slavery

On the morning of September 6, 1853, Thomas Sudler rode slowly along the sandy highway in his carriage towards a solemn and unwelcome duty in Princess Anne. On this day he had the distasteful task of having to sell one of his deceased cousin's slaves on the steps of the courthouse to settle the estate. There had been problems. Grace, the slave of the former Eleanor Sudler Hall, had waged a bitter struggle and escape attempt when she learned that her fate and that of her eleven-month child would be determined by the auctioneer's hammer. To prevent Grace from escaping, Sudler had confined her in the Princess Anne jail – a customary procedure when the settlement of an estate involved slaves.[19]

A few minutes before noon, Sudler arrived at the courthouse where he was met by Mr. Edward Wainwright, the town printer and auctioneer. The slave and her child were brought to the courthouse door by the sheriff and the sale commenced promptly at 12:00. "Selling off Negroes" was a nasty business that put Sudler's conscience in unresolved conflict with his family's financial obligations. While the slave auction attracted a curious crowd of onlookers, the actual bidding was desultory. Many planters in the county were already "slave poor" and had no use for another female and child. Finally Thomas Overly, a slave trader for the firm of Woolfolks, Sanders and Overly, purchased the two Blacks. It is most likely that Grace and her child were subsequently shipped overland by slave coffle to the firm's slave jail in Baltimore at Eutaw and Camden streets and then transported by schooner to New Orleans.[20] Thomas Overly and Richard Woolfolk enjoyed considerable notoriety in Princess Anne as suppliers of slaves to the labor-starved plantations of Louisiana and Mississippi. An unprecedented boom in cotton prices in the deep South in the 1850s spurred brisk trading on the New Orleans slave market as thousands of planters became possessed by the "Negro fever." Cotton was king. "Top prices paid for likely young Negroes!" slave traders advertised. In order to prepare slaves for the market it was usual to have them greased and rubbed to make them look bright and shining. Prospective buyers often stripped females naked for inspection.[21]

At his office in Princess Anne Thomas Overly posted the latest market prices on the Richmond and New Orleans exchanges:[22]

Table 2

Market Prices	Slaves	Richmond and New Orleans
Best men	18-25 Years	$1,200-$1,300
Fair men	18-25 years	$950-$1,050
Young Women	16-25	$750-$850
Boys	Four feet tall	$375-$400
Girls	Four feet tall	$350-$450

During the 1850s slavery was in decline in Somerset County. Soil erosion and falling commodity prices forced Somerset to yield its slaves to other regions of Dixie where the peculiar institution enjoyed a more vigorous existence. Somerset's slaves amounted to little more than half of the county's Black population, as Negro emancipations were a frequent occurrence. Also planters were repelled by news coming from Dorchester County of a band of raiders led by Patty Cannon and Joe Johnson that kidnapped free Negroes and spirited them off to the slave auction blocks of Florida and New Orleans. Kidnappers often stole away carpenters and other skilled Black craftsmen that were of value to the community.

Prominent Somerset families considered selling off their slaves to what they called "nigger traders" to be bad business, to be entered only for the direst of economic reasons. Their attitudes towards slavery were complicated by the fact that many of their slaves were quadroons and mulattoes related by birth to the families that owned them. Occasionally when slaves were auctioned off at an estate sale, courthouse onlookers would gasp and point when a young mulatto girl, who bore more than passing resemblance to her late master, mounted the auction block. Here was human testimony to the hidden sexual element in the slaveholder's power over bondwomen.

While much has been written about the physical pain experienced by Black men on the plantation, slave women could suffer galling abuse. Life on an isolated farm and the many responsibilities of a planter's wife could result in outbursts of temper against Black maidservants. Sometimes an angry planter's wife would attack her "Negress" with a frying pan, fireplace tongs, or any weapon within reach. Occasionally a fiery-tempered wife would order her husband to whip the unfortunate slave. And pity the mistress' wrath that could fall on a Black woman discovered to be having an illicit relationship with her husband.

Planters often resorted to a kind of moonlight and magnolias sentimentality in defending their "peculiar institution." A good example of this can be found in the writings of John Pendleton Kennedy (1795-1870), a popular Maryland novelist. In *Swallow Barn*, Pendleton wrote affectionately of educated aristocrats, gentle masters with wives brimming with affection for their slaves. In turn "the darkies" were loyal to the planter's family. Stout Black women minded the White children and old male slaves named "Jupiter" mixed drinks and cleaned master's guns. As one White narrator put it in *Swallow Barn*, "I should not hesitate to pronounce slaves a comparatively comfortable and contented race of people with much less of the care and vexation of life I have often observed in other classes of society."[23] Many planters opposed manumission for their slaves because they thought that freedom would put them in even a worse condition.

Given the proximity of the Mason-Dixon line and freedom in northern territory, slave escapes, however, bedeviled planters. To counter this, planters told their slaves that Canada was a frigid barren place – much too cold for horses, cattle, and hogs. Not many slaves believed this, however. "Anyplace but here" was always the mantra of the potential fugitive slave.

Winters on the Eastern Shore could be fierce and Somerset planters provided, for the most part, clothing made from used burlap salt bags. Slaves received one pair of shoes per year made of crude oxhide in one large "fits all" size for men and women. Forced to live in one story log or board structures, slaves rested on beds of straw while the cold winds blew across the marsh from Chesapeake Bay. Food rations consisted of a peck of corn and five pounds of meat or salt pork per slave per week. Slaves supplemented their diet by fishing, hunting rabbits and working small vegetable gardens.

The Entailed Hat as Social History

In 1883, George Alfred Townsend published *The Entailed Hat*, a novel that encompassed his experiences in Princess Anne and the Eastern Shore of Maryland when he was a young Eastern Shore-born writer living in the Snow Hill area before the Civil War. The plot centers on Meshach Milburn, a man who believed that he was condemned to wear an oddly shaped hat that had been passed down to him from the times of the 17th century English colonists. Milburn, a man of lower caste, surmounts his difficulties to become a rich Somerset merchant The novel also details the "Negro stealing" exploits of Patty Cannon (an actual historical figure) a vicious hard knuckled criminal operating out of Dorchester County.[24] During his career as a famous war correspondent, novelist, and lecturer, Townsend recapped in this novel the observations of Somerset from his youth.

What is of interest here is Townsend's social analysis of Princess Anne and its immediate environment. In this case, his fiction deftly resembles the social reality of that time. Judge Custis, the lordly proprietor of Teackle Hall, a mansion the size of three local churches, is financially ruined by bad investments in the Nassawango Iron Furnace Company in the nearby county of Worcester. The judge's daughter, Vesta Custis, knew the family would be social outcasts in Princess Anne without money. At stake was a privileged life of dress balls, picnics, hunting parties, and shot guns and muddy leather boots strewn about for Black servants to clean and place in their closets and gun racks. Their ancestors were painted by Rembrandt Peale! To save the family house and fortune, Vesta resolves to accept Milburn's marriage proposal. The Judge, however, is revolted by the idea of Vesta's marrying Meshach Milburn, his social inferior, and pleads to have her appeal to their extended aristocratic family in Delaware. But there would be no redemption, as Vesta knew her avaricious and sour relatives would take advantage of their situation, grab Teackle Hall at auction and have the Custis family as dependent boarders. Thus against the judge's will, Vesta marries a man she does not love and saves the family from disaster. As Judge Custis and his family learn in Princess Anne, "Money is becoming a thing and not merely a name and it captures every reputation, landholding – even personal beauty."[25] The Custis's in their lifestyle and prominent position had "seen everything but the humiliation of their own selves."

The scene shifts to the dilemma of Roxie and Vergie, two light-skinned mulatto house servants. It is well known among the slaves of Teackle Hall that Vergie is the daughter of Judge Custis and Vesta's half sister. But such matters are not discussed in the White side of the family. The Custis and other families of the Eastern Shore would tell you who had sired light-skinned slaves in every family but their own.

Townsend writes at length of the delicate quadroons of Princess Anne—"gals with White beauty in colored skin, graceful with willowy figures." These women were the maids and skilled hairdressers of the county. Townsend described them living in a parlous state: "She can't marry a White man, she despises Black ones."[26]

In a fit of financial panic Judge Custis's wife sells off Vergie, her mulatto maid. Vergie escapes, only to fall into the clutches of Patty Cannon and the slave raiders and dies. Roxie, the other Custis, maid meanwhile survives by taking on a White lover named Jack Wommel, the cook and woodchopper of Teackle Hall.

The casual way that Townsend portrayed interracial sexual relations suggests two conclusions: Black women, if they chose, took poor White men as lovers. And those who submitted to their master's desires did so out of either affection or saw their sexuality as a ladder out of oppression. Further, mixed race offspring often gave slaves access to White economic privilege. Interracial sex happened. For the most part, though, the idea that southern plantations were red-hot Negro brothels for the masters was more in the imagination of New England abolitionists unfamiliar with the actual workings of slavery. Planters functioned in a world where diligent White wives and Protestant ministers policed somewhat the sexual life in the quarters. (Even today readers of Kyle Onstott's novel *Mandingo* (1957) thrive on imagined plantation lust.) Marriage, however, between Whites and Blacks was such a social taboo, writes Sidney Norton in *Maryland Public Health Reports* that it took over 300 years to remove from the statutes the law banning interracial marriages in 1967.[27] Thus in *The Entailed Hat*, George Alfred Townsend casts light on the social, economic and racial complexities of Somerset County in the antebellum period. Somerset made a deep impression on him as essentially an oppressive society.[28]

(As an additional note: In the Chesapeake, there are ample records of Black men and women who were free becoming slave-owners of their spouses to protect them from being sold off down to Mississippi. Those Blacks who owned slaves were usually quadroons or octoroons.[29])

Problems of Slaveholding

Regardless of their personal convictions, Somerset Whites knew well the problems of slaveholding. Accordingly Blacks were crafty, insolent, and rebellious – not only a source of boastful paternalism but also a source of infinite exasperation. Occasionally an Eastern Shoreman would speak plainly on the frustrations of slaveholding:

> *"What is slavery worth to us. ...Fields, corn, hogs, niggers. It takes a big field to raise a little corn*
> *The hogs eat up all the corn; the niggers eat up all the hogs; and what do you have at the end of the year? Just what you had to begin with – fields and niggers. I'd rather have a string of a dozen herrings than a dozen Negroes!"*[30]

In the late antebellum period the Federal Census recorded 747 slaveholders in the county with most owning five slaves or less, about 5 percent of the total population of Somerset County. Slaves in Somerset in the 1850s were but one or two generations removed from the heritage and memory of Africa. While the international traffic in slaves was outlawed by federal statute in 1808, sea captains during the troubled times of the War of 1812 smuggled Blacks into the Chesapeake from the Guinea coast and Senegambia of Africa. Also Somerset's ocean commerce put it in contact with the Afro-Caribbean culture of Trinidad, Tobago, and Barbados with its "coasting captains" carrying lumber and foodstuffs and returning with molasses and an occasional contraband slave. Frederick Douglass, the famous Black abolitionist and fugitive slave from Talbot County, Maryland, noted in his youth the presence of many Guinea Negroes with their African accents and transmogrified English. Further, a discerning observer could note the pervasiveness of African folkways of Yoruba, Ibo, or Bantu origin.[31] On the Eastern Shore conjurers, root doctors, and others versed in the arts of "Hoodoo" provided leadership to the slave community of Somerset. Root doctors were the traditional healers and conjurers of the rural, Black South. They used herbs, roots, potions, and spells to help and sometimes to hurt recipients of their ministrations. . The practice of "working roots" was familiar to many slaves in the South during the antebellum period.[32]

Most slaves worked as farm hands harvesting wheat and corn and occasionally tending to large herds of pigs that roamed through the pine forests of the county or dug sweet potatoes in the fields for eventual shipment by boat to the Gulf Coast states. Many were "hired out" for cash when their services could provide their masters with extra income. The Handy family of Princess Anne and Brinkley's District was a large extended family of cousins with extensive slave holdings that were often rented out.

Some slaves developed craft specialties like blacksmithing that Whites valued. On weekdays after harvest time, slaves could be seen loading lumber on schooners moored at Salisbury or Whitehaven on the Wicomico River or in Somers Cove on the Chesapeake's Tangier Sound. Many slaves had small gardens and chicken coops and often swapped vegetables and eggs for coffee, tobacco and small amounts of cash. Some slaves in good physical condition earned money by prizefighting. The rough crowd of planter' sons that frequented Theodore Dashiell's Somerset Hotel wagered on bare knuckle fights involving Blacks from surrounding farms. Thus in bondage did many Blacks show an enterprising spirit that contradicted the White stereotype of the lazy slave.

Table 3: Largest Slave-owners in Somerset County in 1850		
Name	District	Number of slaves owned
George E. Austin	Quantico	28
Joseph Cottman	Trappe	45
John Crisfield	Princess Anne	30
John Curtis	Brinkley's	18
James Dashiell	Trappe	80
George Davy	Brinkley's	38
George R. Dennis	Brinkley's	28
John U. Dennis	Hungry Neck	24
John Gale	Hungry Neck	25
George Handy	Princess Anne	30
Mary Jones	Tyaskin	33
Levin Riggin	Trappe	27
George Todd	Salisbury	26
Elijah Williams	Princess Anne	28
John Woolford	Hungry Neck	26

Source: Slave Schedules, Somerset County, Maryland, **U.S. Census of 1850.**

Slaves ultimately were a kind of speculative financial capital and even those critical of the institution knew the latest prices for Negroes on the New Orleans market. Mindful of their investment in Blacks, Somerset slaveholders subscribed to the Slaveholders Insurance Company of Maryland against possible losses from runaways. Also, with a flourishing southern market for corn, sweet potatoes, and pork, the county saw its agricultural destiny linked with Dixie's.[33] Slavery was a matter of social control as it was a labor system. It also gave planters a measure of social control over free negroes who could be easily kidnapped and sold into slavery in the far south and gave the local elite a crude regulator of the community's racial and political climate.

When it came to matters of racial control, Somerset Whites had no illusions about their slaves. As a boy, Frederick Douglass saw a slave woman being whipped because she consorted with a man the master did not approve of. Most likely she had consorted with someone from poor White trash, which was dangerous to the maintenance of the social order. When they let her down from the whipping post. Douglass reported, "she could hardly stand."[34]

In many ways Whites found themselves living in a slave community that could be dangerous. Since slavery's inception in colonial times, Somerset has recorded incidents of Black arson, murder and rebelliousness. Historian Herbert Aptheker documented at least 18 slave revolts in Somerset County beginning in 1680 and continuing to an uprising and mass disobedience in 1861.³⁵ Somerset's White community often had jitters about the prospect of a "Negro rising." After the Nat Turner uprising in Virginia in 1831, slave-owners took deliberate steps to make certain that Blacks would not bring about a racial apocalypse in Somerset County. Slave curfews were rigorously enforced. In Princess Anne, church bells rang at 9:00 p.m. in winter and 10:00 p.m. in summer for Negroes to go indoors. Blacks who violated the curfew risked a whipping. Local militia units such as Company 23 of Potato Neck occasionally patrolled the highways at night and stopped Blacks with the intimidating question: "Boy, who do you belong to?" County authorities forbade the sale of alcoholic beverages to Blacks – whether free or slave.³⁶

John Brown's raid at Harper's Ferry, in October, 1859, tapped a deep vein of fear in Somerset slaveholders. Although he was captured and convicted in Virginia for conspiracy and racial insurrection, John Brown raised again the nightmarish visions of Nat Turner and the terror of Santo Domingo in the Caribbean when Whites were ruthlessly slain by mutinous Blacks. Shortly after Brown's capture, a rumor of a Black rebellion in the county spread through the community. A group of Somerset citizens alerted at church rose from prayers and broke up the benches to provide themselves with weapons. A posse later canvassed the neighborhood and found nothing. At night armed Whites searched the houses of several free Blacks for weapons. Later a slave believed to be an insurgent was killed by an enraged crowd of Whites.³⁷ Fear, racial prejudice, economics, and the weight of social custom caused the White community to identify strongly with the ideals and values of the slaveholding South.

Resistance and Flight

In everyday life Somerset slaves had their own forms of resistance to their oppression. Protesting against the monotonous diet of black-eyed peas, corn, and bacon, Blacks staged work slow-downs. They sabotaged equipment and feigned illness during the labor-taxing harvest season. Slave resistance was tolerated to a point. Whites could accept Black "laziness." Talking back to a master, however, could result in a whipping or even death. Sometimes planters who had trouble with their spirited horses gave stable slaves unpredictable whippings and kickings. "Uppity niggers" occasionally were turned over to slave breakers whose whips and chains adjusted many a Black attitude. They also instilled in beaten Blacks a sorrow of the heart that could not be relieved by tears. Sometimes Blacks drowned themselves in the Pocomoke River to resist the personal degradation of slavery. Others fled. As a border state, Maryland was close to free territory and a cause for worry among Eastern Shore slaveholders. Pennsylvania, for example, in the 1850s had "personal liberty laws" – statutes that made the recovery of fugitive slaves legally difficult and expensive. The number of slaves who escaped from Maryland during the antebellum period is not clear. According to the Census of 1850, 279 slaves escaped from Maryland between June 1849 and June 1850. Of those, 49 were captured and imprisoned in Baltimore to await their masters. In many cases free Blacks aided and abetted slave resistance. Despite their general state of deprivation and illiteracy, Eastern Shore Blacks had a sophisticated knowledge of Canada and routes of escape northward. Black fugitives armed with pistols and knives had the best chances of escape. Blacks on steamboats were closely watched with suspicion by White crewmen eager to get a bounty on capturing a fugitive. William Still in his book, **Underground Railroad**, (1872), estimates that about 800 slaves escaped from Maryland during the antebellum period.

Slaves who ran off from plantations on the Eastern Shore often suffered from geographic illiteracy. What was North? Who could they trust to guide them through the swamps and forests of the region? On the Eastern Shore, Harriet Tubman, herself an escaped Maryland slave from Dorchester County, repeatedly returned on missions to conduct Blacks across the inlets and the forests that she knew so well. Tubman was tough and resourceful. Once after a daylong wait in a swamp without food one of her fugitive Blacks stated that he was willing to take his chances back on the plantation. Tubman pointed a loaded pistol to his head and told him to "Move or die."[38] Tubman led her party of fugitives northward crossing the Niagara River from New York into Canada to a refugee center at St. Catherine's, Ontario. The St. Catherine's center, established by Tubman and William Hamilton Merritt, a wealthy White abolitionist, was 35 miles from Toronto and the terminus of the Underground Railroad. In 1856 St. Catherine's had a population of 6,000 Whites and 800 Blacks who had at some time been slaves. Most of the fugitive slaves who resided there were males aged twenty-five to thirty-six years of age.[39] Once arriving in Canada, fugitives received the following advice from their Black colleagues: "Change your name. Never tell anyone how you escaped. Never let anyone know where you came from. Never write back to your wife. You can do your kin no good. You are free, well, be satisfied then."[40] At St. Catherine's Blacks walked into another life. As the days and seasons turned in Canada, freedom seemed like a thing a fugitive slave could live with.

State officials estimated that slave-owners in Maryland lost $80,000 worth of slaves through runaways each year.[41] High rewards of $500 to $3,000 were posted for escaped slaves – bright mulatto slaves were highly valued. Slaves were often mortgaged and part of an estate. Their escape was a financial calamity for their White owners. Escaped slaves from the Eastern Shore often melted into the Black community of Philadelphia and the protection of Quaker abolitionists.

Escape from the Eastern Shore, however, was fraught with peril. Slave agents resident in Seaford, Delaware, kept a wakeful eye for fugitive Blacks. Those Negroes who escaped to Dover were often aided by sympathetic Whites and a mysterious Black woman named "Moses" (Harriet Tubman). A few Blacks escaped by boat and made a difficult crossing of the Delaware Bay from Worcester County to Cape May, New Jersey. Often runaway slaves received money and support from local free Negroes.[42] The decision to flee a plantation or farm for an unknown and ill-defined North and freedom was a momentous one. What dangers would befall the fugitive in flight? Would they be captured or even killed? Would they use their freedom wisely or foolishly? To a great extent fugitive slaves were assisted by the Vigilance Committee of the Underground Railroad. Located in Philadelphia, the Committee was comprised of abolitionists and church leaders who maintained an extensive network of anti-slavery contacts in the south and worked with Harriet Tubman. One such contact was Sam Green of Somerset County.

Sam Green was a free Negro who worked at blacksmithing and carpentry. He was a secret correspondent of Harriet Tubman. Green worked at smuggling runaway Blacks off the Eastern Shore until his arrest by county authorities in 1856. Green had a son living in Canada and local authorities had long suspected Green of being part of the Underground Railroad. In the spring of 1857 a posse went to Green's house and made search. The posse found abolitionist pamphlets and promptly indicted him for aiding runaway slaves. The Court, however, could not prove its case and the indictment was quashed. Green, however, was found to be in possession of a volume of Harriet Beecher Stowe's **Uncle Tom's Cabin** and found guilty by the court of sedition with intent to overthrow the Constitution of Maryland which guaranteed slavery. Green was sentenced to ten years in the state penitentiary until, May 14, 1867. Fortunately for Green, the Civil War and Emancipation ended his incarceration.[43]

Slave escapes should be placed in the context of a monolithic system of racial oppression in the South from the colonial period to the outbreak of the Civil War. It was an unusual planter who could boast that none of his slaves had fled or "gone off" during the course of a year. Most returned after a short period and were often flogged or branded. The time and expense for retrieving runaway slaves was considerable and slave catchers usually demanded five dollars a day plus expenses for their efforts. Planters usually limited their rewards for common field hand runaways to thirty-five dollars or less.[44]

Historians of the South estimate that only about 50,000 slaves successfully escaped their masters out of a total slave population of 3.5 million. This amounts to less than two percent. This offers perspective on the fact that it took considerable courage and planning to escape slavery. It more or less required the same kind of abilities of Jewish escapees from a Nazi World War II concentration camp.

III
"Free Negroism"

In the last years before the Civil War, Somerset citizens believed themselves to be more afflicted by the curse of "free Negroism" than by slavery. In 1860 there were 4,483 free Negroes living in the county. According to Federal Census schedules of that year, free Blacks worked as blacksmiths, carpenters, skilled tradesmen, oystermen and laborers cutting timber and working in shipyards. Many had amassed considerable property. One free Black owned a restaurant that served Whites. Free Blacks owned an aggregate wealth in the county of $23,500. On the average they owned over $200 in personal property.

From the Census Schedules of 1850 and 1860 one can observe the free Black community's upward economic climb in the county. So prosperous did some Black watermen become that Whites demanded that Blacks be legally prohibited from harvesting and selling oysters in Somerset.[45] Mrs. Virginia Underhill, a 70-year old Black "laborer" listed assets in 1860 amounting to $19,000 – a fortune by the standards of her day. George Ballard, an enterprising woodcutter, Raymond Miles, an oysterman, and George Green, a successful farmer, were part of a moderately prosperous group of free Blacks in the county. Free Negroes worked as farm hands and earned fifty cents a day. By 1861 the annual average wage for free Blacks in the county amounted to $100. Farm work was rigorous and a fifteen-hour day was not uncommon.[46] The work schedule went "from Christmas to Christmas." Also free Blacks were required to donate three days a year to the county for road maintenance. Farm work ceased at noon on Saturday. In the afternoon Blacks rested and prepared for the long walk into Princess Anne or other villages to buy food and clothing from local merchants. Blacks were good customers and White storeowners depended on their trade.

Black preachers did not fare as well, especially those like Rev. Frost Pollitt who preached spellbinding sermons on the Day of Judgment when all men would be free. Pollitt led his flock in a joyful refrain of a better life: "Yes childring we'll be free when the Lord do appear. Wid a mighty hand he free us; and old Satan neber tease us when the Lord do appear." Pollitt's sermons displeased local authorities with their political and racial overtones. In 1856 Pollitt was arrested and jailed for incendiary preaching in nearby Accomac County, Virginia, spent time in jail and was subsequently prohibited from preaching anywhere on the Eastern Shore. Judicial authorities ultimately deported Pollitt from the region with orders not to return. [47] Although free Blacks enjoyed some freedom of movement in their own community, that freedom did not go beyond county lines.

Free Negroes in the county were objects of White contempt. As one historian put it, "Reliance on Black workers gave free Negroes a measure of power which Whites found intolerable. Whites disliked the fact that free Negroes referred to themselves as "Free men of Color." Also as we have seen, many free Negroes had assets and lived better than some Whites. This only increased Whites racial antipathies. The Census of 1850 revealed that free Blacks comprised thirty-three percent of Somerset's population.

Over time the Eastern Shore transitioned from a tobacco economy that required constant Black slave labor to wheat, corn, and vegetables where Black labor was only critical at harvest time. Slave labor could be hired out after the harvest and free Blacks could sell their labor to shipyards, timbering, and other personal service activities.

Throughout the 1850s, the South enjoyed a period of almost continuous economic expansion and labor scarcity forced Somerset planters to attempt to control and dictate the use of the local free Negro labor force. Authorities increasingly made it difficult to manumit slaves and free Negroes were required to carry county permits that authenticated their status or else risk being sold into servitude. For local planters free Negroes were "an incubus on society."[48] Planters demanded that Blacks sign "iron clad labor contracts tying them effectively to the land. A free Negro peonage, so familiar in the post-Civil War South, loomed large in the county during the late antebellum period. Blacks resented labor contracts that made their condition as odious as slavery and balked at the system. John Duffy, a free Negro, sued Benjamin Lankford in court to have his labor contract voided. After a lengthy and unsuccessful suit, Duffy was fined $100 and remanded to Lankford's custody.[49] Free Negro farm workers who were "uppity" often found themselves arrested on trumped up charges.

Washington Mosley, a free Negro, was indicted for robbery in circuit court. Although he was acquitted in the ensuing litigation, he was forced to pay $91 in court costs. Indebted for such a heavy sum, Mosley became a very cooperative farm worker. Mosley, like most free Blacks knew, that Negro debtors could be sold into slavery to settle outstanding financial obligations. Idle free Blacks with no visible means of support were compelled by law to leave the county within fifteen days or risk being forcibly hired out to a local planter.

By 1850 Maryland counties with slaves and free Blacks were fearful of unfolding demographic consequences. Free Blacks in the state were increasing at a rate of 1,000 per year. Notes historian Jeffrey Brackett, "If that rate continued, the free Blacks would exceed the Whites in number in eleven counties."[50]

Table 4

Somerset Population in 1860
15,332 Whites
5,089 Slaves
4,571 Free Blacks

Maryland Population in 1860
515,918 Whites
87,189 Slaves
83,942 Free Blacks

Disturbed by the presence of large numbers of free Blacks in their midst, delegates from Caroline, Talbot, Worcester and Somerset Counties met in Cambridge in September, 1858, to adopt a common plan of action. The delegates feared free Blacks and thought them responsible for a number of barn burnings on the Eastern Shore. Many of the delegates advocated the reenslavement of free Blacks. Somerset County representatives passed a resolution at the meeting declaring that "free negroism" and slavery were incompatible and that Negroes should be made to go into slavery or leave the state.[51] The Maryland legislature tabled a free Negro expulsion measure, thinking that expulsion would anger public sentiment in counties with large anti-slavery voters. In western counties like Frederick there was little complaint about free Blacks in their midst. But this did not prevent planters addressing the Committee on Colored Population with long-winded complaints against the free Negro.[52] This pro-slavery militancy was probably in direct response to the growing reluctance of the free Black community of the Eastern Shore to acquiesce to the White-inspired contract labor program. In the January session of the Maryland state legislature, Somerset delegates supported the Jacobs Bill, a plan to reenslave all Blacks with less than $150 and who refused to be hired out on labor contracts. Although the bill was defeated in a November statewide referendum, Somerset supported the bill. Undaunted, Somerset County authorities offered Blacks over eighteen years of age the right to renounce freedom and take masters.[53] Forced to choose between a bi-racial society and an inhumane and increasingly problematic slave labor system, Somerset County chose the latter.

IV
Proslavery Politics

Somerset's proslavery politics was reflected in the county's support of Henry Clay, a much vaunted Whig Party presidential candidate whose views on the "peculiar institution" found resonance in Somerset. In state politics Somerset citizens were loyal to their United States Senator, James Alfred Pearce, a wealthy conservative lawyer from Chestertown. Until its collapse in the 1850s, the national Whig party was a slaveholder's party. During the period 1836-1848, Whigs polled 62.3 percent of the vote in presidential elections and 56.6 percent in gubernatorial contests. Whig delegates from Somerset advocated internal improvements to the region's bridges and roads and militantly defended slavery. In the legislature, Somerset representatives joined their Eastern Shore colleagues to oppose all measures that would dilute the power of the Eastern Shore in Maryland.[54]

In 1850 the Constitutional Convention assembled in Annapolis to consider the question of reapportionment. Western counties in the state and Baltimore were growing in population and demanded greater representation in the government. This issue caused great apprehension in Somerset and other tidewater counties as reapportionment on the basis of population would decrease their membership in the legislature and wrest political control of the state from the Eastern Shore. Many Eastern Shoremen feared that if they lost control of the legislature, Baltimore and the western counties with their large foreign-born populations would advocate the abolition of slavery. The staunchly anti-slavery German farmers of western Maryland particularly frightened Somerset politicians. Writing from the Maryland Constitutional Convention to his wife in Princess Anne, John Crisfield worried that Maryland was in a state of upheaval. A "wild spirit of radicalism," he complained, pervaded the convention. He feared "mischievous consequences."[55] His fears soon materialized.

The pro-slavery Somerset delegation comprised of John Dennis, James U. Dennis and William Williams found itself on the losing side of the reapportionment struggle. The new state constitution which was quickly ratified reduced Eastern Shore representation in the General Assembly from 40 to 29 seats and shifted power in the legislature to Baltimore and the western counties. In the taverns of Somerset disappointed lawyers and planters engaged in highly emotional talk about the secession of the Eastern Shore of Maryland and the formation of a new state.[56]

Other political shocks to the county came from the Whig Party itself. To the consternation of Somerset conservatives, many Whig leaders were speaking out against slavery. According to one historian, by 1855 antislavery was making itself felt in national politics and "many of the radical anti-slavery voices in Congress were embarrassingly Whig."[57] Disillusioned with political developments, Somerset voters embraced the American Party, a nativist political movement that was vociferously anti-immigrant and anti-Catholic. Somerset County embraced nativism not out of contact with foreigners but as an attempt to check what it perceived to be the evil course of American politics in the 1850s. Inasmuch as Somerset residents disliked Germans because of their outspoken hostility to slavery, it was easy to blame immigrants for the reversal of political fortunes affecting the Eastern Shore and for the mob violence in Baltimore that was so widely reported in tidewater newspapers. In the 1856 presidential election Somerset voted for the nativist American Party candidate, Millard Fillmore, by a majority of 54.6 percent.[58]

In the late antebellum the issues of slavery and "free negroism" emerged in a county whose economic and cultural identification with deep Southern states had grown stronger. Slaves were in demand in the cotton fields of Mississippi and Alabama and foodstuffs ranging from potatoes, wheat and corn linked Somerset's prosperity with a burgeoning southern market. As a border state, Maryland stood at the critical edge of northern antislavery politics. The large population of free Blacks in the state posed a threat to the continuation of Somerset's slave-holding way of life that had been in continuous existence since the seventeenth century. As the country lurched towards a hotly contested presidential election in 1860, Somerset residents contemplated their social and political future with fear mixed with anger.

1. Harriet Tubman, Conductor on the Underground Railroad in Maryland.

38   *Strange Fruit*

2. Cape Palmas, Maryland Colonization Settlement for Expatriated Slaves in Africa.

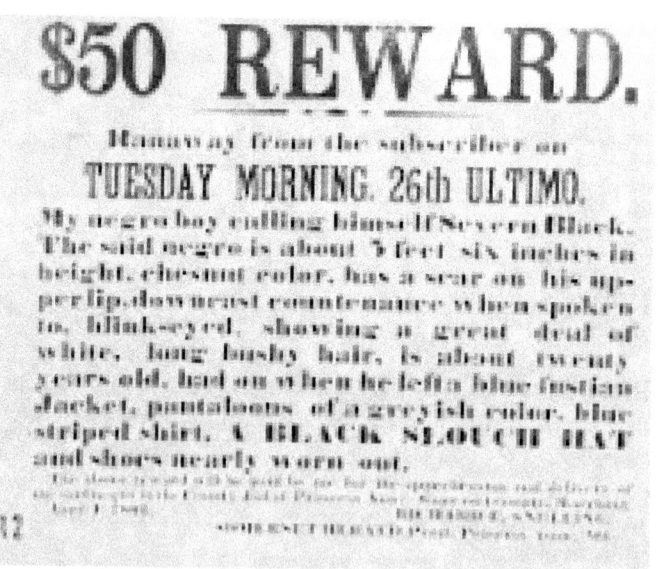

3. Fugitive Slave Ad Somerset County

4. George Robertson Dennis of Kingston Hall Plantation, physician, member of House of Delegates and a pro secession slaveholder

40   *Strange Fruit*

5. Fugitives escaping from the Eastern Shore of Maryland. Illustration from William Still, *The Underground Railroad,* Porter and Coates, 1872.

6. A sheet music cover illustration with a portrait of prominent Black abolitionist Frederick Douglass as a barefoot runaway slave.

Notes

1. Jeffrey R. Brackett, *The Negro in Maryland; A Study of the Institution of Slavery,* (Baltimore: 1889), 265.
2. *History and Statistics of the State of Maryland,* (Washington, D.C. 1852); *Worcester County Shield,* January 29, 1850
3. *Chancery Records, 1851,* Somerset County, Princess Anne, Md. Et. passim.
4. *Certificate of Indenture,* August 6, 1856, Thomas Sudler MS, Maryland Historical Society.
5. James Murray, *History of Pocomoke City,* (Baltimore: 1883), 153-155.
6. *United States Census of 1850,* (Washington: 1852) Somerset County, Maryland; Benjamin Dashiell, *Dashiell Famiy Records,* (Baltimore: 19290, 409-413.
7. *U.S. Census of 1860,* John Upshur Dennis, *Genealogical of the Paternal Line of the Dennis Family,* (Baltimore:1890). 9-12; Clarence Eugene Collins, *Brief History of Somerset County Physicians, 1751-1959,* (Crisfield, Md) 4.
8. *Biological Encyclopedia of Representative Men of Maryland and the District of Columbia,* (Baltimore: 1879), 297-298.; Somerset County Deed Book WP2, May 26,1847, 122 LW4, March 19,1856, 382; William R. Byrd, Will, August 6, 1855, Somerset Records.
9. Thomas Sudler MS, Maryland Historical Society.
10. Administrative Accounts, Somerset records, October 29, 1856.
11. Hulbert Footner, *Rivers of the Eastern Shore,* (New York: 1944),102.
12. Property Schedules, *Census of 1850 and Census of 1860,* Somerset County, Md.
13. Administrative Accounts, Somerset Records, 1853.
14. Jeffrey E. Brackett, *The Negro In Maryland,* 142
15. Manumission Lists, Somereset County, Maryland, Maryland Colonization Society MS, Maryland Historical Society.
16. Charles B. Clark, ed. *History of the Eastern Shore of Maryland and Virginia,* 2 vols. (New York: 1950 Vol 1, 8
17. John H. Latrobe, *Maryland in Liberia, Cape Palmas, Africa 1833-1853,* (Baltimore: Maryland Historical Society, 1885).
18. I.K. Sundiata, "Prelude to a Scandal: Liberia, and Fernando Po, 1880-1930," *Journal of African History,* XV,1974, 97-112.
19. General Advertisement for September 6, 1853, Thomas Sudler MS, Maryland Historical Society; administrative accounts, Somerset records, 1853
20. Frederick Bancroft, *Slave Trading in the Old South,* (New York: 1931),120-121
21. William Still, *The Underground Railroad,* , reprint, Boston, 1960, 76.

22 Lewis C. Gray, *History of Agriculture in the Southern States to 1860,* (Gloucester, Massachusetts, 1958),665.
23 John Pendleton Kennedy, *Swallow Barn,* 2 vols. Vol, 2 , 57,225,227.
24 Patty Cannon was a serial murderer. See Michael Morgan, *Delmarva 's Patty Cannon, Devil on the Nanticoke,* Charleston: History Press 2015.
25 George Alfred Townsend, *The Entailed Hat,* 122.
26 Ibid. 215
27 Sidney M. Norton, "Interracial Marriage in Maryland, A Statistical Report," *Public Health Reports,* vol 85,August, 1970, pp739-747.
28 In its time *The Entailed Hat* was an extremely popular novel, a precursor of that bosom-heaving novel of the 20th century, *Gone With the Wind.* As a reporter for northern newspapers like the *New York Herald,* Townsend covered McMillan's Army of the Potomac during the Civil War as well as the capture of John Wilkes Booth and the Lincoln assassins In the 1880s and 1890s Townsend was one of the most successful journalists in America, often earning $50,000 a year. He built a lavish estate near Frederick, Maryland and a memorial to Civil War newspaper reporters called Gathland. It is now a state park.
29 Calvin Dill Wilson, "Black Masters: A Sidelight on Slavery," *North American Review* vol. 181, 1905, 685-698.
30 Robert W. Todd, *Methodism of the Peninsula,* (Philadelphia: 1885), 175.
31 Michael Morgan, *Patty Cannon, The Devil of the Nanticoke,* Charleston, 2015
32 Frederick Douglass, *My Bondage and My Freedom,* reprint, (New York: 1968), 76; Newbell Miles Pickett, *Folk Beliefs of the Southern Negro,* reprint (Montclair, New Jersey: 1968), 5; "Root Doctors" Encyclopedia.com
33 Clark, *Eastern Shore of Maryland and Virginia,* Vol. 1, 520; Bancroft, *Slave-trading in the Old South,* 120-121
34 Frederick Douglass, *Narrative of the Life of Frederick Douglass,* reprint, Boston, 1960, p.38.
35 Herbert Aptheker, 374. *American Negro Slave Revolts,* 374
36 Jeffrey Brackett, *The Negro in Maryland,* (Baltimore: 1889), 106, 213
37 *Somerset County Union,* November 4, 1859.
38 Earl Conrad, *Harriet Tubman,* Washington, D.C. 1943, 63.
39 Benjamin Drew, *The Refugee or Narratives of Fugitive Slaves in Canada,* Boston, 1856, 17.
40 William Still, *The Underground Railroad,* reprint, Boston, 1960, p.38(Chicago,1970),
41 Wilber H. Siebert, *The Underground Railroad, From Slavery to Freedom,* (New York: 1968,) 189
42 Still *Underground Railroad,* 552-553.
43 Still, *Underground Railroad,* 246

44 Loren Schweinger, "Counting the Costs: Southern Planters and the Problem of Runaway Slaves, 1790-1860, *Journal of Business History Conference* 28, winter 1999, 267-76.
45 Property Schedules, Somerset County, *U.S. Census of 1860*.
46 Clark, *Eastern Shore of Maryland and Virginia*, I, 516.
47 Todd, *Methodism of the Peninsula*, 189-193
48 Brackett, *The Negro In Maryland*, 240
49 Circuit Court of Somerset County, *Lankford v Duffy*, May 29, 1860; Washington Mosley Case, Circuit Court Papers, Thomas Sudler MS, Maryland Historical Society.
50 Brackett, *The Negro In Maryland*, 251.
51 *Baltimore Sun*, January 20,1860
52 Brackett, *The Negro In Maryland*, 259
53 *Baltimore Sun*, June 20, 1860
54 William J. Evitts, *A Matter of Allegiances*, (Baltimore: 1974), 51.
55 John Crisfield to Mary Crisfield, January 13,1851, Crisfield MS, Maryland Historical Society.
56 W.Wayne Smith, "Politics and Democracy in Maryland, 1800-1854," in Richard Walsh and William Lloyd Fox ed., *Maryand, A History, 1632-1974*, (Baltimore: 1974), 282-283.
57 Evitts, *A Matter of Allegiances*, 51.
58 *Ibid.* 106

Chapter Two

War and Emancipation

"In giving freedom to the slave, we assure freedom to the free."
Abraham Lincoln

National Overview

The election of Abraham Lincoln to the Presidency in 1860 traumatized the South. Dubbed a "Black Republican," Southerners saw Lincoln as an agency for the extinction of their way of life. After the election southern states seceded from the Union and formed their own Confederate government in Richmond, Virginia. Despite intense pressure from many of its citizens to secede and join the Confederacy, Maryland remained tenuously in the Union. Its Eastern Shore region and the port of Baltimore were occupied by federal troops. The Eastern Shore remained a hotbed of pro-rebel sympathizers while its leaders sought to make a deal with the federal government that would protect the institution of slavery and prevent the hemoraging of fugitive Blacks. "Fugitive Negroes" were a problematic presence in the Unionist states of Maryland, Delaware, Kentucky and Missouri. Following Lincoln's Emancipation Proclamation, slavery began to crumble in these border states during the Civil War; and the enlistment and use of Black soldiers from these states helped to sound the death knell of slavery.

I
John Crisfield's Dilemma

In the spring of 1860, John W. Crisfield, the peripatetic lawyer and businessman from Princess Anne, spent weeks in Annapolis lobbying vigorously for state funds to complete the Eastern Shore Railroad in Somerset County. Crisfield and his partners had taken over the bankrupt railroad and were trying to obtain a $112,000 loan from the state to begin construction. Crisfield had traveled extensively the previous year in New York and New England and had seen northern enterprise at first hand. The future, Crisfield believed, would be determined by industry and railroads were the key to Somerset's economic development. Rented slaves and free Blacks were a convenient cheap labor force for the railroad's construction.

The national debate on the future of slavery, however, complicated Crisfield's business plans. Anti-slavery delegates in the Maryland legislature were not inclined to support a railroad construction plan of a lawyer/planter who owned and trafficked in Negroes.[1]

Newspapers in the state were filled with ominous accounts of the bitter national debate over the future of slavery and Crisfield followed events with growing apprehension. In the South nationalist firebrands called for disunion and the creation of a new nation based on slavery. Meanwhile northern abolitionists aroused sectional passions by denouncing "the peculiar institution" and disobeying laws that sanctioned it.

Crisfield knew all about southern firebrands. He had one stirring up secessionist trouble back in his own Somerset County. In his mind's eye he could see Major Alexander Hamilton Handy holding forth at the Washington Hotel with a whiskey in hand and dressed in expensive riding clothes, and boots freshly cleaned and polished by the Hotel bootblack. Major Handy was related to most of the Somerset gentry. The extended Handy family owned over thirty slaves in the county ranging from children to young Black boys being ready for sale. The family patriarch, Littleton Dennis Handy and his wife Sophia owned nearly two dozen slaves. But the family grandee was cousin James Upshur Dennis whose many slaves at Beverly Plantation were treated well with six pounds of meat per week and ample supplies of corn. Dennis was active in the Maryland Colonization society.

Handy spent his early years in Somerset at a plantation called "Salisbury" in Westover on the Manokin River. His was a family of lawyers and his brother was Clerk of the Somerset County Court. Alexander Handy read law at Washington Academy in Princess Anne and after achieving the bar took his young wife, Susan Wilson, to the Mississippi cotton frontier of the Yazoo Delta in Madison County, a classic case of second sons pursuing life elsewhere. Carving out a career for himself as a lawyer, jurist and businessman, Handy became rich in dealing with Boston cotton merchants and trading in slaves, cattle and horses with slave dealers like Nathan Bedford Forrest.

In those days cotton planters in Madison County eagerly imported slaves from Maryland and the upper South. The Mississippi Handy owned over a dozen slaves. In his Madison, Mississippi county on the eve of the Civil War 18,118 Black slaves outnumbered 5,260 Whites. Little wonder that Madison County worried constantly about a possible slave insurrection and wanted strong laws to control their "servants."[2]

Alexander Handy ultimately was appointed Justice to the High Court of Appeals and Errors of Mississippi. In 1860 he was appointed by the Mississippi legislature to be Special Commissioner to Maryland as an emissary of the secessionists who wanted their own separate nation. During much of 1860-1861, Handy proclaimed that secession was the wave of the future. Handy painted a glowing picture of an independent nation that would eliminate tariff restrictions and allow people on the Eastern Shore to purchase European goods at cheaper rates than they paid for northern manufactures. Also, Handy claimed that there would be a ready market for Maryland agricultural produce in the South and that Baltimore would become a major commercial entrepot for a new and vigorous nation. In December, 1860, Handy made several pro-slavery addresses in Somerset County that were well received. The North, Handy argued, was "ready to destroy our own property. Are you ready for this?" As Handy was to argue later, the question of slavery had to be settled "now or never. . . . We can't do without slavery and we will not do without it."[3]

In his travels throughout the state Major Handy drew throngs of proslavery men as well as a share of detractors. In his major speech to a large and cheering crowd in Baltimore defending the right of the southern states to secede from the Union, Handy said, "we are here not to sow discord but to arouse a feeling for the preservation of liberties which our fathers fought for."[4] Handy had two key allies for secession in Somerset: Edward Long and James Upshur Dennis. Both men served in the Maryland legislature and were considerably influential on the Eastern Shore.

Secessionists in the community, however, faced the determined opposition of John Crisfield. Crisfield believed that if the South were allowed to secede the romance of southern rights would pale before the cold economic and military realities of an expansive North. In public comments Crisfield stressed the fact that the North was eager for Maryland timber and foodstuffs and the U.S. Navy would easily establish naval supremacy on Chesapeake Bay. Throughout the election of 1860 Crisfield campaigned for the moderate Constitutional Union Party of presidential candidate John Bell of Tennessee. Abraham Lincoln who was viewed as a "Black Republican abolitionist" and anathema on the Eastern Shore received only two votes in Somerset during the national election.

Shortly thereafter southern states began to secede and establish their own government, the Confederate States of America. When Virginia issued an invitation to all states in the Union to send commissioners to a Peace Conference to secure a compromise with the secessionists on February 1, 1861, Maryland Governor Thomas H. Hicks chose "strong Union men" to represent Maryland. Among those commissioners chosen by the governor, Crisfield was the most outspoken. At the conference at the Willard Hotel in Washington, D.C., Crisfield denounced secession and attempted to find a satisfactory platform for saving the Union. Secession was not warranted by the Constitution and while Crisfield criticized Lincoln and the Republicans for their lack of prudence, he nonetheless supported the Federal government.[5] After the peace meeting failed, the Unionist commissioner sadly returned to the Eastern Shore.

And the war came. Early rebel victories caused political panic in Washington and the government began to arrest those people with pronounced Confederate sympathies. Among those imprisoned at Ft. McHenry in Baltimore were the two Maryland legislators from Somerset.

Though Maryland was rife with secessionist oratory, Unionists in Somerset County found encouragement in the election of John Crisfield to the United States Congress for the First District on a platform of loyalty, peace and "fraternal accord." In a communication with newly elected Maryland Governor Augustus Bradford, Crisfield wrote, "I would treat with severity all who hereafter shall attempt to disturb or corrupt the loyalty of our people."[6] Crisfield, however, failed to consider the danger of his situation. He was representing a region with strong Unionist sympathies while at the same time full of secessionists and rebel sympathizers who arrogantly flew the Confederate flag. All of his constituents, however, were united on one thing, the perpetuation of slavery and the subordination of the free Negro.

During the Civil War, the federal government began drafting men for military service. The federal troop quota for Somerset was 660. As only 157 men had volunteered for the Union Army by the spring of 1862, the remainder had to be conscripted. Believing that they had no quarrel with either the North or the South, the men of Somerset bitterly resented the draft. Further, if Somerset's men went off to war, who would keep watch on the county's increasingly restive Black population? At first many men avoided the draft by purchasing substitutes, men who would for a fee serve in their place in the military. Thirty-six county residents contributed $105 each for a safety fund to hire a substitute in the event that one of their number was called to serve.[7] In the beginning it was relatively easy to hire a substitute in the county and many Irish immigrants were imported to Somerset for this purpose. But following the horrible carnage of the Battle of Antietam, the price for hiring a substitute for the Union Army soared to $500. Those who were not financially able to purchase a substitute often fled the county to avoid the draft. Two officials in Somerset resigned as soon as they were appointed as conscription enrolling officers. One of the reluctant officers explained that his acceptance of the appointment would endanger his life and property. J.B. Melvins, a conscription officer in the Dublin District, had his wheat and oats put to the torch by Levin Roland, Albert Parsons, and Francis Milburn, well-known draft resisters. One undaunted draft resister broke into the office of the conscription agent, stole the draft books, and buried them briefly in the yard of the Episcopal parsonage.[8] Given the local resistance to the draft, the Union regiment at Camp Bradford was not disposed to treat the populace charitably. Local leaders who expressed hostility to Union officers had their horses and cattle confiscated for use in the war effort by a squadron of First Connecticut Cavalry.[9]

Throughout October and November, 1862, five hundred substitutes from various counties registered for military service at Camp Bradford, a Union military installation south of Princess Anne. It was a motley crew of immigrants and natives of mixed ethnic backgrounds. A large percentage of these men were characterized by local authorities as men of vicious habits who planned to desert with their substitute's bounty at the first opportunity.[10]

Washington, fearful of pro-Confederate movements on the Eastern Shore, dispatched several union army regiments to the area under the command of General John A. Dix to disarm Confederate sympathizers and to prevent locals from enlisting in the Confederate Army. Secessionists in Somerset were disarmed and the plans to form a local Confederate militia company were foiled. To prevent smuggling of military contraband to the rebels, General Dix had a small fleet of government steamboats and tugs for use in patrolling the rivers, inlets and bays of the Eastern Shore.

Arresting Eastern Shore secessionists or armies clashing, however, would not determine the fate of Somerset County. It would be determined by struggles taking place in the halls of the United States Congress.

Throughout the spring and summer of 1862 Congressman John Crisfield had been dismayed by the recalcitrance of Confederate sympathizers in his home county and by the general inability of the Lincoln administration to bring the war to a speedy and victorious conclusion. On the floor of Congress abolitionists like Owen Lovejoy minced few words when it came to linking Maryland's "slaveocracy" with the rebellious south. A bill introduced in Congress on December 16, 1861, to emancipate slaves in the District of Columbia brought the slavery question sharply to Crisfield's attention. Passing the House and Senate in April, 1862, the bill compensated loyal slaveholders up to $300 per emancipated slave and appropriated funds for the voluntary colonization of emancipated Negroes in either Haiti or Liberia. This emancipation measure resulted in the massive slave flight into Washington out of Prince George's and Montgomery counties and a political crisis for Maryland's congressional delegation.[11]

II
The Specter of Racial Emancipation

The specter of racial emancipation deeply disturbed many Maryland leaders. In wealth alone, emancipation in Maryland would result in a loss of property amounting to over a half a billion dollars and would raise the question of Black equality in southern Maryland and the Eastern Shore. Most Maryland politicians feared that the District emancipation bill would be the first step of a general emancipation of slavery. Attempting to strike a psychological blow at the Confederacy, President Lincoln asked all the loyal slave states to abolish the institution with the help of federal compensation. The offer went forth as a war measure, which would save money and lives by shortening the conflict.[12]

In March of 1862, President Lincoln sent for Congressman Crisfield to sound out the Maryland delegation on the idea of emancipation. During his chat with Crisfield, Lincoln spoke about the terrible war affecting the nation and how inevitably slaves came to the army camps. The radical group in Congress, Lincoln said, protected Negro fugitives while slaveholders complained that their rights were denied. Lincoln's comments prompted Crisfield to ask the president whether it would be an act of cruelty to emancipate the slaves. The choice Crisfield argued was "between slavery on the one hand, and the degradation, poverty, suffering, and ultimate extinction on the other."[13]

Lincoln respected Crisfield, though he disagreed with him on emancipation. A man of unquestioned courage and patriotism, Crisfield was an articulate spokesman for the border slave states in the union that Lincoln was loathe to alienate. Shortly after Lincoln signed the bill for compensated emancipation in the District of Columbia, he made a peace overture to the Maryland delegation that would allow the Maryland delegation to have a major voice on the issue of emancipation in their state. Crisfield and his allies rejected this overture. Finally in July, 1862, after the passage of the Second Confiscation Act, which forbade the army from chasing runaway slaves and sanctioned the enlistment of Negro soldiers, Lincoln met again with Crisfield. Lincoln assured Crisfield that he would guarantee Maryland slave-owners $300 for each emancipated slave and colonize the freed Negroes at government expense in Latin America. "You had better come to an agreement," Lincoln warned Crisfield. "Niggers will never be higher."[14] Thus by placing himself squarely against emancipation, Crisfield lost an opportunity to direct the process of Black liberation in a manner that would least disrupt the social, political and economic life of the state. Conditioned to maintaining a racial caste system that had been in continuous existence for over two centuries, Crisfield and other Marylanders stood immobile as the winds of social change swirled about them.

Shortly after the battle of Antietam, Lincoln issued the preliminary Emancipation Proclamation. Crisfield, while visiting friends in Philadelphia, was surprised by the measure. He told colleagues that he felt cheated and betrayed by Lincoln. Such an act could only encourage outraged Whites to engage in "indiscriminate butchery" of emancipated slaves. In Somerset County, slaveowners soundly denounced the Emancipation as a "paper manifesto."[15] Although the Emancipation Proclamation freed slaves only in those states in rebellion against the federal government, slavery was doomed in Maryland. Throughout 1862 and 1863, the exodus of fugitive slaves from Maryland plantations continued with increasing tempo.

III
The Great Unraveling

By the summer of 1863, the Union army was pulling Blacks off Maryland farms and plantations and putting them into uniform; and the old plantation society of the Eastern Shore began to unravel. Following the passage in Washington of the Second Confiscation Act which allowed Negro enlistments in the Union army, the recruitment of Negro troops began in earnest. Lincoln's decision to allow free Negroes to enlist in the Union Army was prompted by the all-consuming manpower needs of the army during that critical summer. With military casualties reaching record proportions and given widespread resistance to the draft in the North, Lincoln viewed the Negro as the best available source of men for the Union military machine.

The plan to use Negro troops, however, was vigorously opposed by the Maryland legislature. Leading the protest were Somerset delegates William T. Lawson and Edward Long who had earlier objected to the War Department's use of Delaware Negroes in the war effort.[16] A storm of indignation raged throughout Somerset County and the region in 1863 and 1864 following the arrival of the infamous Colonel William Birney, the son of the great abolitionist and presidential candidate James G. Birney, on the Eastern Shore.

In July, 1863, Colonel William Birney was attached to the Maryland Department of the Union Army and given the task of organizing a Negro regiment in the state. Sharing his father's hatred of slavery, Birney made little distinction as to whether free Blacks or fugitive slaves joined his regiment. Birney saw his position as a military commander as an excellent means of striking a blow at slavery and the tidewater elite that controlled the legislature.[17] Colonel Birney's men conducted enlistment raids on the Eastern Shore to get slaves to desert the plantations. A steamer with an officer and armed guards aboard would sail into one of the many rivers that flowed into Chesapeake Bay and Blacks would slip away into the night. The steamer would weigh anchor and head towards a camp in a different part of the state. During that summer over two hundred Negroes from Somerset and Worcester counties fled to the Snow Hill dock on the Pocomoke River on October 31, 1863, to board a boat they called "Jesus" (*The USS John Tracey*) that would take them to paradise. On board the steamer were a Negro brass band, Colonel Birney and some Negro soldiers. The Black soldiers paraded the streets of Snow Hill with fixed bayonets while Blacks flocked to the boat.[18] Somerset provided 395 Black troops as the war broke all rules and standards. As President Lincoln famously said, "You can't mend broken eggs."[19]

As Blacks increasingly deserted the Eastern Shore, farmers blamed Lincoln for Birney's actions and claimed that Negro enlistments in the army induced free Black desertions. They believed that if the free Blacks were taken out of the state, they would be forced to hire slave labor from planters at ruinous rates. Furious at the thought of being dependent on slave owners, many Somerset residents pressured the state legislature to enlist slaves rather than free Blacks. Thus one of Colonel Birney's recruitment efforts was to divide Eastern Shore Whites on the issue of Negro enlistments. Meanwhile, in Somerset, many of the voters who otherwise would have stubbornly defended the slave owners were mollified by the fact that slave enlistments relieved the county of further conscription of Whites into the Union army. Anti-planter forces in the county lead by William Parsons, kept the pro-slavery forces off balance by referring to Negro enlistments as "poor men's substitutes."[20] Not only could the county use the Negro to meet the draft quota, but they could also be rid of a racial problem, they argued. Appeals to racism and self-interest in Somerset County gave anti-slavery spokesmen respectful audiences that before the war would have lynched those who tried to tamper with slavery.[21]

Deferring to his pro-slavery supporters, John Crisfield vainly attempted to prevent Negro enlistments in the Union army. In a major address to his constituents in the First Congressional District, Crisfield argued that a Negro army would weaken the nation and hinder the return to tranquility at war's end. Also, as he had done in the past, Crisfield raised the specter of a racial insurrection that would be the inevitable result of arming the Negro. Capitalizing on local racism, Crisfield urged the involuntary deportation of all Blacks from the Eastern Shore so that the counties could remain exclusively White preserves.[22]

Despite Crisfield's best efforts Negro enlistments continued. In late October, 1863, 140 slaves left Princess Anne to enlist in the Union Army and boarded the armed steamer *Meigs* on the Pocomoke River. Of these slaves, six belonged to John Crisfield.[23] Attempts by owners to recover fugitive slaves had become increasingly futile by this time as federal officials and Union Army commanders were reluctant to deal with a problem whose magnitude and complexity they were incapable of handling. The slave auction, once a flourishing activity on the steps of the courthouse in Princess Anne, was halted for fear that slaves who were sold would merely join the army. While a few die-hard slave-owners shipped their slaves to Baltimore to be housed in a special slave jail to prevent their escape to freedom, most owners stoically accepted the changing social and racial scene in the county.[24]

By January, 1864, a "colored squadron of soldiers" was permanently encamped in Somerset County and Black recruiting officers were at work in the towns of Whitehaven, Salisbury and Princess Anne. In one month recruiters enlisted fifty-five Black men. In the ensuing months over 270 slaves in Somerset were manumitted on the condition of their enlistment in the Union Army. The Crisfields, Dashiells, and Robertsons freed some of their slaves for military service in order to allow their sons to remain at home. Most of these slaves joined the 9th and 19th Regiments of Colored Troops of Maryland. Somerset Blacks who served in the 9th Regiment engaged in some of the bloodiest fighting of the war at Petersburg, Virginia, in 1864. Afterwards the 9th Regiment participated in the military occupation of Richmond following the Confederate surrender. According to one historian, "the gallantry of the 19th Regiment at the battle of Cemetery Hill near Richmond, was conspicuous and losses severe. Of the over 700 men in the unit, 360 were killed in the first thirty minutes of the fighting." After the war the Somerset County Board of Commissioners paid enlistment bonuses of $100 to $300 to its combat- hardened Black veterans.[25]

9th Colored Maryland Regiment 1863-1866 Enlisted African Americans From Somerset County, Maryland[26] This regiment was recruited initially by Colonel William Birney in 1863.[27]

Last Name
Acty	Robert
Ballard	Isaac
Baptist	Charles
Boston	Ambrose
Bowling	William H.
Britman	Levi
Brittman	Henry A.

Burroughs	Rufus
Carroll	David
Church	Littleton
Collins	James
Costin	Charles
Costin	Richard
Cottman	Robert
Cottman	Samuel
Covington	George
Dashiell	Alfred
Dashiell	Benjamin
Dashiell	James W.
Dashiell	John
Dashiell	Joseph
Dashiell	Wainwright
Dennis	John L.
Dennis	John T.
Dennis	Littleton
Dennis	Samuel
Deshields	Ephraim
Deshields	George W.
Deshields	Joseph
Deshields	Samuel
Deshilds	George
Deshon	William
Dixon	Cornelius
Douglas	Ishmael
Elzey	Daniel
Elzey	Dennis
Elzey	George
Evans	George

Evans	Samuel
Fooks	William
Gale	Francis
Gale	James
Gale	Joshua
Givins	Samuel
Gosley	Albert
Gosley	Levin
Gould	Samuel
Grayson	Dennis
Hall	Thomas
Hamlin	Noah
Hamon	George
Hamon	Harrison
Handy	George
Handy	Henry
Handy	Hiram
Handy	John
Hargus	Charles
Hargus	George T.
Hargus	Henry
Hargus	Littleton
Harris	Isaac
Haymon	Harrison
Haymon	Levin
Hayward	John WS.
Hicks	Laban
Highes	Robert
Hitch	Benjamin
Horsey	Columbus
Horsey	Selvey

Ht	Rufus
Hughes	Levin
Hughes	Nelson
Hull	Sidney
Humphreys	Solomon
Jackson	Gorge
Johnson	Elijah
Johnson	George
Johnson	George II
Johnson	Major
Johnson	Sandy
Johnston	Charles H.
Jones	George H.
Jones	Henry
Jones	Jackson
Jones	James
Jones	John A.
Jones	Perry
Jones	Purnell
Jones	Robert
Lafewell	Alfred
Langford	Charles
Larmer	Alfred
Leatherbury	Charles
Leatherbury	Eban
Leatherbury	John
Leatherbury	Samuel
Leonard	Joshua
Lewis	Robert
Mattox	Alfred
Miles	Lewis

Miller	Lewis
Mitchell	Charles
Moore	William
Morris	John P.
Myers	Francis
Nutter	Dennis
Parsons	Charles
Pinckett	Wilson
Polk	Alfred
Price	Horace
Proce	Charles
Pullett	Elsey
Pullett	Joseph
Pullett	Joseph
Pullett	Washington
Richards	Jenkins
Roberts	David
Robinson	Joseph
Roixbury	George
Ryder	Levin W.
Scott	James
Selvy	Francis
Smith	Francis
Smith	George
Smith	Jeffrey
Smith	Peter
Steward	Peter
Stewart	John
Stewart	William
Swilson	Franklin
Taylor	George

Taylor	George Ed.
Taylor	John
Thoms	Charles
Trader	Edward
Turner	John
Wainwright	Alfred
Wainwright	Arthur
Waller	Samuel
Washington	Grayson
Water	Benjamin
Waters	George
Waters	John
Watgers	Robert
Wetherly	James
Whalen	Joseph
White	Edlzey
White	Festus
Wilkins	George
Winder	Samuel
Winder	Sidney
Wller	Alfred
Wood	George
Wood	Thomas

In Somerset John W. Crisfield was the most illustrious victim of the shifting political allegiances of Marylanders and the changing necessities of the Union war effort. Although Crisfield argued that he had remained constant in his politics, his relationship with President Lincoln had reached its breaking point. On several occasions Crisfield had joined other Democratic congressmen in protesting against the dictatorial tendencies of the Lincoln administration. When Crisfield accused Lincoln of using emancipation for selfish political purposes in January of 1863, the Eastern Shore

Congressman became *persona non grata* at the White House. During the summer of 1863, Henry Winter Davis and other prominent anti-slavery leaders in Maryland launched a campaign to run candidates to defeat pro-slavery politicians like Crisfield in the November elections. Anti-slavery unionists nominated John A. Creswell of Harford County to oppose Crisfield for Congress. Anxious to insure Crisfield's defeat, Henry Winter Davis asked General Robert Schenck, Commander of the Military Department to issue a military order that would virtually guarantee the election to Creswell. Accordingly, Schenck issued General War Order No. 53, which was designed to prevent pro-Confederate voters from using the November election to "foist enemies of the United States into power." Schenck decreed the arrest of all rebel sympathizers in the vicinity and ordered election judges in Somerset and the other counties to require an oath of allegiance from citizens and to swear that he was not in communication with anyone in the Confederacy – a considerable hardship for those with relations in the South. Also Schenck sent soldiers to every political subdivision in the First District and placed federal marshals at the polling stations with power to arrest those at the polls whom the soldiers identified as "disloyal."[28]

Throughout his campaign for reelection to Congress, Crisfield suspected that underhanded devices would be used against him. Attempting to speak in Salisbury and other places on the Eastern Shore, Crisfield encountered hostile groups of Union soldiers who hooted and jeered him. Also the election ballots were printed on colored paper to allow soldiers to follow the voting at the polls. Crisfield and his ticket were placed on a white ballot while his anti-slavery opponent's name was printed on the yellow ballot. In Somerset Union troops were ordered to make sure that county residents would either vote the yellow ballot or be disqualified. Throughout the county Union soldiers dominated the election. Union soldiers waved yellow ballots and exclaimed, "This is the only ticket that shall be voted today!"

John A. Creswell, the pro-emancipation candidate defeated Crisfield 6,742 to 5,482 and military interference in Kent and Somerset counties determined the election. Without arbitrary closing of polls and the use of military force in these counties, Crisfield would have carried the election. Afterwards Crisfield appealed to the Maryland House of Delegates, which had jurisdiction in state election matters. The House Committee on Elections of the Maryland Legislature, counting a majority of Creswell and Lincoln supporters, defended the use of the military in the election as necessary and proper. The minority report of the Committee, though, took a radically different position. "In a majority of the districts," the committee claimed, "soldiers in organized military force appeared at the polls . . . .. and the evidence is conclusive that there was an organized and predetermined effort to use military force and intimidation to affect the result of the election."[29] Crisfield appealed both to Governor Bradford and to President Lincoln but his case came to naught. John Crisfield the redoubtable slave-owning businessman and railroad entrepreneur would spend the remainder of the war as a private citizen.

Meanwhile a large contingent of Irish and White vagrants gravitated towards Somerset county to take work in the shipyards, docks and farms that had been left short of workers owing to the military draft and emancipation. James Phoebus, President of the Somerset County Board of Commissioners led the county in raising money for a new seaport in the county. Phoebus, a Unionist, counseled his fellow citizens to think less of race and more of a steamboat terminus, good roads and pier construction.[30]

In September, 1864, the State of Maryland organized a convention for the express purpose of outlawing slavery and reducing the representation of the Eastern Shore and southern counties in the House of Delegates from 34 to 17. When the delegates from Somerset County arrived, journalists noted that they were the elite of Somerset's slaveholding society. Delegates Isaac Jones, William Gale, Andrew Crawford and John Horsey acceded to the leadership of James Upshur Dennis, the delegation's most sharp-tongued and talented orator. Hotspur of the powerful Dennis family and brother of George R. Dennis, one of the largest slaveholders in the county, James U. Dennis was one of the most articulate defenders of slavery at the Constitutional Convention.

When the delegates from Somerset arrived in Annapolis there was much controversy on the question of their political loyalty to the Union. Anti-slavery men at the convention accused Isaac Jones and James U. Dennis as being little more than unregenerate secessionists. Jones' namesake, they pointed out, was an officer in the Confederate Army. Jones, in fact, narrowly escaped arrest by virtue of the fact that he was the Attorney General of Maryland. Dennis, however, was arrested and only after a fierce legal battle was he allowed to attend the convention. As the debates of the Constitutional Convention were seriously disturbed by the daring Confederate raid on Washington led by Jubal A. Early on July 9, 1864, Unionist factions closed ranks and assailed the slave power for trying to conquer a peaceful state. Thus the debate on slavery, the primary reason for the convention, would become a largely one-sided affair with the spokesmen for slavery in a decided minority.

Inasmuch as slavery appeared doomed, the strategy of the Somerset delegates was to press for compensated emancipation. Isaac Jones and William Gale claimed that a program of compensated emancipation coupled with the forced deportation of Negroes to South America was the only way to avert racial antagonisms between Whites and Blacks. "Who but the abolitionists of the North," argued Isaac Jones, "has ever supposed it possible that the (Negro) population remain on our soil in any other relation than that of master and slave."[31] James U. Dennis, however, was more vociferous in debate. Aware of being on the losing side of the emancipation issue, Dennis nonetheless sought to make his position clear. In the debates Dennis pointed out the hypocrisy of Marylanders who had bought and sold slaves before the war and now had become abolitionists because it was to their political advantage. The South, said Dennis, had before the war been one of the best customers of the industrial North and northern banks had given mortgages on slaves in Maryland. How odd it was that these elements should be great defenders of human rights. Dennis preferred political and moral consistency to wartime expediency. On the subject of owning chattel property, Dennis intoned, "my conscience is perfectly at ease." While he recognized that the federal government could take his Negroes if it chose to do so, Dennis warned that emancipation would be a "sudden shock" that would "shake to the very center all the interests of the state, and for a while at least, tend very nearly to their prostration."[32]

Despite protests from the Eastern Shore delegations, the Convention moved relentlessly forward on the emancipation issue. From a social and demographic viewpoint, the Convention was dominated by the northern counties of the state which were composed of immigrants, small farmers, and businessmen who viewed slavery as harmful to the economic development of Maryland.

In September, 1864, a new Constitution was formally adopted by the Convention. It contained several provisions that the Somerset delegation had opposed. The new constitution outlawed slavery and reduced the representation of the Eastern Shore and southern counties in the House of Delegates from 34 to 17.[33]

The new constitution also provided for the introduction of public schools throughout the state. Isaac Jones, a convention delegate from Somerset, worried that this measure would be used to educate Blacks and attack the social structure of the Eastern Shore.[34] On October 12 and 13, 1864, voters throughout the state went to the polls to vote on the new constitution. Somerset voted 464 for and 2,066 against. Unregenerate on the slavery issue, Somerset would see its peculiar institution die as Marylanders voted for the Constitution 30,174 to 29,799 against. Were it not for a heavy turn out of Maryland soldiers voting and casting 2,633 Unionist votes, the new document would have failed ratification.

Although federal commissioners had been appointed in Maryland and Delaware to dispense over twelve million dollars in compensation to former slave owners, Congress balked at approving the sum. Compensation was never authorized and slave-owners suffered a property loss valued in pre-war dollars at $30 million.[35] Angry voters in Somerset vented their wrath later that fall in the presidential election by voting heavily for General George B. McClellan, the Democratic candidate. Race seems to have been the principal factor for Somerset residents as McClellan was generally known for opposing emancipation and Negro equality. The county voted 2,100 for McClellan and 644 for Lincoln.

A product of war-time necessity, self-interest and humanitarianism, emancipation brought to a close a chapter in Somerset's centuries-long racial and social history. Shortly after the new constitution went into effect, large numbers of Black troops in federal uniforms could be seen in Princess Anne preparing for transportation to the Virginia front. Throughout the county the news of emancipation had been greeted by a massive outburst of rejoicing by several thousand Blacks. Hailing their new liberation, Black people went to church to thank God and pray for wisdom in the trying days that were to come under freedom. Reverend Stephenson Whittington, a Black Methodist preacher who had been a free Negro in slavery days summed up the occasion of what he called "Jubilee": "De blessed Jesus mended the old constitution and sine and seal it wid his blood; and he open the do, and say come forth..."[36]

1. Anna Ella Carroll, who freed her slaves in Somerset County and joined the Union war effort as a journalist and spy.

2. John W. Crisfield of Princess Anne, slaveholding Congressman and railroad entrepreneur.

3. Black Soldiers in the Union Army from Maryland's Eastern Shore

4. Refugee Slaves During Civil War in Maryland

Notes

1. John Crisfield to Mary Crisfield, February 25, 1860, Crisfield MS, Maryland Historical Society.
2. Tom Blake, Madison County, "Mississippi Largest Slaveholders from 1860 Census Schedules," Rootsweb.Com
3. George L.P. Radcliffe, *Governor Thomas H. Hicks of Maryland and the Civil War*, Baltimore: 1901,26;
4. Judge Alexander Hamilton Handy, "Address to the Citizens of Baltimore," Baltimore Daily Exchange, December 20, 1860
5. *National Intelligenser*, June 1, 1861; Charles B. Clark, ed. *The Eastern Shore of Maryland and Virginia*, Vol. 1 (New York: 1950),545.
6. Crisfield to Augustus Bradford, November 10, 1861, Bradford MS, Maryland Historical Society.
7. J. Thomas Scharf, *History of Maryland* III, Hatboro Pa., 518. *Baltimore Sun*, November 21, 1862.
8. *Baltimore Sun*, November 7, 1862.
9. *Baltimore Sun*, August 14, 1863.
10. A.M.S. Reese to Brigadier General Shriver, November 9, 1862, Adjutant Generals Papers, Miscellaneous Letters on Military Subjects, 1862, Maryland Hall of Records.
11. Harold Manakee, *Maryland In the Civil War*, Baltimore: 1959,119; Charles B. Clark, *Politics in Maryland During the Civil War*, Chestertown, Md: 1952, 163.
12. Charles Lewis Wagandt, *Mighty Revolution: Negro Emancipation in Maryland*, Baltimore: 1964, 42 et passim.
13. Quoted in Clark, *Politics in Maryland*, 146.
14. Ward Hill Lamon, *Recollections of Abraham Lincoln, 1847-1865*, Washington: 1885, quoted in Wagandt. *Mighty Revolution*, 190.
15. Remarks of Mr. Crisfield, *Congressional Globe*, 37th Congress, 3rd session, vol.3, part 1, 147-151.
16. Maryland House of Delegates *Journal*, May 7, 1861,73.
17. Wagandt, *Mighty Revolution*, 126-128; Clark, *Politics in Maryland*, 179-180.
18. *Baltimore Sun*, November 11, 1863.
19. For an extensive overview of the Union Army in Maryland at this time see, Brian Thomas Dunne, "Rifles, Residents, and Runaways: The Conflict Over Slavery Between Civil and Military Authority in Maryland, 1861-1864," MA Thesis, Florida Atlantic University, 2011.
20. *Baltimore American and Commercial Chronicle*, October 5, 1863.
21. Wagandt, *Mighty Revolution*, 149.

22 John W. Crisfield, "To The Voters and People of the First Congressional District of Maryland," October 10,1863, in *The National Intelligencer*, October 17, 1863.
23 *Baltimore Sun*, October 30, 1863.
24 *Ibid.*
25 Agnes K. Callum, *9th Regiment of United States Colored Troops, Volunteers, Maryland* , Baltimore, 1999.
26 Ibid.
27 *U.S. Colored Troops Military Service Records, 1863-1865*, National Archives, Washington D.C.
28 Wagandt, *Mighty Revolution*, 159.
29 Minority Subcommittee Report, Document J, "Report on the Committee of Elections on Contested Elections in Somerset County," February 26, 1864, *House of Delegates Journal*, February 26, 1864.
30 *Proceedings of the Somerset County Board of Commissioners*, April 7, 1862, Maryland Hall of Records.
31 *Debates of the Constitutional Convention of 1864*, Annapolis, 1864 II, 595.
32 *Debates*, I. 637-644.
33 Wagandt, *Mighty Revolution*, 229.
34 State of Maryland, *Debates of the Constitutional Convention of 1864*, II, 595, I, 637-644.
35 Wagandt, *Mighty Revolution*, 264.
36 Robert Todd, *Methodism of the Peninsula*, Philadelphia, 1886, 232-233.

Chapter Three

The Freedmen's World

"Colored churches have been burned in Somerset County . . . . to prevent Negro schools from being opened in them, all showing that Negro hate is not by any means confined to the lower South."
J.W. Alvord, Freedmen's Bureau

National Overview

The most difficult task confronting the South at the end of the Civil War was one of constructing a new system of labor to replace the political economy of slavery that had been lost. In many ways, the economic lives of planters, former slaves and nonslaveholding Whites were transformed. Planters throughout the South found it hard to adjust to the end of slavery and sought to devise methods of labor control that were little more than de facto servitude. Farms and plantations in the South were often crucibles of conflict as Blacks expected that the federal government would confiscate southern land and give them "forty acres and a mule." Out of these conflicts on tobacco and cotton plantations emerged a new form of labor called "sharecropping", a kind of agrarian wage labor. Freedmen during this time were especially active in civic affairs after the passage of the Fifteenth Amendment to the Constitution which gave them the right to vote. While the Freedmen's Bureau (Bureau of Refugees, Freedmen, and Abandoned Lands) gave Blacks in the former Confederacy agency in the form of military protection, clothing and fuel, the Bureau met with determined resistance from planters and politicians in border states like Maryland. Because of the resistance of President Andrew Johnson to the Freedmen's Bureau and others in Congress who believed that the Bureau encroached on states rights and relied inappropriately on the military in *peacetime, the Bureau lost most of its funding. In 1872 Congress abandoned the program, refusing to approve renewed legislative appropriation. Blacks made social gains through the introduction of White missionaries who established "Freedom Schools" in the South.*

I
Social and Economic Adjustments

Of the numerous social and economic adjustments confronting Somerset County in the post Civil War era, none was as painful as the task of assimilating over 2,000 emancipated Blacks. As historian Barbara Fields has noted, "the rise of two free populations in Maryland, one White and one Black challenged the political and moral and ideological coherence" of former slaveholding counties.[1] Blacks in the county faced myriad problems such as protecting themselves from violence, guarding their new-found legal rights, establishing schools to surmount illiteracy, and making the painful emotional transition from slavery to freedom in a very troubled time. Many scholars have suggested that the actions of rural Blacks in places like the Eastern Shore resembled those of a peasant-like society in search of whatever it could find amidst the opposing forces of the free market and regulated labor. Somerset's Black experience does not fit into any well-ordered pattern.

II
The Apprenticeship System

Fearful than the new freedmen would be an unreliable labor force as well as a civic problem for local authorities, Whites resorted to an apprenticeship system that until outlawed by the Constitution of 1867 was a *sub rosa* continuation of slavery.[2] Within days of emancipation planters across the state seized the labor of some 3,000 Black minors under the provisions of an unrepealed section of the state's Black Code. Apprenticeships for Blacks was not a new development after the war. Since 1843 the children of free Blacks ages 8 to 18 had been customarily bound out by the courts.[3] John Horsey and Edward F. Duer were two of the most outspoken advocates of Negro apprenticeship in the county. At the Constitutional

Convention in Annapolis in 1864 delegate Horsey had supported a successful movement to have Negro males apprenticed by the Orphans Court to the age of twenty-one and Negro females to the age of eighteen. As Justice of the Peace in the county, Edward Duer bound out Blacks to White farmers to "learn labor and the habits of industry." During the period 1864-1870 Duer and other peace officers in the county bound out over three hundred Black children to hard labor in the fields of Somerset. This action continued well after the new Maryland Constitution of 1867 banned such involuntary servitude.

The apprenticeship system as it operated in Maryland was a deterrent against the implementation of civil rights for Negros. This was a source of grave concern to Republicans in Congress and military authorities on the Eastern Shore who regularly sent reports to General Oliver O. Howard, head of the newly created Freedmen's Bureau. Other problems were equally pressing for Blacks. Specifically, these problems in Somerset involved protecting freedmen from violence, establishing and guarding their legal rights and establishing schools to train a largely illiterate Black population. Black transition from slavery to freedom would not be easy. The newly established Freedmen's Bureau at the end of the war was only minimally successful in protecting Blacks in Maryland. The Bureau's main concern was in helping Blacks in the former Confederate states rather than in border states that had remained "loyal" during the war. There was strong sentiment in Maryland during the war against "vagrant" and "freed" Negroes, writes historian W. A. Low, that the law provided for a monetary fine or enslavement of any free Negro who entered the state. In the early years of the war Maryland authorities could easily "jeopardize the precarious position of free Negroes through a mal-interpretation of the law."[4] Much of the work of protecting freedmen on the Eastern Shore was left to junior army officers with little knowledge or experience of the racial complexities they encountered. After many officers in Maryland's military district had been mustered out to return home in 1867, General Howard selected Henry Stockbridge, a Baltimore lawyer, to aid the Freedmen's Bureau in its fight against the apprenticeship system and to secure the release of "Negro children illegally bound by former masters" after freedom had been proclaimed. Stockbridge argued against Negro apprenticeship before the Supreme Court and won in the case of *Turner v. Hambleton* (1867). But as Stockbridge soon found, it was one thing to win a court case and another to see it enforced in society. The freedom granted by the Constitution of 1864 soon proved to be an empty legal expression. During the period 1866-1878 the entire Eastern Shore was without permanent Freedmen's Bureau field agents. Visits of temporary touring agents helped a little, but not much. Also, many field agents, like their ex-Confederate sympathizers, had a restricted view of what freedmen were capable of achieving.[5] Given the open hostility of White judges on the Eastern Shore, the Freedmen's Bureau lacked the legal power to enforce contractual agreements among its people. One Freedmen's Bureau agent, Edward O'Brien, said of the apprenticeship system, " a better embodiment of slavery under the guise of freedom I ever saw."[6]

III
The Freedmen's Bureau and Civil Rights

Many Blacks in Somerset and elsewhere on the Eastern Shore feared the dark rumors that slavery was being reenacted under a different name. Freedmen were sometimes whipped, jailed, threatened or confined to limited areas, restricted by curfew, or forbidden to hold unapproved meetings after "freedom" had been legally granted by the Constitution. In reality, many of the old slave codes remained in force. What Whites soon realized, and it took Blacks a while to ascertain was that the Federal Government could not easily and readily enforce emancipation or civil rights granted by Congress. This problem was particularly acute in Somerset County as the post-war Orphans Court used its authority to bind out hundreds of Blacks under age twenty-one as apprentices to local farmers. The work of the Freedmen's Bureau was closed in August 1868, at a time when the problems of the freedmen on the Eastern Shore were becoming acute. White leaders in the county rationalized the apprenticeship system for Blacks on the grounds that unskilled and illiterate freedmen were a public charge and a burden to taxpayers. Apprenticeship, they argued, upheld local custom and gave the county a reliable labor supply, a primary concern for former slave owners. Blacks, of course, resented the system. Many made direct appeals to the Freedmen's Bureau for protection, even though there was danger of White reprisal in their doing so. Historian W.A. Low estimates that it may be that statewide in Maryland some ten thousand Black youths were bound out as apprentices in the post-war period.[7] At least 2,000 complaints were lodged with the Freedmen's Bureau office in Annapolis during 1866-1867 by parents of apprenticed youth. Somerset County at this time bound out more Black youths than any other county in the state.

Further, the Freedmen's Bureau supported the contract system of agricultural labor that bound Blacks to the soil. It did little to facilitate the principle of Black land acquisition. Blacks, however, rapidly developed skills in negotiating labor contracts that allowed for family gardens; and Blacks who were cheated in payment refused to sign additional contracts and worked with White farmers on shares. Between 1860 and 1870 the number of Black landowners in Somerset remained small and their property often consisted of no more than a few acres. But the fact that the freedmen owned property at all during this time is impressive. Blacks exerted extraordinary efforts, sometimes at great personal cost, to maintain control of their families. As one historian put it, "In the control of provision for, and deployment of their children, freed parents sought to wrest this important aspect of rural economic control from the hands of Whites."[8]

The Hayman, Costen, and Lankford families, for example, bound out their former young slaves in the first month of emancipation. Between April, 1865, and October, 1867, over 275 Blacks were bound out. An examination of Somerset Orphans Court apprenticeships in the Maryland Hall of Records reveals that between 1864 and 1874 over 537 young Blacks were bound out.[9] Many Blacks fled the county to avoid being coerced into involuntary servitude. Others protested to the United States Army and the Freedmen's Bureau that Somerset was attempting to revive slavery. When N.J. Lankford of Princess Anne attempted to have Joseph Hyland apprenticed to him, Hyland's mother complained to federal authorities and Lankford was forced to release the young Negro. Blacks risked violent physical harm if they complained to federal authorities. While the Bureau was too preoccupied with the enormous problems of post-war adjustment in the former Confederate states to give the Eastern Shore of Maryland much supervision, it did nonetheless intervene in behalf of William Tilghman after he appealed to General Howard to rescue his son from an unscrupulous White man. Tilghman's appeal was courageously forthright:[10]

> Burnettsville,M.D (Now Marion Station) Somerset County, M.D.
> October 30, 1865
>
> Major General Howard
> My dear friend would you be so kind to me and my son as to ade us out of dense trouble there is a certain Mr. Edward Howard of this Somerset County,M.D. that taken my son John Edward during my absence and had him unlawfully bound to him by the seceash (secessionist) court I have been instructed to call on you that you had the power and disposition to Due me and him both justice I had just got my son so that he was able to be of some help to me and then and not till then did they the seceash take him away MY Dear General be on the side of us poor darkies and I pray God be on your side …..
>
> Your obediance Servant
> William Tilghman

Somerset Blacks feared the Justices of the Peace. These men could apprehend "rogues," "vagrants," and "other idle and dissolute persons" who had no visible means of support and bind them out at hard labor for three months. Similarly, convicts could be leased out at hard labor to local farmers. Later as federal authorities overruled involuntary apprenticeships, White farmers avoided the law by apprenticing the children of Negroes in jail or prison on the grounds that the children were wards of the county and had to earn their keep.[11]

Throughout Maryland in the post-war period about 10,000 Negroes were bound out as apprentices. Although Black families occasionally apprenticed their children voluntarily to White tradesmen so that they might learn a craft, the law worked against the apprentice, regardless of condition. A comparison of White and Black apprenticeships in the county at this time is illustrative. While the local Orphans Court stipulated that White apprentices had to be taught reading, writing, and arithmetic by their master, Blacks were not protected by this requirement. Also, unlike Whites, Black-apprenticed children could on the death of the master be transferred to another White in the county without the knowledge or permission of the Black child's parent. The Orphans Court stipulated that Black apprentices could be whipped, restricted by curfew and forbidden to engage in public meetings. If a Black apprentice ran away, he could be sold to anyone in the state. Few of these restrictions applied equally to White apprentices. Under the laws of apprenticeship, Whites were required not only to educate their White wards and train them in a skill, but were required to provide them with clothes and fifty dollars pocket money upon completion of their apprenticeship.[12] On the Eastern Shore, marshes were everywhere and it was difficult to expect that this easy escape route would not be utilized by runaway apprentices. Further some indentures forbade apprentices to swear, to drink intoxicating beverages, to play cards, throw dice or other unlawful games. Those Whites who held apprentices thought of themselves as being benevolent masters, who taught submission to the laws of the state of Maryland and to the higher law of morality.[13] By planters tightly controlling the labor market on the Eastern Shore, the freedmen had initial difficulty in seeking non-farm employment.

Neither Whites nor Blacks, however, fared well under this system. Apprenticeship victimized the poor of both races. In 1872 Elizabeth Gullet, a White woman unable to provide for her child, was compelled to apprentice her son James Edward, aged six, for fifteen years to Richard Darby of Somerset to learn "the art, trade, and mystery of farming." White children whose parents were in the county almshouse were also bound out and females were usually apprenticed to learn "housewifery." One of the last apprenticeships in Somerset County was recorded on January 27, 1908, in which Jennie Smith of Worcester County bound out her three year old son to Jacob Smith of Princess Anne to learn to be a paperhanger. For Whites, apprenticeship was a callous method of exploiting the children of the poor but for Blacks apprenticeship was slavery in new guise. Thus did both poor Whites and Blacks fear the awesome power of the Orphans Court and the Justices of the Peace in Somerset County?[14]

Somerset had always been as much a pro-slavery county as any county in Mississippi. The system was advocated and enforced by some of the leading citizens who were pro-southern in sentiment and temper and formerly some of the largest slaveholders. Abraham Lincoln received only two votes in the entire county in the election of 1860 from a total of three thousand votes. And only 644 out of a total of 2,754 four years later. Bluntly put, Whites in Somerset did not like the new order of Black freedmen. A Negro church, housing the first Black school in the county in Princess Anne, was burned at the close of the war.

The Somerset delegation to the Constitutional Convention of 1864 was composed of slaveholders vigorously opposed to the abolition of slavery and the introduction of Negro schools. The delegates were Isaac Jones, James U. Dennis, William H. Gale and John C. Horsey. Of this group Dennis was the most radical in secessionist leanings and was imprisoned by federal authorities during the war. He was also the largest slaveholder in the county and one of the largest holders of real and personal property. (Ironically, a portion of his land, a house called Olney and one hundred acres would become the home of what today is the University of Maryland, Eastern Shore.)[15] During its short period of existence in Maryland, the Freedmen's Bureau was overextended and understaffed and the Bureau found it difficult to prosecute cases brought before local courts because of the entrenched racial attitudes of magistrates, judges, sheriffs, and local White witnesses. Yet the Bureau was not totally ineffective and secured the release of many illegally bound Negro youths. One Somerset White offered a telling perspective on freedmen: "They can all get their living if they have a fair chance .... If they had their large children they could make as good a living as they got from their master, and much better .... Some of these children could bring into their mothers 15 to 20 dollars a month if they had them to themselves."[16] Others were not so enthusiastic about "colored labor." One farmer argued that the ambition of the Negro does not arise beyond the meager necessities of life. And yet,

Maryland planters actively pursued Blacks as farm labor. Perhaps they were better workers than Whites dared to admit. Yet even with steady work Black freedmen found it difficult to get by. They were easily hired and easily fired; and they faced the stubborn refusal of rural Whites to adjust their racial attitudes. As historian Richard Fuke has commented, "whatever they might accomplish in terms of family autonomy, their efforts remained confined by a White society determined to regulate them in other ways."[17]

Emancipation also forced county residents to change the code of racial etiquette that prevailed for centuries in the community. Intimacy between Whites and Blacks diminished after the war. Earlier social courtesy was based on a patriarchal slave-master relationship and White fear of equality tended to reduce interracial social contacts and excite racial antagonism. Racist tracts warning of the menace of emancipated Negroes enjoyed wide currency on the lower Eastern Shore. In one such warning to Somerset farmers, Maryland's Secretary of Labor and Agriculture advised that "Our African laborers have ceased to be reliable or profitable, and that as tenants or permanent settlers upon your lands are not to be desired." Both the state legislature and the Department of Agriculture urged Somerset residents to bring in European immigrants to solve the local labor problem. Also in a highly popular book entitled *The Plantation Negro As A Free Man*, Philip A. Bruce warned his fellow Virginians and Marylanders that Whites could handle Blacks only by applying the "pressure of a stern and exacting watchfulness." In Somerset and throughout the Eastern Shore the public whipping post was a familiar sight and Negroes and vagrants received the harsh discipline of a whip called the "the Sheriff's Cat."[18]

IV
Black Politics

Following the passage of the Fifteenth Amendment to the Constitution enfranchising the freedmen throughout the South, Blacks voted freely in Somerset County elections. Most of Somerset's Black voters joined the ranks of the Republicans and gave the county its first strong minority party. Federal supervisors were present at all federal elections in Somerset and made it the only county on the

Eastern Shore to vote Republican in a majority of state and federal elections during the period 1870-1895. Determined young Black men such as Armstrong Upshur, Henry Ballard, Isaac Cottman, David King and George Pollitt were among the first Black registered voters in Somerset and worked to assure the political participation of Black people in county life. One of the most prominent leaders of Somerset's Black community was Edward Wilson. Born in 1852 of free parents, this light complexioned oysterman served as a power broker between Whites and Blacks and guaranteed the Black vote in hotly contested elections. Wilson supervised Black patronage matters for the state Republican organization for over thirty years and was subsequently rewarded by President William McKinley in 1897 with a sinecure in the Baltimore Customs House. Wilson was a man widely respected in the community and Blacks always thronged to Ford's Wharf in the Fairmount District when "Captain Ned's" oyster boat came in from Baltimore.

While both political parties worked to expand Somerset's commercial development after the war, Democrats and Republicans differed strongly on the issue of racial accommodation. After 1864 county Democrats supported White supremacy and defended their position by asserting the inherent inferiority of the Negro and his incapacity for self-government. Democratic efforts to prevent Blacks from speaking out on issues and voting in local elections were challenged by Republicans who saw the Negro vote as indispensible to their political survival. With a strong White and Black political base in the Fairmount District (then known as Potato Neck) the Republicans supported public education, opposed Black disenfranchisement schemes, and generally served as spokesmen for the unpropertied working class voters in the county.

The stewardship of local government also included the supervision and care of the poor. The county maintained an Alms House and appointed three men annually to serve as "trustees of the poor." They appointed an overseer for the Alms House, kept a list of all paupers, vagrants and vagabonds and supervised the work of the residents. To make the Alms House self-sufficient, the county spent $1,237.47 for a farm. Both White and Black paupers were admitted to the Alms House as no color line separated the poor in Somerset. Many paupers were superannuated Negroes who had spent most of their lives as slaves and were now unceremoniously dumped on the county by White planters who did not want the expense of supporting them. Emancipation eliminated traditional social pressures on White farmers to maintain aged Blacks on their lands. The Board of Commissioners annually appropriated $2,500 which allowed only the barest maintenance of the Alms House. Like most rural counties in the late nineteenth century, Somerset was neither ideologically nor financially prepared to deal with the poor in its midst.[19]

Many Blacks left Somerset County after 1870 because of racial harassment, fear of forced apprenticeship and uncertain economic opportunities. The phenomenon of Blacks "voting with their feet" was not lost on the *Salisbury Advertiser* which reported in 1873 that large numbers of Negroes were leaving Princess Anne to seek homes in Philadelphia.[20]

V
A New Rural Economy

The Civil War also forced radical adjustments in Somerset's agricultural system. Before the war Somerset sold massive amounts of corn, wheat, sweet potatoes and cured hams to slaveholders in the deep South whose prime farm lands were heavily committed to cotton production. The collapse of the southern market forced a deemphasis on large-scale wheat and corn farming based on slave labor and accelerated the development of small labor-intensive family farms in the county which produced truck crops for local markets. Emancipation forced down agricultural land values and Whites formerly excluded from farming took up a new occupation, truck farming. The switch to growing melons, strawberries, cantelopes, and grapes transformed Somerset's agricultural base. These new products could be handled by small family units and shipped by sailboat up the Chesapeake to Baltimore. At the war's end planters like Joshua Matthews of Kingston and Thomas Sudler of Princess Anne wasted little time in contacting commission merchants in the urban north about the practicability of truck agriculture in Somerset. In turn Blacks in Somerset found jobs in local sawmills and boat yards and expanded their seafaring activities on the Bay that had been part of African-American life on the Chesapeake since the colonial period.

VI
"Will the Negro Work?"

The prevalent White racist view in the region was that Negroes were degraded, lazy, and improvident beings dependent on charity and what they could steal. Blacks in their everyday life, however, contradicted this stereotype. Blacks went into teaching, preaching, carpentry and blacksmithing and Negro women secured employment as cooks, midwives and washerwomen. In Somerset, the White community depended on Black common and skilled labor more than it cared to admit. Whites knew that if they made the social and economic situation absolutely intolerable, the burgeoning industrial labor markets of Baltimore beckoned. Most White farmers gave their "colored help" in addition to wages, a bushel of meal and twenty pounds of meat per month. Barbering on the Eastern Shore was almost exclusively a Black occupation that enabled some freedmen to pull themselves out of poverty. In the 1870s and 1880s one of the best restaurants on the Eastern Shore was owned by a Black man in Princess Anne. Post emancipation Blacks were able to buy and hold on to land during the period 1865-1870 in Worcester, Somerset, and Wicomico Counties. Much of this land was purchased with enlistment bounties that 2,700 Blacks had received for enlisting in the Union Army during the war.[21]

VII
Blacks, Hunting and Guns

Since the early colonial period Eastern Shoremen had hunted and fished in the woods, marshes, and rivers of the region for sport and market. Hunting and fishing provided Blacks with jobs as guides and gun bearers. As guides for duck and goose hunting, Blacks earned extra cash from wealthy sportsmen and market hunters who came to the region in the post-war period. Also, freedmen took their free time to hunt on common lands and these activities were symbols of economic, cultural, and spiritual separation from Whites.

Black hunters often infringed on White designated hunting preserves. To regulate these "interlopers," Eastern Shore county governments forced Blacks to purchase hunting licenses to regulate their activities and made guns difficult to obtain. Ironically Blacks who in slavery had access to guns and hunted freely in the marshes and woods of the region were denied those privileges in freedom.[22] Blacks, however, held firearms in the post-war period. Some guns were had by theft while others were entrusted to them by former masters who used their guide services. Meanwhile state gun-control laws said Negroes could not carry guns without licenses from their former masters or employers. They also used trespass laws to curtail the hunting activities of Blacks and poor Whites as well. In 1866, the *Richmond Times* charged that White communities in the tidewater "suffer great annoyance and serious pecuniary loss from the trespass of predacious Negroes and low pot hunters with dogs and guns live in the field . . . . as if the whole country belonged to them."[23]

In the aftermath of the Civil War and emancipation, a new breed of agricultural realism took hold on Maryland's Eastern Shore that stressed "farming without Negroes." Specifically, White planters shifted from wheat, corn, and tobacco staples to truck agriculture such as peaches, strawberries, and nursery operations. Former slaveholders like Thomas Sudler and John Crisfield were active in constructing a rail line that would connect the county with urban markets in Baltimore, Philadelphia and New York where demand for fresh produce was exceptionally strong. Establishing Riverside Nurseries near Newtown, Sudler quickly secured from Baltimore County fruit growers the exclusive right to sell peach trees on the lower Eastern Shore. Sudler also experimented with agricultural machinery and other labor saving devices to reduce costs.[24] As early as 1865 Sudler joined with other former slave-owners like Crisfield and George R. Dennis, to revive a defunct Eastern Shore railroad and extend rail service to Princess Anne and other parts of the county. These men had most of their available capital tied up in extensive landholdings and some like the Dennis family owned estates of 2,000 acres or more. Utilizing new farm technology and sound marketing techniques, these men worked to revolutionize county agriculture. Somerset farmers, because of the war, had largely lost their southern market and they could not compete against the large grain operations in the Midwest and West that came into being with the Homestead Act and the building of the transcontinental railroad. Neither the equipment nor the techniques of Great Plains grain farming could be profitably used on the Eastern Shore. Thus the opening of the West and racial emancipation confronted Somerset planters with their most serious challenges since the decline of tobacco farming in the late 18th century. Planters readily invested in reviving the Eastern Shore Railroad and by 1866, the rail line would extend from the Delaware line to Somers Cove on the Bay. The town would soon grow into a bustling maritime city and be renamed Crisfield in honor of the railroad's chief promoter and backer, John Crisfield. From a paper organization with few assets, the railroad became a reality. Civil War veterans toiled at rail construction and by Christmas of 1866 the railroad extended from Delmar on the Delaware border to Somers Cove.

The completion of the Eastern Shore Railroad had an immediate and dramatic effect on Somerset's economy. The railroad linked the county with the markets of the urban northeast and precipitated a boom in seafood and fresh produce. As a commercial venture, the rail line was immediately profitable. In a report to shareholders, George Dennis reported that despite the heavy indebtedness, the railroad enjoyed total revenues between 1869 and 1875 of $443,905.27 with a net profit of $143,125.89. George Dennis, formerly the feudal slaveholding planter and his firebrand associates who once traded in Negroes were now trading in strawberries and peaches. Hamden Dashiell, another former slaveholder and businessman pursued economic activities that ranged from railroading to truck produce to timber sales. And during the critical emancipation period Dashiell served as the unofficial banker of the Somerset gentry.[25]

As Somerset County's economy changed, so did its population. Despite the flurry of agricultural and railroad entrepreneurship, the county suffered a net population loss of 27 percent. This is partially explained by the creation of a new county out of the northern districts of Somerset that came to be called Wicomico County with its county seat in Salisbury. It can also be explained by an out-migration of Blacks who had been reduced to the status of temporary farm labor picking fruit and digging sweet potatoes. Baltimore beckoned the freedmen with the promise of work at better wages in the city's industrial sector.

Those Blacks who remained in Somerset had to endure a number of economic restrictions that had been in place long before emancipation. After 1865 in Somerset and Worcester counties Blacks were excluded from merchandising and liquor trades and prevented from selling tobacco, beef or pork. There was an unwritten law in the county that Whites should not sell their farmland to Blacks and large tracts of forest and open land lay idle. Blacks in Somerset were also prohibited from buying lottery tickets. Despite the economic changes taking place in Somerset at this time, the old slaveholding gentry still wielded all the power in the county and steered the course of its development.

VIII
Somerset's Black Oystermen

When the first European settlers arrived in North America they found oysters along the entire Atlantic coast.. The oysters were most abundant in three areas: Chesapeake Bay, Cape Cod, and the Long Island Sound. Constant dredging for oysters in the northeast however had so depleted the supply of the latter two areas that by the 1860s Maryland became the principal supplier of the coveted bivalve.

Work on the water has been a long tradition among African-Americans. Enslaved Africans brought many maritime skills with them from working on African coastal waters including oystering, crabbing, boat-building and netmaking. Blacks were working on Chesapeake waters long before the Emancipation Proclamation. After 1865 newly freed Blacks flocked to the water for opportunities as sailors and oyster harvesters. Meanwhile in the post war era, Eastern Shore counties tried to lock them out of practically all maritime trades. These efforts were unsuccessful largely because in the 1870s there was an oyster boom on the Bay. Though oystering was only of local importance on the Eastern Shore, it would soon become a major industry in Maryland and the United States.

Labor was scarce and much needed to supply the tons of oysters demanded by expanding seafood markets in the West and Northeast. Next to President Abraham Lincoln, Diamond Jim Brady, the celebrated gourmand and champion oyster eater, did much to guarantee Black economic freedom on Chesapeake waters. Rich and famous with Lillian Russell, the renowned actress and singer on his arm, Brady was known for what would be fashionable and imitated by the American middle class. In the post-Civil War era the rich classes of the Northeast set the tone for status goods and especially status foods.

With the expansion of railroads and the development of canning processes, oysters made their way across the United States. Canned oysters were shipped to Europe and as far away as Australia. The rich oyster beds of Tangier Sound turned the city into a seafood mecca from which rail carloads of oysters were daily shipped by train in kegs packed with ice.

Blacks had a high degree of freedom on the Bay that they did not have on the farms of Somerset. They were skilled sailors and oyster tongers in an economy plagued by maritime labor shortages from tonging to oyster shucking. Many sea captains resorted to White slavery on the Bay by impressing German immigrants to work on oyster boats. Black oystermen were smart enough to resist the blandishments of many White oyster boat captains who were only interested in working their crews under wretched conditions and "paying them off at the boom" by violently rotating their ship's tiller and having the sail boom knock the unsuspecting sailors into the icy waters of Chesapeake Bay.

Oystering paid well and enterprising Black sea captains could earn as much as $2,000 a year at a time when back farm hands earned $15 a month. Ironically, one of the principal benefactors of Black oystermen in Somerset was John Crisfield. Crisfield and his partners bought the Eastern Shore Railroad company and extended its line to Somers Cove which was renamed Crisfield in his honor. Entrepreneurs built seafood packing houses and hired Black and migrant oyster shuckers to process the new seafood bonanza. Many of the old restrictive laws governing the occupation and movement of Blacks did not apply in Crisfield. Within a short time most of the White and Black breadwinners in Crisfield owed their livelihood to various aspects of the oyster trade. The percentage of Black involvement was higher than that of Whites. Blacks were more skillful at shucking oysters which paid them on a per gallon piece rate.

Crisfield in the 1870s and 1880s was a rough and dangerous town with ample saloons and bordellos. The docks stank of fish offal and unwashed deck hands and marsh mud. It was a town that allowed tough Negro oystermen a wide-open environment.[26] Some of the whorehouses admitted Black watermen with money. Here in the bustle and clatter of a busy oyster port, both men and women, Black and White, chased profits from the almighty oyster, shucking and packing oysters midst the noise and hollered casual profanities.

The rising price of oysters after the Civil War brought criminal behavior to the Chesapeake. Watermen fought over access to oyster beds and violence escalated to such a level that the State of Maryland created an Oyster Navy commanded by Captain Hunter Davidson to bring law and order to the Bay. Black and White watermen often quarreled on the amount paid for their share of oyster cargoes. One such argument resulted in tragedy that enflamed local White feelings towards freedmen. On March 5, 1869, the county executed four Black men charged with the murders of a White oyster boat captain, Benjamin F. Johnson and his mate Henry Cannon and stealing his oyster schooner, *Brave*. William Wilson, William Wells, Frank Rounds, and George Bailey were arrested on the boat as they attempted to leave Crisfield. After a speedy trial, these men were marched to the scaffold. The **Baltimore Sun** reported the grisly story: "The rope and Black caps were adjusted. The sheriff shook hands with them, and, for a few seconds they had left, and the drop fell precisely at forty minutes past one o'clock. Three men died instantly but William Wilson got his hands free, grabbed the rope, drew himself up, and got on the scaffold again. "The jailer ascended, tightened the noose again, and pushed the wretched man off, jerking the rope violently as he fell. Williams struggled for five minutes, "some of the crowd yelling, 'that's right you ought to suffer."[27]

Despite a welter of legal prohibition against Black entrepreneurs, free Negroes before the war and after engaged in the maritime trades and oyster business. Attempts to prevent Blacks from oystering or captaining vessels, and serving as chief navigators, largely failed because the work was hard and Blacks were skilled at it. Further, Blacks worked on local steamboats. They also excelled as ship caulkers. This occupation came under fire by rioting racist Whites during the 1850-1870 period and after in Baltimore and other shipyards in Maryland because Blacks had a monopoly on this lucrative profession.[28]

IX
Black Churches and Education

As in most areas of the post-bellum South, freedmen responded to racial and economic oppression by turning to the church. In the critical years after emancipation the Black churches would serve as important social and political centers for the advancement of the race in the county. The most heartening development for Blacks on the lower Shore generally was the founding of the Delaware Conference for Colored Methodists in 1864. Except for the Episcopy itself, Blacks dominated the ecclesiastical management of this organization and the Conference proved to be a fertile training ground for Black ministers and lay leaders of the Eastern Shore. By 1886 there were 15,334 Blacks in the Conference and Black-owned church property amounted to $250,160. Placing heavy emphasis on hard work and self-help the Conference sparked church-building campaigns for local congregations that formerly met in pastures and private houses.

On April 5, 1866, a group of Black Methodists in Princess Anne filed incorporation papers in court for the establishment of the "Wesley Chapel for men of color." The first trustees were Freeborn Allen, Isaac Stewart, Edward Dennis, Samuel Miles, John W. Gale, Hanson Handy, George Jackson, David Rich, and Alexander Smith. Though poor, these men were not without resources, marshalling small savings and earning from their trades to build a dream. This chapel was the forerunner of the Metropolitan Methodist Church, the building of which was a point of great pride to local Blacks. Located on the site of the old slave jail, the church was constructed by devoted parishioners using hand made bricks. Significantly, the first major accumulations of real estate by Blacks in the county were in the form of church property. From the outset Blacks had flocked to the Methodist Church because the church in the antebellum period had denounced slavery.

In the post-war period the Delaware Conference conducted large-scale public revivals and camp meetings for the freedmen that were very popular and Black church membership in the Delaware Conference on the Eastern Shore increased from 6,651 in 1864 to 14,055 in 1880.[29] Inevitably at church meetings the congregation would discuss politics and Sunday evening torch light mass meetings on questions of suffrage and civil rights were a common occurrence in the county.

The Constitution of 1864 established public schools in Maryland. Rural areas were underfunded and it made no provision for Black education. Believing that education would lead to racial equality, most of the delegates at the Constitutional Convention had opposed Black schools. Uttering a lonely dissent at the Convention, Joseph M. Cushing of Baltimore argued that "Negro education in the state was inevitable" and inasmuch as "the free colored population of this state shall remain in our midst, it seems to me incumbent upon the state to educate them, even as a mere measure of safety to the state." Cushing's ideas on Black education were distasteful to Eastern Shoremen who needed Black labor in the fields and not in schools. Although the Freedmen's Bureau attempted to bring schoolteachers into Somerset County to teach the Blacks, it had to contend with local racial animosities. J.W. Alvord, the Bureau's Superintendant of Education, wrote in 1865 that "colored churches have been burned in Somerset County . . . . to prevent Negro schools from being opened in them, all showing that Negro hate is not by any means confined to the lower South."[30]

Within two years, however Cushing's position on Black education was vindicated in Somerset County. This change in public attitude was largely the result of increasing local prosperity and the work of the Baltimore Association for the Moral and Educational Improvement of the Colored People, a biracial organization that established schools for Black children in the county in 1866. The Association centered its activities on teaching Blacks the rudiments of reading and writing and did not mix political and racial ideology with instruction. The Association scored a notable success when it persuaded Dr. Henry Monroe to emigrate to Somerset County in 1870. Monroe, a Massachusetts educator with a contempt for racism, toured the county as a circuit rider working with Blacks and

Whites to establish one room Negro schools. During this critical period Monroe would not have succeeded in his work without the financial support of the Black community.[31] From the start Blacks played an important role in the struggle for their own education in Somerset County. As early as 1867, travelers noted the presence of Black schoolteachers on the Eastern Shore, several of whom resided in Somerset County. Blacks throughout Maryland by 1870 had contributed over $23,371.11 to the cause of Negro education in the state, a stupendous achievement for a people barely three years out of slavery. Two Black organizations, The Freedmen's Union Association and the African Methodist Episcopal Church Zion channeled a portion of these funds for Black schools in Somerset. Following the ratification of the Constitution of 1867 in Maryland, the state provided for Black public education in the counties. The manner of financing Black education, however, was most peculiar. According to the new school law, Black schools in the counties were to be financed out of total school taxes paid by Blacks. Given the meager tax base for Negroes in Somerset, this meant that the community would be able to sustain only one school for the entire county. Sensing the folly of this approach, the state in 1872 mandated the establishment of a Negro public school in every election district in the counties. In this year Black schools of Somerset came under the same regulation as the White schools and the school board demanded a certificate of qualifications from the county examiner for every Black teacher. By 1874 the county had built a new schoolhouse for Blacks in Princess Anne and had embarked on a modest program of Negro school construction. Although racism and poverty plagued the schools of Somerset, public instruction in the county was a bold innovation. There were no precedents to go by and the school board, led by businessman Henry White, built a segregated school system out of sweat, anger, anguish, and hope. Future educational leaders in the county would build upon its foundation.[32]

1. First Negro Vote in Maryland

2. Black Oystermen on the Bay

The Freedmen's World 93

3. Black oyster captain and crew

Notes

1. Barbara Jeanne Fields, *Slavery and Freedom on the Middle Ground, Maryland during the Nineteenth Century*, New Haven: 1985, XI.
2. Public Local Laws of Maryland, Article 20, 1-28, *Annotated Code of Maryland*, (Annapolis: 1888), 1769-1775.
3. James Martin Wright, *The Free Negro in Maryland*, 530 *et passim*
4. W. A. Low, the Freedmen's Bureau and Civil Rights in Maryland," vol. 37, *Journal of Negro History*, July, 1952
5. Richard Paul Fuke, Planters, Apprenticeship and Forced Labor. Maryland Hall of Records, US Colored Troops30.
6. Fuke, 26.
7. Low, 233.
8. Richard Paul Fuke, "Planters, Apprenticeship, and Forced Labor: The Black Family Under Pressure in Post-Emancipation Maryland," *Agricultural History*, vol. 62, 1988, 62.
9. Somerset County, Indentures and Recognizances, *1864-1870*, Maryland Hall of Records, 1-266, Debates of he Constitutional Convention of 1864, III, (Annapolis: 1865), 1601.
10. The Highland and Tilghman Cases are cited in W.A.Lowe, "The Freedmen's Bureau and Civil Rights," *Journal of Negro History* vol. 37, July, 1952, 140, 236-237
11. Somerset County, Certificate of Indenture, Benjamin Harrison, *Indentures and Recognizances*, November 18,1873, Maryland Hall of Records, 94; Herbert Gutman, *The Black Family in Slavery and Freedom, 1750-1925*, (New York: 1976), 402.
12. *Ibid.* Certificate of Indenture, James Edward Gullet, January 2, 1872.
13. James Martin Wright, *The Free Negro in Maryland*, 535.
14. Somerset County, Certificate of Indenture, Charles Smith, *Indentures and Recognizances*, January 27, 1908, Maryland Hall of records, 468.
15. John R. Wennersten and Ruth Ellen Wennersten,"Separate and Unequal: The Evolution of a Black Land Grant College in Maryland, 1890-1930," *Maryland Historical Magazine*, 1977.
16. Quoted in Fuke, "Planters, Apprenticeship, and Forced Labor" from Maryland Hall of Records, US Colored Troops.
17. *Ibid.* 74.
18. George Alfred Townsend, "The Chesapeake Peninsula," *Scribner's Monthly*, III, (March, 1872) ,518; *Report of the Superintendent of Labor and Agriculture to the General Assemblu of Maryland*, (Annapolis: January, 1868),4-5
19. *Proceedings of the Somerset County Commissioners*, June 12, 1866, Maryland Hall of Records; Salisbury Advertiser, October 19, 1872.

20 *Salisbury Advertiser,* April 12,1873
21 Fuke, 40
22 Scott F. Geltner, *Hunting and Fishing in the New South, Black Labor and White Leisure After the Civil War,* (Baltimore: 2008) 2-5.
23 Steven Hahn, *Hunting, Fishing, and Foraging: Common Rights and Class Relations in the Postbellum South, Radical History Review,* 26, 1982, 37-64; See also Nicholas Johnson, *Negroes and the Gun, The Black Tradition of Arms,* (New York: 2014).
24 Silverthorn and Company to Joshua Matthews, June 3, 1882, Lengler MS, Salisbury, Md.; William M Schoolfield to Thomas Sudler, April 24, 1873; Sudler Receipt Book, Thomas Sudler MS, Maryland Historical Society.
25 Charles A. Clark, Eastern Shore of Maryland and Virginia, II, (New York: 1950). 589-590. "Hampden Polk Dashiell," *Portrait and Biographical Record of the Eastern Shore of Maryland,* (New York: 1889), 654-655.
26 Lamont W. Harvey, "Black Oystermen of the Bay Country," *Weather Guage,* Spring 1994, pp4-13 Vol. 30.; John R. Wennersten, *The Oyster Wars of Chesapeake Bay,* (Centreville, Md.), 1981.
27 "Schooner Brave Tragedy, Execution of Four Colored Men at Princess Anne," *Baltimore Sun,* March 6, 1869.
28 Frank Towers, "Job Busting At Baltimore Shipyards: Racial Violence in the Civil War Era South," *Journal of Southern History,* vo. 66, May, 2000.
29 Certificate of Incorporation, Wesley Colored Church, April 5, 1866, Somerset County Land Records, Princess Anne, LWB,652-653; Robert Todd, *Methodism of the Peninsula,* (Buffalo:1870), 316
30 **Debates of the Constitutional Convention of 1864,** II (Annapolis: 1864), 1234; W.A. Low, "The Freedmen's Bureau in the Border States," in Richard O. Curry, ed., *Radicalism, Racism, and Party Realignment in Border States During Reconstruction,* (Baltimore: 1969), 249.
31 Richard Paul Fuke, "The Baltimore Association for the Moral and Educational Improvement of the Colored People, 1864-1870, *Maryland Historical Magazine,* (Winter 1971) Vol. 66, 386.
32 *Proceedings of the Somerset School Commissioners,* January 24, 1872 and March 9, 1880. Maryland Hall of Records. Frank William Delaney, "Negro Education in Maryland, 1865-1870," University of Maryland, 1969, 91Unpublished Master's Thesis, University of Maryland 1969.

Chapter Four

Part Arcadia, Part Wolf Pit

"The South is brutalized to a degree not realized by its own inhabitants."
Ida B. Wells

National Overview

The northern abandonment of southern Blacks and a willingness to forget many of the positive accomplishments of the Civil War and Reconstruction constitutes a major theme of national development well into the twentieth century. After the war Republicans in Congress through passage of the 14th and 15th Amendments to the Constitution sought to impose liberal Black and White political regimes in the former rebel states. Many Blacks had important roles in elective office and used their power to build schools, protect civil rights and resurrect the South's shattered economy. In response terrorist organizations like the Ku Klux Klan emerged in the South to intimidate Blacks and force them out of politics. During the contested presidential election of 1876, Rutherford B. Hayes and his Republican allies promised that if Hayes were elected, federal troops would be withdrawn from the South and Reconstruction, in effect, nullified. The North would no longer interfere in southern elections to protect Blacks and that southern Whites would again take control of their state governments. From 1877 onward the South became known as a vacation land for nostalgic Americans rather than a hostile region of racial segregation and lynch law. The passage of the Morrill Land Grant Act of 1890 was the one major bright spot for Black advancement in the Jim Crow South. Under this legislation Congress established a network of Black agricultural schools in the South which, while often underfunded, allowed Blacks to study farming, learn a trade or become a teacher.

I

Nostalgia

During the 1870s a number of businessmen and journalists visited the Eastern Shore to assess the potential of the region. Perhaps the most perceptive of those visitors was Howard Pyle who wrote for *Harper's New Monthly Magazine.* Pyle found the region to be stuck in "a Rip Van Winkle Sleep." It was a place where modernity remained unclaimed – "sleepily floating on the indolent sea of the past, incapable of crossing the gulf which separates it from outside modern life." Pyle deplored the legacy of a woefully ignorant "poor White class and an unproductive upper class." Pyle, however, was struck by the region's rich natural beauty that seemed at times to counterpoint ways in which people hung on to the legacy of antebellum slavery. Concluded Pyle, the region was "part Arcadia, part wolf pit."[1]

By 1877 steamboats began to call at the smaller docks and ports along Chesapeake Bay filled with tourists and "day-trippers" on excursions to beaches and picnic grounds. The Oxford Inn in Talbot County and the Washington Hotel Inn in Somerset County became popular tourist destinations. At the Washington Hotel Inn visitors could still see the scrapes on the fireplace where planters in slavery days warmed their boots in winter and the double staircase that allowed women their own private passage in hooped skirts down to the dining room. It was a chance to savor the days of the rich planters and their "darkies" at "the old home place" and find temporary relief from the frenetic pace of emerging cities like Baltimore and Philadelphia.

Magazines like *Lippincott's* and *Century Magazine* cultivated this new wave of nostalgia for an older way of life with its plantations and ancestral families. Rich families from New York City and Wilmington quietly bought up old estates from families on the Eastern Shore that could no longer maintain them. Perhaps the most illustrious of these was the purchase in 1938 of the Clifton estate in Somerset at Revell's Neck by Mary Carpenter, the wife of Walter S. Carpenter, the President of the DuPont Corporation. Located on 68 acres on the water with a private beach on the banks of the Manokin River, outbuildings and servant quarters, the house had seven bedrooms and a dining room that sat twenty guests.

Those less wealthy than the Carpenters could revel in the nostalgia of the Bay by reading Paul Wilstach's *Tidewater Maryland* which explained the region's history and traditions.[2] Wilstach's work was highly popular in the 1920s and 1930s and helped to make the Eastern Shore of Maryland a desirable playground for rich businessmen, baseball team owners, and Hollywood actors. The fact that Wilstach also managed New York actors on Broadway may have had a bearing on this. What visitors failed to see, however, was a remarkable development in the area of Black higher education in Somerset.

II
The Travail of Princess Anne Academy

The establishment of Princess Anne Academy, a small college "for the instruction of persons of African descent in agriculture, mechanic and liberal arts and their application in the industries of life" in the late nineteenth century was a direct result of segregated public education on the Eastern Shore. Princess Anne Academy was located a short distance from town on the grounds of an old plantation known as Olney once owned by the Dennis family. From its inception the school was plagued by a chronic lack of funds and community hostility. Today the University of Maryland, Eastern Shore traces its heritage back to those uncertain times experienced by the Black school.[3]

Originally founded as a Methodist Institution by the Centenary Bible Institute of Baltimore and the Delaware Conference Academy, the school had become a state and federally supported land grant school after the Morrill Act of 1890.[4] John A. Wilson, a White Methodist preacher originally bought the land in 1886 and turned it over to his Black friend, Reverend John R. Waters for schooling purposes. The White community of Princess Anne was outraged when it learned what Wilson had done to the old plantation. Local Whites believed "that the only education a Negro needs is how to find the back end of a mule."

In 1890 the school had 16 acres, a few rough buildings, three teachers and 37 students. Though state-controlled, the school continued to maintain its Methodist orientation. The principals of the academy were strong-willed Black Methodist preachers who made religious life an integral part of the institution. Churchgoing was an established practice for students and faculty alike. By 1897 the school consisted of six faculty, 93 students and a curriculum that included liberal arts as well as instruction in shoemaking, cooking, tailoring and blacksmithing.[5] This curriculum reflected the "Tuskegee Model" of practical African American education in the South advocated by Booker T. Washington at this time.

Relations between Princess Anne Academy and the local White populace were not cordial. When Louis Morris, a local White physician, deeded additional land to the school, a popular uproar ensued. Afterwards the financial value of school-held land fell precipitously as Whites condemned the school as a blight on their community. John Wilson, a prominent White minister from Wilmington, Delaware, who was actively involved in the school, found himself ostracized by the citizens of Princess Anne. On numerous occasions Wilson had violated local racial etiquette by eating with Blacks and addressing them as "mister." Reverend Wilson was also one of the few Whites in the county who would shake hands with a Black man.[6] Thus in the early years of the school, social practice dictated that Princess Anne Academy be treated as an alien and potentially troublesome institution in the community.

Although there originally may have been hopes among the Black and White Methodist leadership in the Delaware Conference that the economic and educational fortunes of the institution would improve with the conferring of federal land grant status, actual practice proved otherwise. Like other Black land grant schools in the South chartered by the Morrill Land Grant Act of 1890, Princess Anne Academy was sorely neglected by state and federal agencies. In perspective, the 1890 Morrill Land Grant Act created a dual land grant system in the South that would keep Blacks out of the new emerging White state universities chartered under the Morrill Act of 1862.

The term land grant college or university originated from the wording of the first Morrill Act of 1862 which provided for a grant of 30,000 acres of land or its equivalent in script to the states for instruction in agricultural and mechanical arts as well as scientific and classical studies. A brief overview of the development of the 1890 institutions in the South during this time will put the dilemma of Princess Anne Academy in clearer perspective. The second Morrill Act passed by Congress on August 30, 1890, institutionalized then current practices regarding the education of African Americans in agriculture and the mechanic arts. While the law ostensibly forbade appropriations to any college where racial distinctions were a criteria of school admission, it did sanction the establishment of separate institutions for Whites and Blacks. Specifically, the law stated that the 1890 schools were to receive "a just and equitable division" of federal funds and each school would be entitled to the same benefits "as it would have been if it had been included under the act of 1862 . . . . ." This law would be another example of the tragic irony of the separate but equal philosophy of race relations.

The practice of appropriating federal and state funds for Black schools was not new in 1890. Prior to the passage of the second Morrill Act, many southern legislatures had Black elected officials who had influenced their states to interpret the 1862 land grant law to include Black schools. In the 1870's the legislatures of Mississippi, South Carolina, Virginia and Kentucky gave a fixed percentage of their 1862 funds to Black schools.[7] The 1890 law merely codified the practice for the entire South. State legislatures in the region selected seventeen Black schools as recipients of federal funds. Among those were: Delaware State College, Princess Anne Academy, Kentucky State College, West Virginia State College, Virginia State College, North Carolina A&T University, Arkansas State College at Pine Bluff, South Carolina State College, Southern University of Louisiana, Prairie View A&M College, Lincoln University, Tennessee State College, and Langston University.

Maryland negotiated with the Delaware Methodist Conference and Maryland Agricultural College (the 1862 institution) to have Princess Anne Academy designated a state supported school for Blacks in agriculture and general education. The legislature gave oversight of Princess Anne Academy to Morgan College in Baltimore and appropriated $3,000 for the salaries of a superintendant, two instructors and equipment.[8]

Despite the rhetoric of the 1890 law, the Black land grant schools would not enjoy the same financial largesse from the public purse as the 1862 schools. According to Dwight Holmes, the 1890 schools suffered severe discrimination in funding. As late as 1928 West Virginia State University (hardly a well-funded White 1862 school) received $1,419,732, which was slightly more than the total received by ALL the 1890 schools in the South combined. ($1,379, 484 for the 17 Black land grant schools).[9] Other White 1862 schools received as much on an individual basis.

Throughout the decade of the 1890s the funding of Maryland Agricultural College in College Park increased significantly while that of Princess Anne remained static.[10] By 1900 the Academy could have received $25,000 annually in state and federal funds, an admittedly small amount. It received less than this sum, however, due to the fact that funding was based on the number of Black farmers in Maryland. With only 6,000 Black farmers compared to 36,000 White farmers in the state during this period, Princess Anne Academy seldom received more than 39 percent of its allotted appropriation.[11]

The period 1890-1917 was one of great uncertainty for Black land grant institutions in the South. They had to struggle against both illiteracy and inferior public school training of youths in the Black community as well as compete with private and better-established "Reconstruction Colleges" that had been founded by White Protestant church organizations after the Civil War. Although the heads of the 1890 schools were reluctant to admit it, private Black colleges provided the main thrust of Black higher education in this era.[12] Unlike their 1862 Land Grant counterparts, the Black land grant colleges had to start from zero, materially and educationally. Additionally, the 1890 schools like Princess Anne Academy were expected to be multi-purpose institutions on meager funds and limited resources. Princess Anne Academy, for example, was supposed to train schoolteachers, provide instruction in agriculture and offer a liberal arts curriculum.

During this time the Black illiteracy rate in Maryland was high, especially in the rural areas. In 1910 over twenty-three percent of the Black population over the age of ten was illiterate. Throughout the 1920s the statewide illiteracy rate in this category remained at eighteen percent.[13] As there were few Black high schools in the state other than in Baltimore, Princess Anne Academy out of necessity had to provide students the important basic instruction in reading, writing and mathematics. Federal money and some support from the Freedmen's Aid Society of the Methodist Episcopal Church kept Princess Anne Academy alive but did not allow it to fulfill is land grant mission.

The Phelps-Stokes Fund Survey of Negro Education, led by the famous educator Thomas Jesse Jones, described Princess Anne Academy in 1916 as "a small well-managed school of secondary grade with a few pupils in elementary classes. Effort is made to adopt the work to the minds of rural schoolteachers. Manual training and agriculture, though well taught, are subordinated to literary studies." Jones was surprised to find the inclusion of Latin in the general curriculum.[14] Jones, a Welsh immigrant, taught at Hampton Institute, an African American college for several years before becoming a researcher in educational statistics on Black schools. This probably reflected the views of principals at the Academy like Frank Trigg and Thomas Kiah, that while industrial and agricultural training would help students survive hard times, a literary education was also desirable.

The state of Maryland declined to establish an agricultural experiment station at the Academy, which squeezed out Black students from the field of research and extension work dealing with livestock and crop maximization. Dr. John W. Davis, the celebrated Black defender of the 1890 schools, found that with Black people comprising 18.5 percent of the farm population in the state. Princess Anne Academy should have received $69,000 for extension work alone. It received, however, only $10,000 to cover extension, endowment and instruction.[15]

On the state level, many legislators in Annapolis thought Princess Anne Academy hopelessly backward, even though by the 1920s the school was turning out a much needed cadre of Black school teachers and artisans. Its dairy farm was well equipped and maintained and a source of profit for the Academy. In response to community reluctance for having Black faculty live in town, teachers and students in industrial arts built faculty dwellings on campus. Students performed all janitorial work and visitors found the campus in good condition.[16] By the early 1930s two separate viewpoints seem to prevail about Princess Anne Academy. White officials in the state viewed the college as largely a failing enterprise while Blacks were becoming increasingly aware of the great educational advantages the school offered Black people. Princess Anne Academy came into existence during a critical period in the county's racial history. The social and educational life of Somerset reflected the prevailing segregationist doctrine of "separate but equal" as enunciated by the Supreme Court in *Plessy v Ferguson* (1896). Black education, especially, was molded by Somerset's racial policies. Yet, despite the harsh environment of Jim Crow, Somerset's Black community survived largely around the twin bastions of the Metropolitan Methodist Church (situated on an old slave auction block) and Princess Anne Academy. Black teachers continued their fight against illiteracy and Princess Anne Academy trained young African Americans in agriculture and the industrial arts.

III
Race and Politics

Journalists often described the region as a "wood economy," referring to the flourishing lumber industry in the region that was deforesting Somerset and other counties. The nation needed wood for its pulpwood industry, lumber and wooden barrels for packaging oysters and crates to ship record harvests of white and sweet potatoes. Black laborers found jobs in the burgeoning lumber industry as lumberjacks. Others found jobs as farm laborers and tenant farmers. Given the price of investment capital in the area, few Blacks wanted to take on indebtedness to buy a farm.

Although law and social custom placed the Negro in a subordinate position, the Black community was politically active, property conscious and oriented towards educational advancement. White politicians appealed to the newly enfranchised freedmen for votes and without Black support the existence of the Republican Party in the county would not have been possible. As we have already seen, Blacks were involved in numerous Chesapeake Bay occupations in the oyster and steamboat industries. According to the Census of 1880, Somerset had a large class of independent Black artisans who worked mostly as shoemakers, carpenters and blacksmiths.[17] Somerset Blacks were well aware of class differences in matters of racial prejudice and enjoyed the protection of the gentry from hostile poor Whites.

During the period 1888-1917, however, race relations in the county deteriorated. This change may be attributed to a falling off in the local agricultural economy. In addition to competition from midwestern farms, Texas, Louisiana and North Carolina began to severely undercut the price of white and sweet potatoes and reduced Somerset's profit margins. When local Black workers threatened to boycott White farmers who wanted to introduce European immigrant labor on their land, local demagogues and a new generation of self-made men scapegoated the Negro for the ebbing of Somerset's economic fortunes. They seized upon the Black quest for equality as an excuse for violence.

In many respects Somerset County in these years was a microcosm of race relations in the American South. Somerset, similar to its southern counterparts, would experience the tragedy of lynchings as well as other forms of racial subordination and see justice pale before rigid segregation. Local Democrats would lead a movement to disenfranchise the Negro and many of Somerset's most talented Blacks would "leave all that behind" for lucrative employment in the shipyards of Chester and Philadelphia.[18] The "separate and unequal" approach to race relations sanctioned by the U.S. Supreme Court in 1896 in *Plessy v. Ferguson* would have a profound impact on Black life in the county from civil rights to education.

Several developments in the county and beyond in the 1890s worsened the Negro's position. The old gentry that had owned slaves and controlled county life for decades was dying out. The proud Dennis family no longer dominated the county's social life. Hampden Dashiell, the aristocratic chieftain of the local Democratic Party, died in 1895 and John W. Crisfield, the most outstanding member of the old business and slave owning elite, was in retirement. While they ruled, these men viewed themselves as patriarchs responsible for the safety and welfare of Blacks. Their departure from Somerset's political and social life left a serious leadership vacuum that would be filled by the sons of the old guard who did not share their fathers' paternalistic outlook on racial questions. The newly affluent businessmen were often grasping and short-sighted. The shock waves of the nationwide economic panic of 1893 reverberated throughout Maryland's Eastern Shore and a poor corn crop in the following year hurt many local farmers. Most important, the decreased demand in Europe for American wheat forced Somerset farmers to compete in an already tight national grain market that was dominated by the giant farms of Kansas and Iowa. With county farms only averaging seventy acres at this time, local agriculture was severely depressed and increasingly Somerset farmers irrationally blamed Blacks for their economic woes. In state politics the problems of urbanization and industrialization commanded the energies of legislators and agricultural regions like the Eastern Shore were left to their own devices. As Republicans equated the political control of Baltimore with the survival of the Party, they deemphasized their support of the Blacks in the rural counties.[19]

The Republican Party's change of emphasis was keenly felt in Somerset County and a short sketch of local politics is illustrative of the emerging racism in the state at this time. From 1870 to 1885 Blacks comprised the strongest voting bloc in the local Republican organization. Blacks consistently voted for Abraham Lincoln Dryden, a prominent White Republican, and sent him to the state legislature for several terms. The Dryden family commanded a strong Black and White coalition of Republicans in Fairmount. Active in the crab and oyster business, the Drydens had extensive commercial dealings with Black watermen. Dryden's father, Littleton T. Dryden, served twelve years as a Deputy United States Marshall and United States Commissioner for the Eastern Shore. While in power, the Dryden's resisted attempts to disenfranchise Negroes and made sure that Blacks received occasional patronage appointments in the Baltimore Customs House. In 1894, Lincoln Dryden ran for Congress against Joshua Miles, a conservative Democrat, and was defeated. Most likely, Dryden's defeat resulted from a schism within the local Republican Party. Many White Republicans disliked working with Blacks and looked for leadership from men like Edward F. Duer, a local merchant.

A conservative pro-segregation Republican, Duer received a patronage appointment from President Chester A. Arthur and held a $950 a-year job as the Postmaster of Princess Anne. Eager to advance his political fortunes, Duer sought to have his party reflect the anti-Black sector of the state Republican organization.[20]

Somerset Blacks were angered by the Republican de-emphasis of civil rights and switched their allegiance to the Democrats. In 1885, the Democratic Party soundly defeated the Republicans in county elections and the *Salisbury Advertiser* reported that the victory was due to "the great inroads, which the Democrats made on the colored vote." Blacks, however, were uncomfortable in the party of the old slaveocracy and in the 1890's formed their own splinter organization, "the Colored Independent Republicans." From Somerset's scattered political records at this time, it appears that the local Republican Party had set its Black supporters adrift.[21]

Given Somerset's emotional and vindictive level on matters concerning Black people, it was easy for Democratic politicians to capitalize on racism as a vote-getting device. Although Robert Brattan and Henry Page, two prominent Princess Anne Democrats, tried to curb racism in their own party, they were forced to capitulate to men like Lorie C. Quinn, a feisty Crisfield newspaper editor, who used the race issue to challenge the domination of the Democratic Party by Princess Anne politicians. During his brief career in the Maryland House of Delegates and afterwards in county politics, Quinn championed the cause of White supremacy and racial segregation. In 1904, Quinn sponsored a bill to require railroad companies on the Eastern Shore to provide separate cars or coaches for Whites and Blacks "without any difference or discrimination in quality of, or convenience, or accommodation in such cars and coaches." A similar bill for steamboats also had his sponsorship and both measures passed the legislature in the spring of that year.[22]

The emergence of these "Jim Crow laws" for the transportation system of the Chesapeake was in keeping with statewide attempts to restrict Black freedom. After returning to power in 1900, the state Democratic Party launched a powerful movement to abolish Black suffrage in Maryland and for several years Negro disenfranchisement was a critical issue in state and local politics. Although attempts to use a literacy test to deny the ballot to Blacks in Somerset met with failure, racism did have serious consequences in the county. It polluted the local political atmosphere by making race the central issue to the exclusion of others and resulted in a more intensified racial segregation. Local beaches and picnic areas in Somerset became segregated and county authorities negotiated with Wicomico County to allow Somerset Blacks to use Tony Tank's "colored picnic grounds." Each Sunday during summer, Somerset Blacks travelled the "Jim Crow special," an inexpensive 25-mile round trip railroad excursion from Princess Anne to Tony Tank, a large pond formed by the Wicomico River.[23]

Political racism also had a noticeable impact on Somerset's public schools. After 1890 the county became increasingly parsimonious with school funds and Black schools were frequently closed so that White schools could remain open. In 1909 thirty-five Black schoolteachers, performing under adverse circumstances, were charged with educating 1,188 Negro students in schools that were nothing more than one room shacks. In that same year the county spent $391 for books for Black schools and $5,369 for books for its White schools. As the schools were separate and unequal, so too were teachers' salaries. In 1917, for example, White teachers received an annual salary of $400 from the county while Black teachers received an average of only $182.[24]

No one expected things to change much when the Great Depression of the 1930s descended upon the Eastern Shore with its attendant economic misery. A great fear pervaded the region. It would be the hour of the wolf, when men of violence acted upon their most sordid impulses and judges and sheriffs uttered platitudes about the sins of anti-Black rioting and lynching and then went home to their chicken suppers.

1. Shot of Princess Anne Academy 1890s

2. Graduating Class Princess Anne Academy

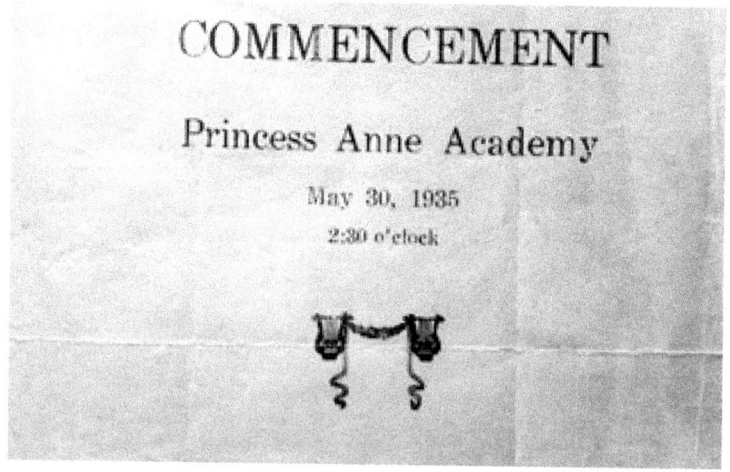

3. Commencement Brochure Princess Anne Academy

Notes

1. Howard Pyle, "Peninsular Cannan," *Harper's New Monthly Magazine*, May, 1879, pp.801-817.
2. Robert Wilson, On The Eastern Shore, *Lippincott's Magazine*, vol. 18, 1875, 73-80; J.W. Palmer, "By the Waters of the Chesapeake," *Century Magazine*, vol. 25, December 1893; Paul Wilstach, *Tidewater Maryland, Its History, its Traditions, its Romantic Plantations, Mansions, and the Celebrated Personages who gave it glamour*, Cambridge, Maryland, 1931.
3. John R. and Ruth Ellen Wennersten, "Separate and Unequal: The Evolution of a Black Land Grant College in Maryland, 1890-1930," *Maryland Historical Magazine*, vol. 72, Spring, 1977.
4. *Princess Anne Academy Charter*, December 31, 1890, Ambrose Caliver, *Education of Negro Teachers*, Washington: U.S. Office of Education, 1933, Jay S. Stowell, *Methodist Adventures in Negro Education*, New York: 1922.
5. W.A. Low, "The Establishment of Maryland State College," in *The Eastern Shore of Maryland and Virginia*, Charles B. Clark ed., 2 vols. (New York, 1950, Vol 2., 752.
6. *Ibid.* 749.
7. Dwight Oliver Wendell Holmes, *The Evolution of the Negro College*, New York, 1968, 151.
8. Op. cit. *Princess Anne Academy Charter*.
9. Holmes, *The Evolution of the Negro College*, 155.
10. George H. Callcott, *A History of the University of Maryland*, Baltimore, 1966, 228-238.
11. John W. Davis, "The Negro Land Grant College," *The Journal of Negro Education*, vo. 2, July, 1933, 25.
12. Rufus B. Atwood, "Origin and Development of the Negro Public College with Special Reference to the Land Grant College," *Journal of Negro Education*, 31, Summer ,1966.
13. Davis, "The Negro Land Grant College."
14. Thomas Jesse Jones, et. al. *Negro Education: A Survey of the Private and Higher Schools for Colored People in the United States*, U.S. Bureau of Education Bulletin, No. 39, Washington, 1916.
15. Davis, *The Negro Land Grant College*, 29.
16. United States Bureau of Education, *Survey of Negro Colleges and Universities*, Bulletin No. 7, Washingto, 1928, 170.
17. *United States Census of 1880*, Schedule 1, Somerset County, Maryland.
18. Interview with Mr. Stanley McCready, July 15, 1976.
19. Margaret Callcott, *The Negro In Maryland Politics*, (Baltimore: 1969), 102.

20 "Abraham Lincoln Dryden," *Portrait and Biographical Record of the Eastern Shore of Maryland*, (New York: 1898), 533; *Salisbury Advertiser*, April 27, 1889
21 *Salisbury Advertiser*, September 11, 1897
22 *Journal of the Proceedings of the Maryland House of Delegates*, March 1904; *Journal of the Proceedings of the Maryland Senate*, January 21, 1904. 110.
23 *Marylander and Herald*, August 17, 1915.
24 *Annual Report of the State Board of Education*, Baltimore 1909, 341-345; *Annual Report of the State Board of Education*, Baltimore 1917, 314-315.

Chapter Five

Strange Fruit

*"Southern trees bearing strange fruit
Blood on the Leaves and blood at the roots
Black bodies swinging in the southern breeze
Strange fruit hanging from the poplar trees."*
Lyrics by Abel Meeropol. Sung by Billie Holiday, 1939

National Overview

The problems of the Great Depression affected virtually every group of Americans. No group was harder hit than African Americans, however. By 1932, approximately half of African Americans were out of work. In some Northern cities, whites called for African Americans to be fired from any jobs as long as there were whites out of work. Young black men, when they could find work in the south, often worked for fifteen cents a day when a loaf of bread cost nine cents. It was easy during the Depression years of the 1930s to make the African American a scapegoat for hard times. Much of the South, including Maryland's Eastern shore had a belated frontier environment where men often took the law into their own hands, Central to southern beliefs at this time was that Whites had unlimited rights to persecute and even murder black criminals. Racists believed that unless a Black man was lynched now and then White women living on isolated farms would be in danger As the Depression lengthened, racial lynchings in the South which had declined to eight in 1932, surged to 28 in 1933 and sparked national protest by churches and civil rights organizations against racial violence. The hate and bitterness that to a great extent had characterized race relations in the South since Emancipation remained a festering wound that would trouble a post-war generation of Americans seeking to resolve the problems of racial segregation and prejudice in the 1960s.

On October 29, 1929, corporate financial reports indicated that the sluggish American agricultural and industrial economy was incapable of sustaining national growth. A record thirteen million shares were sold on the New York Stock Exchange as Wall Street speculators and investors rushed to divest themselves of deflating securities. Wall Street collapsed when corporate financial reports indicated that the sluggish agricultural and industrial economy was incapable of sustaining continued national growth. The Wall Street crash left Somerset County stunned. How could the stock market collapse despite the speculators, asked Somerset? Was not the economy sound? Could not hard work and "Americanism" end the crisis? These questions, unfortunately, were more easily asked than answered.

Shortly thereafter, Somerset's agricultural and seafood economy began to founder. Despite the attempts of local and state authorities to help residents, hundreds were unemployed or worked at low wages. Families were destitute. Desperate men vented their frustrations in acts of racial violence. Adversity often brings out both the best and the worst in people and Somerset's response to hard times sheds light on how many communities experienced the ordeal of the Great Depression.

As the shock waves of the national financial collapse reverberated throughout the county, Somerset authorities took the position that responsibility for relief for the unemployed rested with local charitable organizations. Government relief, they argued would weaken the moral character of the people. Those in need could work for their bread at the Alms House farm. Many Somerset residents believed that the rich and powerful of the nation had been in a conspiracy to manipulate the government against working people. This translated into local hostility against all programs which they believed would only help millionaires.

At this time Somerset's relations with Annapolis were stormy. Albert C. Ritchie, the Governor of Maryland, was widely disliked for his arbitrary manner and insensitivity to the people of the Eastern Shore. Ritchie, they complained, was too allied with the growing urban ethnic wing of the Democratic Party and ignored political leaders from the Eastern Shore. Ritchie also antagonized "dry" forces in the county because of his political position favoring the repeal of Prohibition and his efforts to increase the size of the Baltimore delegation in the state legislature. Further, after the crash Ritchie advocated a luxury tax on the sale of cigarettes, cigars, soft drinks, and chewing gum that infuriated the Eastern Shore. Thus at the outset of the Depression, Somerset considered Governor Ritchie an enemy and residents were not eager to have Annapolis support local relief measures. Somerset struggled to remain solvent until 1931 when a long summer drought ruined local crops. By then most banks in the county had failed as well. Later in 1932 President Franklin Roosevelt gave banks opportunity to reorganize and build up reserves. After reopening, several banks cautiously limited withdrawals to $25; and large depositors could withdraw up to two percent of their account. In a lengthy editorial in the *Marylander and Herald* of Princess Anne, James Byrd urged the people to keep their faith in local banks and not draw out their money. "What we lack is CONFIDENCE," Byrd argued. "Remember all that this nation ever had, she now has – except confidence."[1] Yet by 1933 there was neither confidence nor prosperity in Somerset County. Angry citizens demonstrated before the County Commissioners for a moratorium on property taxes and demanded salary cuts for all public officials. The Commissioners, in response, slashed the county budget and demanded salary cuts for all public officials. People stopped paying their school taxes and teachers went without salaries. Somerset's 1,500 farmers were hard hit by declining commodity prices and nearly every farm had three mortgages. The wholesale collapse in truck crops prompted local farmers to plow up their strawberry crop while others left their fruit unharvested on the vine. Black watermen had great difficulty getting twenty-five cents a bushel for their oysters. One irate White waterman remarked that it was "more profitable to have the Chesapeake product at the bottom of the Bay." Many of Somerset's poor Whites toiled in the forests cutting firewood for sixty cents a day, recalled Somerset resident L.Q. Powell. "We were glad to get the work." Unemployed men dug drainage ditches for farmers, the most exhausting kind of physical labor in the county, at seven and one half cents an hour. As the Depression lengthened many residents hung on with a daily diet of corn bread and a thirty-five cent bushel of sweet potatoes, which could sustain a family for a week. The people also subsisted on white beans and fatback.

The situation for Blacks was even more desperate. Wages for Negroes in local sawmills fell to twenty-five cents a day and there was strong local prejudice against giving Blacks relief of any kind. Hundreds of Blacks stood idle on the street corners in Crisfield and caused great uneasiness among the White seafood packers who owned most of the town. Those few Blacks that received flour from the Crisfield Red Cross had to do domestic service in White families to pay for it. The widespread unemployment of both Whites and Blacks caused great tension in the county and a Baltimore relief worker who visited Princess Anne worried that "we have four or five hundred restless men right here . . . . that have got to be put to work – soon!"[2]

On August 19, 1933, a furious rainstorm lashed the county. After four days of pelting rains, the sky suddenly turned black and a hurricane came howling across Chesapeake Bay. Tides rose sharply, people evacuated their homes as the Chesapeake began to flood the lowlands of the county and make roads impassable. Finally late that night the winds receded and Somerset residents struggled to get home. Boats had drifted on to the roads, trees had fallen everywhere and the air reeked with the stench of dead livestock.[3] Princess Anne lost all telephone communication and the Pennsylvania Railroad cancelled all service in the county.

Governor Albert C. Ritchie, no friend of Somerset, preoccupied himself with protecting the state's credit while the stress of the unemployed in the county grew acute.

Armwood

In desperate times reason often gives way to the passions of the mob and less than six weeks after the hurricane, a wave of racial violence swept the community with gale-like force. The lynching of a young Black man named George Armwood would leave a legacy of racial bitterness in the county and embroil the entire Eastern Shore in a political war with Governor Ritchie.

Race relations in Somerset since slavery days were paradoxical. On the one hand, Black workers were essential to the county's economic welfare; on the other, Whites viewed Blacks as a disturbing and unwelcome presence in the community. Occasionally the tensions fostered by this peculiar relationship erupted in violence. Even during the prosperous 1920s, Whites murdered Blacks on the pretext of upholding law and order and the virtue of White women. Vera Fulton, a visitor to the county during the Depression summed up the matter bluntly when she wrote that during hard times there is no issue in the county but "racial hatred." When bread is scarce, she claimed, "lynchings provide highly satisfactory circuses." The historical social isolation from the rest of the state had given the region a belated frontier environment where men often took the law into their own hands. In 1907, for example, James Reed a Black man, allegedly shot and killed Crisfield Police Chief John Daugherty. Reed was captured while fleeing town. He was beaten to death and hung from a telegraph pole. Later his body was exhumed from his grave and an angry crowd filled the corpse with bullets before throwing it on to a bonfire. In keeping with the lynching tradition of Somerset and other southern communities, there existed a body of public opinion that defended mob violence as the only way to punish guilty criminals. Thus, to a great extent, popular opinion hampered criminal investigation of racial violence and frustrated hopes for justice in cases involving Blacks. Lynchings have been recorded in 18 of Maryland's 24 counties.

Between 1889 and 1930, 3,724 people were lynched in the South; over four fifths of these were Blacks. In practically every case no determined effort for the conviction of the lynchers was made in the community where the lynching occurred. The Depression merely intensified the lynching mania in the south and during the period 1929-1932 forty-five Blacks were murdered. Racial violence spread easily from one community to another. During these times the latent fears of the Black man's sexuality usually surfaced as Whites were driven into a frenzy at the thought of a Negro engaged in sexual intercourse with a White woman. Central to southern racial beliefs at this time was the assumption that Whites had unlimited rights to persecute and occasionally murder Black criminals. For the most part, lynchings in the South provided people an emotional escape from the economically dreary and unilluminated life of isolated rural communities. One baffling aspect of southern lynchings, wrote Arthur F. Raper in his classic study, *The Tragedy of Southern Lynchings*, was that the mob was seldom content with the death of the victim. The mobsters often tortured, mutilated, and burned their victims. "One is forced to the conclusion," Raper asserted, "that their deeper motivation is not for the just punishment of the accused as for an opportunity to participate in protracted brutalities."[4]

In December 1931, the alleged murder of Daniel J. Elliott, a Salisbury lumber merchant, by Matt Williams, a Black former employee, raised a storm of popular indignation in Wicomico County. Although Williams was speedily apprehended by the police and rushed to Peninsula Local Hospital for "self-inflicted wounds," local demagogues screamed for vengeance. Shortly thereafter a mob dragged Williams from his hospital bed and lynched him from a tree on the courthouse lawn. A mobster severed his toes with a knife for a souvenir. His body was subsequently carried to Salisbury's Black neighborhood, saturated with gasoline and burned.[5]

The Williams lynching prompted a national protest as civil liberties groups, civil rights organizations, and churchmen publicized the murder and demanded the apprehension of his killers. Broadus Mitchell, a professor of Political Economy at Johns Hopkins University who investigated the lynching for the American Federation of Churches, urged federal intervention as the only means of protecting the civil rights of Blacks on Maryland's Eastern Shore. The famous journalist, H.L. Mencken, in his column in the *Baltimore Sun* attacked the lower Eastern Shore as a depraved civilization "wherein there are no competent police, little save a simian self-seeking in public office, no apparent intelligence on the bench, and no courage and decency in the local press," Characterizing the shore as an Alsatia of Morons," the combative journalist argued that Williams' lynching was the result of social degeneration that had allowed "ninth-rate men" to come to power. "The gallant Wicomiconians, having butchered a wounded and helpless Black man," Mencken concluded, "seem very likely to get away with it."[6]

The Eastern Shore wasted little time retaliating against Mencken and the *Baltimore Sun*. In one day Salisbury merchants cancelled $150,000 worth of business from Baltimore firms that advertised in that newspaper. Farmers tore up their subscriptions and drivers of Sun news trucks were molested. Salisbury spent so much time denouncing Mencken that Wicomico County delayed bringing the accused lynchers to trial. In the end, a local grand jury found no one guilty of Williams' murder.[7]

A similar crime occurred that year in Worcester County. Green Davis, a White truck gardener with a small farm near Ocean City, his wife and children were murdered in their sleep and Euel Lee, a Negro who was known to have quarreled with Davis over wages, was arrested and charged with the crime. Lee was a sixty-year old wino with a long arrest record in Pennsylvania. Intimidated by the police, Lee promptly confessed that "the Devil and Whiskey" made him do it. After being taken to the Snow Hill jail, Lee was visited by Bernard Ades, a Baltimore attorney representing the International Labor Defense, a socialist organization currently waging an anti-lynching and Black civil rights campaign in the South. Lee quickly changed his plea to innocent and Ades requested a change in venue to Towson outside Baltimore on the western shore. Ades and his associates were attacked by an angry crowd and his car was wrecked. No one in Snow Hill would repair his car and Ades was warned not to return to the Eastern Shore.

The Euel Lee case dragged on for two years because Bernard Ades was able to capitalize on the gross errors made by Maryland judges, which tied up the case in complicated litigation. Also, with the case moved to the Baltimore metropolitan area, the Euel Lee case became a *cause célèbre* for the Socialist Party of Maryland, the NAACP, and the Urban League. Convinced of his innocence, these organizations battled for Lee all the way to the United States Supreme Court. The Court denied Lee's appeal and Governor Ritchie ordered the lower court's verdict of death by hanging to be administered. A last ditch effort to obtain a state pardon for Lee from the Governor failed. In signing Lee's death sentence Governor Ritchie wrote: "I consider the propaganda that he is innocent is without the slightest basis in fact." Ades and Henry Williams, a Black attorney for the Communist Party also defending Lee, charged a frame up and rallies and demonstrations in support of the condemned man were staged all over Baltimore. As popular feelings in the city grew intense, a police guard of sixty state troopers was assigned to protect Governor Ritchie.[8]

The Eastern Shore was outraged by the protracted defense of a guilty Negro criminal by "Communist Jew lawyers." By allowing Lee to be removed to Baltimore, the Eastern Shore had become the object of ridicule and the just punishment of a murderer had been delayed two years. As White men gathered in country stores in the evening across the Eastern Shore, they vowed that that there would be no more Euel Lee cases. The next time they would take matters into their own hands. It was during the dramatic conclusion of the Euel Lee case that the Armwood lynching occurred in Princess Anne.

In late summer, 1933, John Richardson, a White Somerset farmer and George Armwood, a twenty-eight year old Black in his brother's employ, schemed to rob Mrs. Mary Denston. The eighty-two year old White woman was reported to carry large sums of money on her person and often walked alone on the dirt road that connected her home with her daughter's farm. The robbery was to be a simple affair. Armwood would lurk in the woods until Mrs. Denston passed; then he would jump out, grab Mrs. Denston and steal the money. To avoid identification, Arwood was to wear a large woolen cap pulled down over his eyes. After the robbery, Armwood and Richardson would divide the money. As Armwood was slow witted, Richardson rehearsed the plan at some length with him.[9]

On October 16, at 11:00 A.M. Armwood attacked Mrs Denston as she passed a clump of trees near her home. The old woman proved to be more spry than Armwood anticipated and during the scuffle to get the money contained in her bodice, the Negro succeeded in only tearing off her dress before he panicked and fled into the woods. A short time later the half naked and terrified woman was discovered by a State Roads employee who gave her some clothing and notified the sheriff. After calming down, Mrs. Denston identified her attacker, claiming that she would recognize Armwood's face "among a thousand." Armwood's cap, which was found at the scene of the crime, corroborated her testimony.

Rumors of the Denston "rape" quickly spread throughout the county and hysterical farm women gave currency to the wild tale that Armwood had chewed off both of Mrs. Denston's breasts. County Sheriff Luther Dougherty and Lieutenant Ruxton Ridgely of the state police quickly organized a posse of 2,000 men and combed Worcester and Somerset counties for the fugitive. The highway between Salisbury and Princess Anne was also jammed with posse men in cars hunting Armwood. "Armed men," reported the *Baltimore Sun*, stood around stores and filling stations and congregated about policemen whenever they stopped."

Armwood, meanwhile, had fled to the Richardson farm and begged John Richardson and his brother to save him. A small boy, however, spotted Armwood and quickly alerted the police. Within an hour Deputy Sheriff Norman Dryden of Somerset County drove up to the farm with two armed men and arrested the terrified Negro.[10]

Fearing mob violence in Princess Anne, Dryden and his men took Armwood to the jail in Salisbury by way of Snow Hill. At Salisbury, Armwood was turned over to the state police and placed under heavy guard. The men and their prisoner had been in the jail scarcely three minutes before an angry crowd rapidly gathered outside. Wicomico authorities feared that they would be unable to protect Armwood and urged the state police to take him out of the county. As the mob outside the jail grew increasingly unruly, Captain Edwin Johnson of the state police called Governor Ritchie's office and asked for Armwood's removal to Baltimore. Without waiting for clearance from Ritchie, the police rushed their prisoner to Elkton. Finally Ritchie telephoned Johnson and the police transferred Armwood from Cecil County to the Baltimore City jail.[11]

In Princess Anne county law enforcement officials were under considerable pressure to guarantee that the Armwood case would not follow the Euel Lee trial. Both State's Attorney John B. Robins and Judge Robert F. Duer of the First Circuit Court demanded that Armwood be returned for trial in Somerset. At 10:15 p.m. on October 17, Sheriff Luther Dougherty removed Armwood from the Baltimore jail. Later that night a caravan of five police cars escorted the chained prisoner back to Princess Anne. While in Baltimore, Armwood had confessed to the assault and was photographed and fingerprinted. His White accomplice, John Richardson, was charged with being an accessory to the fact and remained in the Baltimore jail.

The caravan arrived in Princess Anne with its weary prisoner at 3:30 A.M. With Armwood secure in the Somerset's jail, State's Attorney Robins told newspaper reporters that his chief wish was "to see justice done as soon as possible." The people of the county were satisfied and would remain satisfied, Robins claimed, "if there was no undue delay in the trial of Armwood." On the afternoon of October 18, Governor Ritchie telephoned Princess Anne and both Robins and Duer assured him that Armwood would be safe in the local jail. Robins predicted trouble only if the state police tried to take him out of the county.[12]

Visitors and curiosity seekers and newspaper reporters thronged Princess Anne. Many came as a result of local radio broadcasts that treated Armwood's incarceration and the mob at the jail as one would advertise a county fair. By four o'clock in the afternoon small groups of men stood on street corners and talked excitedly of the rumor that five hundred shoremen from Accomac County, Virginia were preparing to drive to Princess Anne and lynch Armwood. Captain Johnson later testified the crowd that assembled in front of the jail appeared to be "a friendly gathering." By 7:30 p.m., however, the mood of the crowd turned ugly as men began yelling, "Let's lynch that nigger." As darkness fell, Captain Johnson ordered three police cars in position to focus headlights on the crowd. At 7:45 p.m. men began throwing stones at the police and as the crowd advanced, the police lobbed six canisters of tear gas into the mob and retreated to the front door of the jail. Fearful that the state police would be unable to control the situation, Captain Johnson requested assistance from the local American Legion unit. The Legionnaires, however, informed the police that the laws of their organization forbade their protecting Negroes during riots.[13]

At eight o'clock Judge Duer, accompanied by his friend George W. Jarman, made an impassioned appeal to the mob to let Armwood remain in jail and promised that the grand jury would be convened and the trial would begin promptly. In his appeal Judge Duer said, "I know nearly all of you." Duer's speech annoyed several men in the crowd who resented his aristocratic tone. They yelled out "What about Euel Lee? We ain't going to have no Euel Lee in Somerset County! Yeah and Bernad Ades will defend him. To hell with Ades." After speaking at length to individual members of the crowd, Duer cautioned the men. "Remember, I place you upon your honor. Several men laughingly replied, "All right judge, go home, we'll attend to the matter." After Duer and George Jarmon left the jail to attend a dinner party, a *Baltimore Sun* reporter rushed to telephone Governor Ritchie that the crowd had increased to about 2,000 and was growing more violent. At 8:30 p.m. someone set off the town fire alarm, which further excited the mob.[14]

Soon the crowd began to hurl "an avalanche of bricks and stone at the police." "Captain Johnson was struck in the face with a brick and knocked unconscious. The crowd cursed the state police and warned that they had guns and if the policemen started shooting, they'd shoot back. "That crowd at Princess Anne was sober," a witness reported. "They weren't farm hands in overalls." At nine o'clock a mobsman yelled, "Come on let's get him," and the crowd rushed the jail. Five policemen were beaten to the ground and others were swept away by the fury of townsmen who used a heavy oak battering ram to smash three doors and reach the jail cell of the terrified prisoner. Throughout the intense struggle in front of the jail police did not fire one shot. "It was futile for us to use our arms," Captain Johnson later testified. "We were overwhelmingly outnumbered and we were overpowered." After the jail was forced, Sheriff Dougherty rushed up to the second floor and pleaded with the mob not to take Armwood from his cell. Norman Dryden, the frightened jail warden, turned his keys over to the mob leaders. "There wasn't anything else I could do," he said. "I was just too scared that they were going to get the wrong man."[15]

Armwood put up a desperate resistance in his cell and was only semi-conscious when the mob carried him out of the jail. The mob carried Armwood a short distance before it stopped to figure out what to do with him. One mobsman took a knife and severed an ear from Armwood's head while several others stabbed him in the neck and face. As the mob howled and cheered, a rope was placed around Armwood's neck and twenty men dragged him to death down the gravel street of the main business section. The mob planned to hang Armwood on the courthouse lawn but someone suggested Judge Duer's home and the body was dragged the full length of Main Street to the judge's residence. As there was no suitable tree in Duer's yard, the crowd decided on a tree in the front lawn of a house owned by Mrs. Thomas H. Bock. Flashlights sought out the branches and a ten year-old boy was hoisted up to secure the rope on a sturdy limb. The mob quickly jerked up the body of George Armwood and left it hanging for five minutes. "Here's what we do on the Eastern Shore," the mob cried. The dead Black man was then cut down and the mob dragged Armwood's body to the intersection of Prince William and Main, directly in front of the courthouse, where it was stripped naked, doused with gasoline, and set aflame while the mob howled excitedly. According to William O. Player, a *Sun* reporter who witnessed the lynching, "the rope was measured into five inch lengths and distributed to the mob as souvenirs. A young boy darted about wildly waving a severed ear of the lynch victim. As Armwood's naked body lay in the street, many young White women came to gaze at the charred remains, many on the arms of male escorts." By 11:30 p.m. the streets of Princess Anne were deserted. The shades were drawn at Judge Duer's residence and no one answered the bell. Sheriff Dougherty and States Attorney Robins fled to Crisfield to avoid newspaper reporters.

Right after the lynching, Clarence Mitchell, a reporter for the *Baltimore Afro-American* and other reporters arrived on the scene. Mitchell beheld a ghastly site. Armwood's body still lay smoldering in the street. People eyed Mitchell warily. Later in an interview Mitchell said, "I guess that because I was well-dressed, had a press card and a camera and was with other reporters that we sort of had an immunity. But I was not going to go too far with that. Not with that crowd." Mitchell's boss at the *Afro-American* had given him a loaded pistol for protection. But Mitchell was afraid to have it on his person because he did not know how to use it. And a Black man with a gun in those tense moments might have received a sentence of death. White people who did answer Mitchell's questions about the lynchers' identity claimed that the murderers were "Virginia boys." C.L. Kiah, the Principal of Princess Anne Academy, gave Mitchell supper and a safe bed for the night so that he could leave Princess Anne by train. "That train came once a day and waiting for it to come and take me out of Princess Anne was one of the longest waits in my life."[16]

Around midnight the town garbage truck hauled Armwood's charred remains to a nearby lumberyard where it was left until the next morning. Fearing reprisal from the mob, the town's

Black undertaker refused to take charge of the body. The body was finally removed by Sergeant M.D. Brubaker of the state police and quickly buried by local Blacks. When the *Sun* reporter left Princess Anne the next day, he wrote, "everything was business as usual. There wasn't anything crestfallen about the people you saw on the streets, you'd think that nothing had happened at all."[17]

But something indeed had happened – something violent, grotesque, and evil. The Armwood lynching set off a storm of national protest. Former President Herbert Hoover issued a public denunciation of lynchings in the South and urged Congress to use its authority to curb racial violence in the country. Northern newspapers like the *New York Times* editorialized that the Armwood case would strengthen public awareness of the great injustice done to the Scottsboro Boys and all southern Blacks accused of serious crimes.[18] In New York City, Dr. Samuel M. Calvert, General Secretary of the Federal Council of Churches of Christ, sent a letter to every major newspaper in the country in which he stated that "I have no hesitation in saying that my feelings of utter horror at the atrocious lynching in Princess Anne, expresses the . . . . "Council of Churches as a whole." Calvert asked for a national day of penitence devoted to "removing the blot of lynching from our land." Roger Baldwin, the national president of the American Civil Liberties Union, offered a $1,000 reward for evidence leading to the conviction of any member of the lynch mob. Baldwin also urged the intervention of Homer Cummins, Roosevelt's Attorney General, in the Armwood case.[19]

The Aftermath

Shortly after the murder, Governor Ritchie issued a public statement claiming that "the responsibility for Armwood's being at Princess Anne rests squarely on the shoulders of Judge Duer and State's Attorney Robins." Ritchie stated that he wanted Armwood kept in Baltimore and that Annapolis had done its duty in trying to protect him. In his subsequent 1977 oral interview, Clarence Mitchell, who was present at the scene of the lynching, found Ritchie's argument disingenuous at best. According to Mitchell, Ritchie was very well aware of the Shore's blood lust following the Euel Lee case and the lynching in Salisbury. The Governor could have superimposed his anti-riot power over the local subdivision to keep Armwood in Baltimore. But Albert Ritchie harbored presidential ambitions and did not want to appear in the south to be "soft" on Negro issues.

In New York, Baltimore, and Washington, protesting citizens groups demanded the criminal prosecution of Duer and Robbins. The Socialist Party of Maryland adopted a resolution calling for the impeachment of Governor Ritchie and the trial of Robins and Duer for second-degree manslaughter. Bernard Ades, Euel Lee's attorney, told reporters that racial prejudice was so strong on the Eastern Shore that sending Armwood back to Princess Anne was "like inviting them to lynch him." If Ritchie were sincere in his belief that responsibility lay with Duer and Robins, Ades argued, "Let him order their arrest."

In Annapolis and Baltimore protesting civil rights groups besieged Ritchie's offices and a cordon of state police was ordered to protect the Governor. Looking at the heavily armed state troopers, Charles Trigg, the head of the Baltimore NAACP, complained "there are more police here than you had at Princess Anne to hold back that mob of 5,000." Broadus Mitchell, a distinguished southerner and Johns Hopkins professor, blamed Ritchie for Armwood's death. Taking issue with Ritchie's claims that his powers were weak in this area, Mitchell demanded the removal of Duer and Robins from office. He also condemned the state police for their restraint and added that state troopers seldom showed such equal restraint during labor disorders.[20]

The *Baltimore Sun* was exceptionally vigorous in its denunciation of the lynching, the Eastern Shore and Governor Ritchie. On its editorial page the paper displayed the picture of a dead Black man hanging from a rope. "O Maryland, my Maryland," read the caption. In a lengthy editorial the *Sun* claimed "the original and controlling error was Judge Duer's decision, apparently arrived at with in cooperation with state's attorney Robins to take the Negro back to Princess Anne." Governor Ritchie took too many chances he need not have taken and the state police at a critical moment lost its nerve. When Captain Johnson and his men might have quelled the mob with a single shot, accused the *Sun*, the police "surrendered to blood lust." A day earlier the newspaper had carried an anguished public statement by Judge Duer that corroborated the *Sun's* accusations.

> I received a call from the jail authorities to come down as they were apprehensive of trouble. I met and talked to a crowd of about 200. They did not strike me as being a determined crowd, rather curiosity seekers and I went back still satisfied that there would be no trouble. I was badly mistaken in my judgment and I am deeply grieved that such a thing happened in our county.[21]

Too much trust, the *Sun* claimed, had been placed in Judge Duer. Such was "his excessively amiable opinion of all his neighbors," that he went off to a dinner party after facing the mob. Writing in his column, H.L. Mencken concluded that it was hopeless to expect any positive change on the Eastern Shore. The good people of talent and brains had left and the "riffraff" stayed behind. Anti-lynching legislation, Mencken predicted, would never pass the state legislature. "The only way to clean out the area is to reduce its representation in the legislature and let Baltimore take the lead," he wrote. Thus did the lynchings on the Eastern Shore make Mencken one of the earliest advocates of legislative reapportionment in the state.[22]

The censure of the *Baltimore Sun* was deeply resented in Somerset County. Dr. John J. Bunting, pastor of Immanuel Methodist Episcopal Church in Crisfield, blamed "interlopers" for the trouble. The people of Somerset were "good citizens," proclaimed Bunting and neither the Eastern Shore nor the state were helped by the *Sun's* "inflaming imprecation." According to Sheriff Dougherty, the lynchers were outsiders from Virginia. "I did not see a single man from Somerset County in the bunch," he said. One Somerset woman blamed the lynching on the state police. "If it hadn't been for the state cops," she claimed, "there wouldn't have been any lynching here yesterday." The *Marylander and Herald*, the county newspaper, blamed the lynching on Governor Ritchie's decision to take Armwood to Baltimore. "We honestly believe that had Armwood been lodged in the Somerset County jail that night, without state or local protection, there would have been no lynching. The taking of this man to Baltimore too vividly recalled to the citizens of this section the Euel Lee case ...." *The Salisbury Times,* the largest paper on the Eastern Shore, remained aloof from the controversy. While *Times* editor, Charles J. Truitt could lament in a column that "We're still Lagging In Social Progress," not a single word was uttered by that paper in condemnation of the lynching.[23]

While protest raged in Baltimore over Armwood's murder, Princess Anne prepared to celebrate Founders' Day. Among the floats being prepared for the parade was "a pageant depicting seventy years of Negro progress on the Delmarva Peninsula."

Following the lynching public outrage in Baltimore and western parts of the state was so hot that Governor Ritchie ordered Attorney General Preston Lane to conduct a full-scale investigation of the murder. When reporters asked the Governor if such an investigation would accomplish more than one conducted in Wicomico County after the Matt Williams lynching, Ritchie was non-committal. Lane's only authority was to convoke a Coroner's Jury in Princess Anne to determine how and why Armwood had died. Two days later States Attorney Robins invited Lane to join him in the investigation of the available evidence as a preliminary step to an inquest and grand jury review. On October 25, 1933, the coroner's inquest was held before trial magistrate Edgar Jones and a jury and twenty-one witnesses were summoned.

The courtroom was packed with a jeering crowd and magistrate Jones had to gavel the inquest to order constantly to keep down the hooting and laughter. Throughout the inquest not a single witness was able to identify the lynchers. Sidney Cottman, a Black man who had occupied a cell next to Armwood, looked at the mass of jeering White faces in the room and testified that he had been too frightened at the time to recognize anyone. "I didn't see anyone but a big crowd hollerin," replied Cottman. Pearl Norris, another Black convict, reported that when the mob burst into the jail, he had been "too scared to look." Neither Sheriff Dougherty nor his Deputy, Charles Dryden, could identify anyone. Both men testified that they thought the lynchers were outsiders from Virginia. "I didn't see anyone that I knew," Dougherty claimed.

The coroner's inquest cost the county over $5,000 and there was considerable resentment in the community over how Preston

Lane had "barged in" on a case being handled by local authorities. Many Eastern Shoremen believed that Lane and the Baltimore newspapers were more concerned over "the Negro brute" than they were over "the innocent White woman victim." State's Attorney Robins refused to spend any more money on the case until the grand jury convened. "The investigation so far has not turned up a bit of evidence that implicates anyone in the actual lynching, the overt act," complained Robins. "The only ray of sunshine," claimed the State's Attorney, was that Armwood had confessed to the crime.[24]

In Annapolis Governor Ritchie, worried about his political career, grew impatient for a resolution of the case. In 1931 Maryland had spent several unsuccessful weeks trying to get a grand jury in Salisbury to indict the lynchers of Matt Williams who had been positively identified by the state police and Ritchie and Lane were unwilling to await the convening of a grand jury in Princess Anne. The best strategy, they reasoned, and one often employed in criminal cases was to have the state's attorney use the sworn testimony of the state police who witnessed the Armwood lynching. With these affidavits in hand, the state's attorney could arrest the mobsmen and bring them before a trial magistrate. Only in this way could evidence be introduced against the accused murderers as a matter of public record. Attorney General Lane personally interviewed and accepted affidavits from twenty state troopers who had been guarding Armwood at the Somerset jail and sought to have the following men arrested:[25]

Marby L. Heath of Princess Anne
    He was seen by Judge Duer's car as he made his speech. He was drunk, was in front of the crowd, shoving, yelling and encouraging the crowd, while in front of the jail he was shoving to get on the steps .... He was also seen pulling on the other end of the rope while the Negro was hung.

Irving Adkins of Princess Anne
    He was the leader of the crowd and is the one who yelled 'Let's Go' and led the crowd to the jail .... he was yelling 'Come On, they won't shoot.' It is believed that he is one of the men who had hold of the battering ram at the jail.

William H. Thompson of Princess Anne
   He was in front of the jail, pushing against the police line, yelling to get a pole and had hold of the ram . . . . which crashed the jail door.

Jack "Walloper" Sterling of Crisfield
   Officer Wheeler has known him for some time and positively identified him as pulling on the rope at the hanging.

Shelburn Lester of Salisbury
   Is identified by Officer Bradley before the jail, where he was yelling, going into the police, and in front of the mob. He is supposed to be the man who hit Captain Johnson.

Pete "Big Boy" Smith of Mount Vernon
   Is known as 'Big Boy' Smith. Fights under this name and is registered in the State Athletic Commission under this name . . . . Smith was in front of the crowd. He was later seen at the side of the jail with a brick in his hand, which he refused to drop at the command of Officer Bohler.

   Both Ritchie and Lane hoped this strategy would result in indictments from the grand jury. Since the case was a county matter, there was no chance of securing an indictment in the state except where the murder took place. John Robins was the proper official to investigate the lynching and Governor Ritchie relied upon his cooperation. State's Attorney Robins, however, was not only uncooperative, he used every legal means at his disposal to frustrate the state's attempt to apprehend the lynchers and bring them to trial.[26]
   During the period November 15-20, Preston Lane and Robins engaged in a sharp exchange of letters that detailed each man's legal position. State's Attorney Robins argued that the whole matter should be put before a grand jury. The arrest of the accused lynchers would only inflame local sentiment and Robins doubted that the men would stay in jail for very long. In order to follow the strategy of Lane and Ritchie, Robins complained, the State's Attorney "must necessarily presume that the grand jury will do its duty, and I...refuse to be a party to that." Robins also believed that war-

rants sworn out before a magistrate based on" information and belief" would be void and any person arrested under such warrants could be released under *habeas corpus* proceedings. Robins resented Lane's interference that only arrests could pressure the grand jury into returning indictments of the lynchers. Lane exclaimed: "You have no reason at all for assuming that the grand jury will not measure up to its duty, responsibility, and oath of office," Robins responded that there might be a case of mistaken identity and he did not want to see innocent people "incarcerated in a felon's cage" until a grand jury could determine their case.[27]

In reply Attorney General Lane wrote that the affidavits of the state police were compelling evidence that justified the arrest of several men. "The information that I sent you," answered Lane "is so definite that no magistrate could legally refuse to hold those arrested for the action of the grand jury, and for the same reason the grand jury would not be justified in refusing to return indictments." It was unnecessary, Lane argued, for the State's Attorney to raise the question of mistaken identity, as Robins was a prosecutor and not a defense lawyer. On November 20, State's Attorney Robins informed Preston Lane that he would not arrest the accused lynchers. Robins professed to have no evidence against anyone.

In Annapolis, shortly thereafter, Governor Ritchie and Lane met with Chief Judge Pattison, Judge Bailey, and Judge Duer of the First Judicial Circuit. Lane informed the judges that he had sufficient evidence to arrest from eight to ten individuals as either principals in the second degree or accessories before the fact. Lane doubted that these arrests could be made "without some force as amounts to martial law" in Somerset County. Several state officials at the meeting added that they did not believe that Robins was interested in prosecution. "There would be Hell to pay," Judge Pattison warned if the militia was used. The use of the militia, he believed would cause such resentments that indictments would be impossible. The indictments would be hard enough to get anyway, Pattison said. Judge Duer, sensitive and depressed over Armwood's death, argued that it was important for Lane to become involved in the investigation because he and the other judges were doubtful about Robins.[28]

Governor Ritchie, meanwhile, was under great public pressure to take action against the lynchers. Mail from protest groups all over the country flooded the Governor's office demanding that Armwood's killers be brought to trial. Interracial organizations in Boston, New York, Atlanta, and Washington D.C. called for action. In late October a large demonstration was held in New York City in front of the Black newspaper, *The Liberator*, to denounce the Armwood lynching. Walter White, the head of the NAACP, warned that the lynchings in the south were part of a campaign of terrorism of Negroes "into acceptance of wage differentials and lower economic status." Also, 1934 was an election year and if the Armwood case was not speedily resolved it would harm Governor Ritchie's reelection prospects in Maryland.[29]

On November 20, 1933, Governor Ritchie telephoned Judge Pattison and asked him whether the judges would agree to remove Robins from office. Pattison was surprised by the question and replied that Robins' refusal to follow the Attorney General's advice was no legal cause to remove him from office. Four days later the grand jury convened in Princess Anne to investigate Armwood's death. Although by now Robins had received all the state police affidavits as well as a list of nine participants in the lynching, he refused to order any arrests. Robins was under intense community pressure. In a long letter to Attorney General Lane, Robins warned that any attempt to arrest the accused lynchers on the Eastern Shore would result in riots. As State's Attorney, Robins accused Lane of attempting to deny Somerset's right to self-government by forcing the county to arrest men on evidence that lacked "authenticity."[30]

On November 27, Governor Ritchie conferred at length with General Milton Record, commander of the Maryland National Guard, and Preston Lane about the governor's emergency powers under the state constitution. After a long thoughtful silence, Ritchie turned to the two men and informed them that he had decided to send armed troops to the Eastern Shore to arrest the lynchers. The state constitution, Ritchie claimed, gave the governor power to use the National Guard to quell riots and enforce the law. As Robins had refused to arrest the lynchers, the state would now act with military force. In the early hours of November 28, three hundred soldiers left Camp Meade in buses. Great secrecy surrounded the mobilization of the troops and before anyone on the Eastern Shore knew about the plan, the militia entered Salisbury and Princess Anne and took over the local telephone exchanges. The soldiers dragged William O. Thompson, Irving Adkins, William P. Herm, and William S. McQuay, another accused lyncher, from their beds just before dawn and rushed them to the Armory in Salisbury. Transport problems delayed the transfer of the prisoners to the Baltimore jail and it would be nearly noon before the troops could leave Salisbury.[31]

By this time a large and angry crowd of 2,000 had gathered outside the Armory. As the Attorney General arrived at the Armory to make his formal arrest, the crowd stoned his car. "Let's lynch Preston Lane!" the crowd yelled. The crowd soon began to throw bricks and stones at the troops guarding the Armory and it appeared that the mob would rush the soldiers to rescue the prisoners. During a struggle in front of the Armory, someone pulled the fire alarm and firemen raced to the scene. While they were trying to connect a hose, a nervous soldier threw a tear gas bomb in their midst and the angry firemen turned the fury of their hoses on the hapless militia. As the mob pressed on the soldiers, General Record of the militia shouted to his men "Let them have it!" The masked soldiers hurled tear gas bombs into the crowd and with fixed bayonets the militiamen formed an impregnable line from a side door to a fleet of waiting buses and trucks. As the convoy sped away the mob showered the vehicles with bricks and bottles.

In Annapolis Governor Ritchie issued a public statement on his decision to send the militia to the Eastern Shore. "The state government," Ritchie claimed, " cannot stand by and permit a State's Attorney to decline to arrest persons who are reliably charged with crime, and, as long as neither he nor the judge would act, it became my duty to put in motion the machinery of the law and cause the arrests to be made." Later that afternoon in Salisbury, two newspaper reporters were severely beaten and their automobiles set afire. Angry townsmen seized trucks carrying Baltimore, Philadelphia, and Washington newspapers and their contents flung into the Wicomico River.[32]

Hot on the heels of the state militia came Sheriff Luther Daugherty of Somerset County with a writ of *Habeas Corpus* issued by Judge Duer that demanded the return of the prisoners from the

Baltimore City jail to Princess Anne. Neither the governor nor the Attorney General were informed of Judge Duer's action and the men were whisked away before the state had time to organize its case. Ritchie, furious over Duer's decision, accused the judge of using some technicality to release the men before he received the "evidence, which justifies holding the prisoners on the merits of the charge."

On the afternoon of November 29, a crowd of over 3,000 gathered at the Princess Anne courthouse to await the return of the four men from the Baltimore jail. Some of the waiting men organized themselves into squads and drove the Negroes out of town. At 5:35 P.M the prisoners appeared before Chief Judge John R. Pattison. In the crowded courtroom Calvin Trice, a Cambridge lawyer, represented the prisoners from Dorchester County, and local barristers Edgar Jones and Harry C. Dashiell. Speaking for the defense, Trice approached the bench and asked Judge Pattison if State's Attorney Robins had filed charges against the men. The judge turned to Robins and the State's Attorney shook his head. "We find," Trice then said, " that there appears no warrant for their arrest .... likewise, there are no witnesses to give reasons for their being held. I move that they be released." After eight minutes of testimony and deliberation, Judge Pattison freed the prisoners. As the men left the court, reported the *Marylander and Herald*, "the siren in the fire house was sounded, and for ten minutes, auto horns, fire sirens, and other noise makers added to the din of cheering throngs celebrating the release of the accused men. The celebration was spontaneous and resembled the greetings accorded returning veterans following the close of the World War." A few days later the grand jury failed to return indictments against the accused lynchers and the Armwood case was closed by county authorities."[33]

For Preston Lane and Governor Ritchie, the case had ended in frustration and disappointment. Lane, by going to Salisbury with the militia to arrest the lynchers, had laid his life and career on the line in order to have Armwood's murderers brought to trial. Fully aware of the racial and political repercussions of the case, Ritchie had steadfastly determined to suppress mob violence and lynching in the state of Maryland. There was no way short of declaring martial law in the First Judicial Circuit and suspending civil government that Ritchie could have overridden county officials. One man, State's Attorney Robins, had frustrated the state's case against the lynchers at every turn with delays, legal casuistry, and sentimental appeals to county rights.

Although the discharge of the men helped to cool the inflamed feelings of White farmers and townsmen of the Eastern Shore, there remained great resentment against Governor Ritchie. State Senator Creston Beauchamp of Princess Anne called Ritchie's actions "unreasonable, illegal, and outrageous" and sent a memorial censoring the governor to Annapolis that was signed by every member of the Eastern Shore legislative delegation. Throughout the Shore, residents placed large White initials, NRA, on their cars and trucks – "Never Ritchie Again." Shore legislators also talked of creating a new state in the Union, "Delmarva" out of the Eastern Shore of Delaware, Maryland, and Virginia.[34]

In 1934 Ritchie was soundly defeated in the state gubernatorial election. While it is difficult to pinpoint the exact reasons for his defeat, the Armwood case was certainly a contributing factor. In the ethnic wards of Baltimore, many voters saw Ritchie as being too accommodating to Blacks and left wing groups. In southern Maryland and the Eastern Shore, race was clearly the key issue in the contest. Many people also voted against Ritchie because after several terms they believed he had been governor for too long. Fresh leadership was needed.

In February 1934, Preston Lane testified in Washington at a hearing of the Costigan-Wagner Anti-Lynching Bill. During Lane's testimony, Senator Robert Wagner of New York was astonished by the fact that State's Attorney Robins had refused to arrest Armwood's lynchers when Lane had sufficient evidence to justify their apprehension and trial. Maryland and other states, Lane asserted, were "impotent" to deal with lynching and federal assistance was an "imperative necessity." In the long run, the Attorney General concluded, lynchings in the south could be curbed only by the intervention of federal agencies like the Justice Department and the passage of enforcement legislation. According to Martin Sobelof, United States Attorney for the district of Maryland, new laws were needed, as the federal courts had no jurisdiction over lynchings. As long as the law gave more power to local police and local legal officials than to state government, then lynchers in the south, Lane added, would go unapprehended.[35]

The Armwood lynching was a particularly revolting case. It demonstrated how poverty, racial fear, and geographic isolation from the cultural mainstream could result in acts of horrendous brutality. In 1933, the year of Armwood's murder, there were twenty-one lynchings in the United States. In every instance the lynchers went unpunished.

White hostility towards Blacks smoldered in Somerset. On September 9, 1934 a race riot between 200 White men and from 400 to 500 Blacks raged on the streets of Princess Anne that night. The cause of the riot ostensibly was that a Black man cursed a White man. A fight ensued between the two men and the severely beaten Black man retreated to a nearby Negro restaurant. The White man went off to gather up his friends and the Black men did likewise. A battle raged into the early hours before the heavily armed White mob forced the Blacks to retreat from the town. Fortunately at this time there was no lynching.[36]

Not until after World War II would President Harry Truman sign legislation that would give the federal government the power to apprehend and imprison southern lynchers. In August 1934 the NAACP published a poem, Flag Salute, by Esther Popel in *Crisis Magazine* about the Armwood lynching.

Flag Salute[37]

"They dragged him naked
"Through the muddy streets,
"A feeble-minded Black boy!
"And the charge? Supposed assault
"Upon an aged woman!
""*Of the United States of America*" —
"One mile they dragged him
"Like a sack of meal,
"A rope around his neck,
"A bloody ear
"Left dangling by the patriotic hand
"Of Nordic youth! (A boy of seventeen!)

""And to the Republic for which it stands" —
"And then they hanged his body to a tree,
"Below the window of the county judge
"Whose pleadings for that battered human flesh
"Were stifled by the brutish, raucous howls
"Of men, and boys, and women with their babes,
"Brought out to see the bloody spectacle
"Of murder in the style of '33!
" (Three thousand strong, they were!)
"One Nation, Indivisible" —
To make the tale complete
They built a fire —
What matters that the stuff they burned
Was flesh — and bone — and hair —
And reeking gasoline!
"With Liberty — and Justice" —
They cut the rope in bits
And passed them out,
For souvenirs, among the men and boys!
The teeth no doubt, on golden chains
Will hang
About the favored necks of sweethearts, wives,
And daughters, mothers, sisters, babies, too!
"For ALL!"

    Shortly after Armwood's death, Abel Meeropol, a New York City school teacher was so revolted by the Armwood atrocity that he wrote a poem that began: "Southern trees bearing strange fruit. Blood on the leaves and blood at the roots." The song was quickly set to music and in 1939 the singer Billie Holiday sang "Strange Fruit" to a sympathetic national audience. Both Holiday and "Strange Fruit," however were barred from musical venues in the south. Researchers at the Tuskegee Institute have identified a grand total of 3,437 Blacks and 1,293 Whites lynched from 1882 to 1955 which averages out to over 78 a year for the entire period. The lynching of George Armwood continues to reverberate in the public mind. In modern times citizen groups and civil rights organizations have sought to keep the memory of lynching before the public eye.

"Strange Fruit" has often been called the first Negro protest song. Its poetry of condemnation continues to outlive the rude facts of southern racial violence. Today the Equal Justice Initiative maintains a web site on the terror of lynching.[38] The National Memorial for Peace and Justice has been established in Montgomery, Alabama, as a sacred space for truth-telling and reflection about racial terror in the United States.

Lynching Postscript from the Author

In 1975, I was teaching American History at the University of Maryland, Eastern Shore when I was recruited by the local Bicentennial Committee to write a history of Somerset County. During my research I came across the Armwood Case and wrote about it at length in the manuscript. George Armwood's violent and tragic demise did not sit well with the committee and the book was never published. Later I wrote extensively of lynching on the Eastern Shore in 1991 in my book, *Maryland's Eastern Shore, A Journey in Time and Place*. The Eastern Shore is a fascinating region; but it is not a replica of *Gone With The Wind* which is what the Bicentennial Committee desired.

Armwood's lynching "was carried out before a crowd of some 2,000 people," writes *Baltimore Sun* reporter, Jonathan M. Pitts, "well within the lifespan of thousands of Marylanders.[39] Mary Armwood (a seventy-year-old grandmother in 1993) remembered well as a girl of ten the lynching of her cousin. She recalled a frightened George Armwood running for his life through her house ahead of a baying mob.

Strange Fruit 139

1. Lynched African American 1930s

2. Armwood Lynching Protest Drawing, *Baltimore Sun*

3. Photo of George Armwood's arrest in Princess Anne

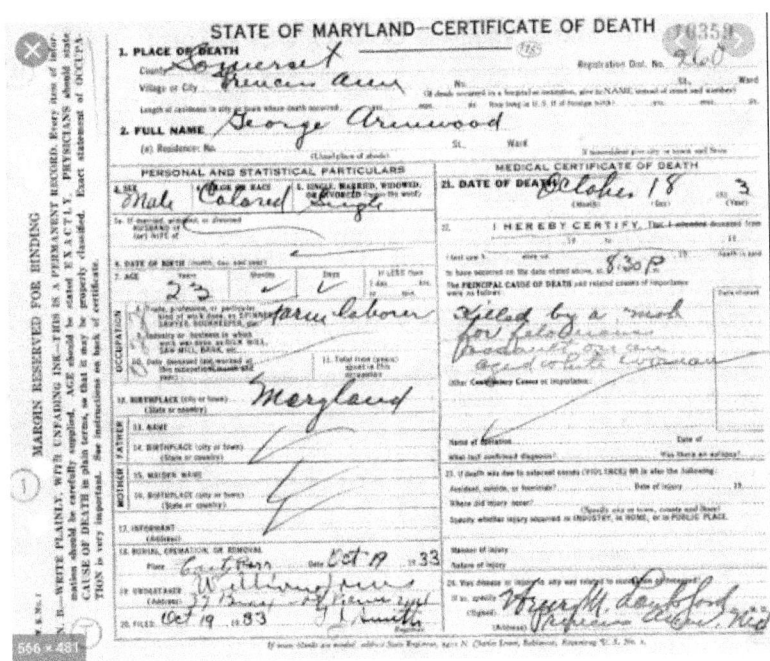

4. George Armwood death certificate

Historians at the Maryland State Archives have documented 38 lynchings in the state beween 1865 and 1935 which took place in 18 of Maryland's 24 counties. Historians have also exposed the canard that lynchings were used to prevent Blacks from raping White women. In most cases in Somerset and other places of the American South interracial sex was consensual.

Finally I should like to mention two things: 1. Every lynching in Maryland in time became wrapped in a code of silence that prevented public discussion, 2.A public mythology has evolved that states that members of Armwood's lynch mob were from the marginal or criminal sectors of the local population or else were "outsiders." In fact, Armwood's mobsters came from established families and the upper class of the county. This may explain why States Attorney Robins used every legal tactic at his command to prevent Armwood's killers from being brought to trial. Historian Samuel Hays has noted that students of politics have "failed to take into account the shared pattern of values and the social organization of community life" as a persistent force in local culture and politics."[40]

Notes

1 *Marylander and Herald,* March 17, 1933.
2 Interview with L.Q. Powell, July, 1977; Rose Bradley, "Back of the Maryland Lynching, *The Nation,* December 13, 1933.
3 Nola Tyler, "The August, 23, 1933 storm," *Baltimore Sun Magazine,* February 16,1975.
4 Arthur F. Raper, *The Tragedy of Lynching,* (Montclair, New Jersey: 1969), 48.
5 *The Worcester Democrat,* December 12, 1931
6 H.L. Mencken, "The Eastern Shore Kultur,"*Baltimore Sun,* December 12, 1931.
7 *New York Times,* January 24, 1932.
8 *New Republic,* December 20, 1933; *Salisbury Times,* October 19, 1933, October, 20, 1933.
9 The reconstruction of this plan is based on confidential interviews in

1977 of Blacks resident in Princess Anne at the time of the lynching. See also *Nation,* December 12, 1933.
10 *Marylander and Herald,* October 20, 1933
11 *Baltimore Sun,* October 17, 1933.
12 *Baltimore Sun,* October 18, 1933; *Salisbury Times* October 18, 1933
13 *Baltimore Sun,* October 19, 1933, *Salisbury Times,* October 19, 1933; *New York Times,* October 19, 1933.
14 *Baltimore Sun,* October 19, 1933; *Marylander and Herald,* October 20, 1933.
15 *Baltimore Sun,* October 20, 1933.
16 Clarence Mitchell interview with John R. Wennersten, July, 1977; Mitchell oral history interview, Maryland Historical Society, 1977.
17 *Baltimore Sun,* October 21, 1933.
18 The Scottsboro Boys were nine Black teenagers accused of raping two White women aboard a train near Scottsboro, Alabama.
19 *New York Times,* October 19, 1933; *Salisbury Times,* October 27, 1933; *Baltimore Sun,* October 21, 1933.
20 "Maryland Lynchings," Clippings File, Pratt Library, Baltimore.
21 Baltimore *Sun,* October 19, 1933; October 21, 1933
22 H.L. Mencken, "Plans to Put Down Lynching," *Baltimore Sun,* October 20, 1933.
23 *Baltimore Sun,* October 23, 1933; *Salisbury Times* October 21, 1933.
24 *Marylander and Herald,* October 28,1933; *Salisbury Times,* October 25, 1933, *New York Times,* October 29, 1933.
25 *Punishment for the Crime of Lynching,* Hearings Before a Subcommittee of the Committee of the Judiciary, 73rd Congress, February 20-21, 1934, (Washington: 1934), 115-118.
26 *Baltimore Sun,* October 21, 1933.
27 *Punishment for the Crime of Lynching,* 118-122.
28 *Ibid.* 124.
29 *Baltimore Sun,* October 20, 1933.
30 *New York Times,* November 20, 1933; *Punishment for the Crime of Lynching,* 121.
31 *New York Times,* November 28, 1933, November 29, 1933;*The New Republic,* December 20, 1933.
32 *New York Times,* November 19, 1933.
33 *Marylander and Herald,* December 1, 1933.
34 *New York Times,* November 30, 1933; *Marylander and Herald* December 1, 1933
35 *Punishment for the Crime of Lynching,* 111-112; *Baltimore Sun* February 22, 1934.
36 "Race Riot Sweeps Maryland Town: 200 White Men Battling 400 Ne-

groes Drive Negro Population Out of Princess Anne, *New York Times,* September 9, 1934.

37 Abel Merropol, A Socialist civil rights activist was the foster father of two boys whose parents, Julius and Ethel Rosenberg had been executed for treason after the atomic spy trials in 1953. *Flag Salute,* Written by Esther Popel and first published in the NAACP *Crisis Magazine,* August, 1934. The poem had wide currency at home and abroad in the 1930s and 1940s.

38 https://lynchinginamerica.eji.org

39 Jonathan M. Pitts, "Bringing a Dark Chapter to Light: Maryland Confronts Its Lynching Legacy," *Baltimore Sun,* September 25, 2018.

40 Samuel P. Hays, "Political Parties in the Community-Society Continuum," in William Chambers and Walter Dean Burnham, eds. *The American Party Systems, Stages of Political Decelopment, Oxford University Press,* 1977, 158.

Chapter Six

These Low Grounds

"Sometimes the sun will come in making a bright yellow day. But then again, sometimes it won't."
Sarah E. Wright

National Overview

Agricultural prosperity in the United States contracted severely after World War I. This was largely the result of the rehabilitation of European farms in the 1920s. When the war ended, supply increased rapidly as Europe's agricultural market rebounded. Increasingly American farmers turned to crops like strawberries, fruit generally and truck vegetables like tomatoes -- all of which could be packed, sold and shipped within the United States. At the center of this economic development were canneries.

Mostly owned by large farms, the canneries offered low wages and when the Depression hit after 1929, wages decreased even further sparking demands for collective bargaining in the canneries through unionization. The quality of farm life in America deteriorated to such an extent that middle class America was shocked by the levels of poverty, poor health and general misery that were reported in American newspapers. While New Deal programs of the Roosevelt Administration in the 1930s sought to ameliorate this situation, farm workers suffered. It was not until the outbreak of World War II that some semblance of agricultural prosperity returned to the nation. Afterwards a tsunami of Black, White and Mexican agricultural workers deserted the truck farms with their shabby houses and company stores for more lucrative employment in cities.

I

Cannery Feudalism

By 1900 the small Eastern Shore "Mom & Pop" cannery packing operations for vegetables and seafood had transformed themselves into successful corporate entities using large amounts of poor Black and White agricultural labor. The fertile farmlands of Chesapeake Bay provided canneries with a continuous flow of food for processing. Crisfield oysters had long been the centerpiece of the canning process and canned oysters from Crisfield found markets as distant as Colorado and California. By 1920 the Eastern Shore counties of Maryland had some 120 canneries that processed fish, pears, tomatoes, snap beans and sweet potatoes just to name a few commercial products. Picking produce or working the hot steamers in canneries was a physically debilitating drudgery. James Wallace, who started a firm in Cambridge in Dorchester County in 1870, was one of the earliest packers on the Eastern Shore. By 1896 he was one of the largest vegetable and tomato packers on the Eastern Shore, producing 25,000 cans a day under the labels *Abbasco Brand* and *Pride of Cambridge*.[1] Local White men and women assembled boxes and unloaded crates of baskets which paid better than "negro work."

Crisfield, a town of 3,000 citizens, was already a thriving packing center. The Crisfield Packing Company, started by Ewing Ward and his brother Vernon processed and packed a variety of seafood. Another thriving company, John T. Handy, canned both seafood and vegetables. The Tawes family and Sterling brothers were also adventurous entrepreneurs and their business involvement included packing, ice plants, banking, a bakery, and the manufacture and sale of electricity. All in all, these packers were a business elite that brooked no interference with "uppity" workers complaining over low wages. The packers dominated the economic, social and cultural life of their communities.

The titan of the packing industry was Albanus Phillips whose Cambridge packing operations of tomatoes, green beans and sweet potatoes made him one of the richest and most powerfully connected men on Maryland's Eastern Shore. Phillips was always referred to as "the King of the Canners." Packers in Somerset took their cue from Albanus Phillips and smaller firms like Kings Creek Cannery in Princess Anne endeavored to pay low wages under strict worker supervision. In the 1930s many canners sought to get rid of local labor altogether by importing gangs of Black farm labor from Florida and Slovak immigrants from Europe. Canners provided their seasonal workers with such miserable housing that the Farm Settlement Administration in Washington sent in photographers to record the plight of this benighted population.

Canneries and packinghouses in Somerset and elsewhere on the Eastern Shore were plagued by discontent over low wages and working conditions. A massive strike occurred in the Phillips plants in Cambridge in June of 1937 when union organizers from the CIO (Congress of Industrial Organizations headed by John L. Lewis) sought to unionize the plants because Phillips planned to reduce wages and the work force. Most workers were Black and stoned the police who tried to prevent union organizers from coming into the plants. The strike against Phillips Packing Company in Cambridge brought Black workers hope that they could achieve racial and economic justice in an area where they were subjected to the worst aspects of Jim Crow. Meanwhile many Black strikers and union organizers in the Cannery Union were accused of being communist troublemakers set on overthrowing capitalism in America.

On the night of June 23, 1937, over 1,000 workers and allies marched through the streets rallying support and overturned trucks carrying vegetables. Shotgun carrying farmers tried to protect their truck loads of vegetables. For a time it appeared that the strikers would carry the day and win a settlement. But Phillips outsmarted them with police intimidation and a quick agreement with the rival American Federation of Labor to increase wages by 10 percent. Nothing was said about work force reductions. The workers joined by migrant farm laborers would have none of it and voted down the proposal. Over the next several days, strikers clashed with police on their picket lines. While negotiations with Phillips and the two rival unions took place, workers fumed and demonstrated in the town. The discontent simmered until Phillips accepted the unionization of his plants. Meanwhile farm and cannery workers struggled to live on wages averaging nine dollars a week. At this time wages in Baltimore manufacturing plants averaged sixty-three cents per hour or about $25 a week.² Unionization of the Phillips plant was a pyrrhic victory. Cannery uprisings and union struggles were not just a Chesapeake phenomenon at this time. They were part of a national movement that stretched from Alaska to the Atlantic. The 1930s were volatile years when agricultural labor in Maryland and throughout the nation attempted through strikes and collective bargaining to find their rightful economic place in the sun.

It is in this context that Black farm and cannery labor worked and sweated. Tomato pickers were required to pick tomatoes all day hauling twenty pound baskets. For that labor they received "tomato tokens" with a dollar value. But when they went to redeem their tokens at the end of a shift, they were often held accountable for incidental expenses of which they had no knowledge. Thus did the tomato token system perpetuate a lifestyle much like that of the company store in Kentucky coal mines.

II
The 1938 Crab Pickers Strike in Crisfield

As the Depression lengthened, many businesses in Somerset County shut down, including two garment factories that employed nearly three hundred women. Local officials estimated that ninety percent of the port of Crisfield's work force was unemployed. County officials, despite its dire economic straits, refused to seek help from President Roosevelt's New Deal Agencies that were likely to upset standing wage policies in an isolated rural county on the Eastern Shore.

The year 1938 was not the first time that crab pickers had resisted packinghouse attempts to reduce their pay from thirty-five cents a gallon to twenty-five cents. In 1931 packers said that the twenty-five cent rate would apply for the entire season. Eight hundred crab pickers went on strike. One hundred were White. The pickers marched through Crisfield. J.C.W. Tawes announced that "rather than submit to the strikers' demands I'll sell out and leave Crisfield." Tawes called for local police and the local militia to break the strike and allow those who wanted to work to enter their packinghouses. The packers broke this strike; but labor unrest sparked inquiries from the National Recovery Agency and the packers raised the rates back to thirty-five cents a gallon.

On April 4, 1938, Crisfield's seafood packers decided to lower the amount paid to over six hundred Black female crab pickers from thirty-five cents a gallon to twenty-five cents a gallon. Taking advantage of hard times, the packers argued that Black women in Crisfield should be happy just to have a job. The women, however, were incensed by the wage cut and two days later went out on a strike that lasted for five weeks. Aided by CIO union organizers, they formed their own union and demanded that the rates be restored to thirty-five cents a gallon and that the CIO be their bargaining agent. Crisfield packers enlisted a band of hired thugs to intimidate the workers but the ladies stood firm. There were long desperate weeks for the women when food was scarce and they were forced to survive on lean diets. After many long weeks, the packers capitulated.[3] Organized Black workers were almost unheard of but by 1938 the CIO Union was a presence in Crisfield and other food packing towns.

The women won their strike and union recognition. County authorities, however, interpreted the crab picker strike as racial radicalism despite its being caused by the greed and mendacity of Crisfield packers. And Blacks aware of the Armwood lynching in the county, had to temper their militancy. To control what large farmers and seafood packers termed "nigger communists" new forms of labor management were introduced in the county. Specifically, the local agricultural elite began to import Black labor gangs from Florida to work in the tomato fields and canneries at wages far less than those paid to local White and Black workers.

III
P.O.W.

On the afternoon of June 24, 1944, a large unscheduled passenger train stopped at a railroad siding near Westover in Somerset County. Heavily armed American soldiers quickly bounded out and placed themselves strategically around the train. Peering out through the heavy oak slats that had been nailed across the car windows were over eight hundred German prisoners of war destined for internment at Camp Somerset. Lightly clad and suntanned, the Germans wore the chevrons of General Erwin Rommel's famous Afrika Korps.

During World War II over 270,00 German and Italian prisoners of war were interned in the United States. Following the surrender of the German Army in North Africa in 1943, the Allies found themselves without facilities to handle the large mass of P.O.W.s and the only solution to the problem was to transport a majority of them to America. Later, after the Normandy invasion, many German P.O.W.s from the French theater of fighting were also shipped to the United States. In Maryland military authorities worked feverishly to convert old National Guard barracks and CCC camps into prisoner of war compounds. The largest P.O.W. installation was located on the western shore at Fort Meade; other smaller facilities were scattered across the state.

By July, 1945, there were over 3,000 German prisoners of war in camps on the Eastern Shore. Camp Somerset, located five miles south of Princess Anne, was the largest of these regional prisons. On May 10, 1944 General W.W. Irvine of the Army Service Forces in Washington, D.C. had Somerset's former National Guard Facility and CCC camp transferred to the United States Army as a prisoner of war camp.

As the German prisoners marched from the train, they saw close by what was to become their home for the duration of the war – a thirty-five acre compound surrounded by an eight foot high barbed wire fence with six guard towers. Given the exigencies of war, Camp Somerset was an excellent facility for the enlisted men of the Afrika Korps. Men were assigned to one story barracks in groups of thirty-eight. The camp had flush toilets, showers, a library containing over 1,300 volumes, mostly in German, and a well-managed dining hall. Each prisoner received rations of 3,400 to 3,700 calories per day and was allotted three packs of cigarettes and three bottles of beer per week. Throughout the German internment, Swiss representatives of the International Red Cross visited the camp and were impressed by its quiet efficiency and discipline. Most prisoners' grievances, the Swiss found were "only trivial."

During 1944-1945, 697 prisoners were forced to work as contract labor at eight cents a day for county farmers. Others were forced to cut wood in the forests and endure swarms of mosquitoes. Of the prison labor force, 113 worked in local orchards; 132 worked for the Somerset Truck Growers Association; and 116 worked in local sawmills. Others worked on small farms, nurseries and also cleared right of way for the Eastern Shore Public Service Company. The Germans quickly established a reputation for being hard workers in the county. A few escape attempts occurred, however, when the soldiers feared that they might be repatriated to the Russian sector as the war wound down.

For farmers in the county who had long been troubled by racial difficulties in the fields and canneries, the German prisoners were a heaven-sent labor force. With farm labor in a time of soaring food demand costing only eight cents a day for German prison labor versus thirty cents a day for African American workers, local agriculture prospered. Further, Camp Somerset with its comfortable facilities and ample food supply seemed to mock poor Black circumstances in the county. It was also an affront to many Blacks who had family members in the military fighting against the Nazis overseas for "equality and Democracy."[4]

Thus did Somerset growers expand truck and vegetable production dramatically. The value of farm products sold in the county soared from $1.5 million in 1939 to $5.7 million in 1944. With the repatriation of the Germans, Somerset grower looked for new sources of a stable labor supply. Local Black labor scarcely filled the bill. By the late 1940s farmers and cannery owners resorted to Caribbean and Hispanic labor imported from Florida to work the harvests. They dealt with labor contractors who managed and controlled the labor gangs. The truck farmers provided housing that were dilapidated barracks. An immigration chain of Hispanic and Haitian labor began at this time and is now a mainstay of local farms, nurseries, and poultry plants.

IV
Somerset's Two Populations

Somerset's agricultural prosperity after the war went into decline. Agricultural extension agents warned that without infusions of federal and state money there could be little community development.

These agents saw at first hand an alarming rise in poverty, stagnation and outmigration that did not auger well for the future. These fears were well-documented by the U.S. Bureau of the Census. Between 1930 and 1970 Somerset's population declined by 19.1% from 23,382 to 18,924; and over 4,000 men and women in the 20-34 age range left the county during the 1950-1970 period. Government officials identified 5,180 residents in the county living below the federal poverty level. The fact that 42.2% of all Black children and 28.8% of all White children in the county were living in poverty was particularly disturbing.

Increasingly demographers also pointed out that Somerset was becoming a county of two populations distinct in age. One population was Black, youthful, and poor, while the other was White, older, and racially conservative. Additionally, the community's ideology of self-help and entrepreneurship went against government-sponsored social and economic innovations. Paradoxically the county would be faced with continued outmigration of local youths while skilled and unskilled jobs went begging for lack of applicants. Given the economic and educational level of the county's population, it seemed doubtful that job-providing industries would be attracted to Somerset. The county appeared to be locked in a tragic cycle: without industry there would be few tax funds for quality education in the schools; without good schools the county could not provide a competent work force; and without this work force the county would be unable to attract the managerial and professional classes that would serve as catalysts for growth and social change. In this environment it would be difficult for local government to be anything more than a watchdog against social discontent.[5]

V
Senator Harry Phoebus

Folks in Somerset County have been conditioned by hard times to accept the fact that life is a matter of unrelenting struggle. Those who have succeeded have possessed a bold vision and a fighting heart. Of all the men in the county who rose out of poverty and aspired to greatness, no one epitomized this indomitable spirit and folk wisdom better than Harry T. Phoebus, a country boy from Oriole. A man whose political outlook was an amalgam of homespun philosophy, native wit and strong religious values, Harry Phoebus was Somerset County's perennial representative in the Maryland State Senate from 1947 until his death in 1964. Phoebus was a serial entrepreneur, failing in several enterprises until he hit it big when he bought up all the junk and used cars he could find when World War II broke out. By 1945 the national shortage of new automobiles would send people from three Eastern Shore counties clamoring down to Crisfield to buy Phoebus' old cars. This was the genesis of several auto dealerships that sustained the Phoebus family.

In the Maryland Senate Phoebus was a crusading populist against what he called "the money boys." As such Phoebus had a strong empathy for Black people in the county and worked for their benefit as much as he did for the struggling farmers and small businessmen. Harry Phoebus was a stalwart of the Republican Party when Republicans, locals said "were as scarce as crab wings." County voters did not care about his party affiliation. They cared for what he stood for even though it was difficult for a Republican minority member in the legislature to reward his followers. As the **Baltimore Sun** noted "The watermen loved him, the Holy Rollers loved him and the old prohibition crowd loved him for his stand against whiskey."[6]

Yet Phoebus's strongest constituency over the years was Somerset's Black community. In an age of racial segregation, he was the Black man's eccentric champion. While Blacks readily admitted that he sold them over-priced cars, he did nonetheless give them credit when no other White man in the county would lend them a cent. He also gave them jobs at his garages fixing tires, running errands and tending to Senator Phoebus myriad business interests. Harry Phoebus was also their "fixer." He got Blacks school bus contracts, helped them find jobs, got college scholarships for their youngsters and bailed them out of jail.[7] Blacks could be seen sitting on the steps of "Mr. Harry's porch" listening to his homespun wisdom and getting much needed information on county politics.

For a long time Phoebus was the only White man in the county who would sit down to lunch with Dr. John T. Williams, the president of Maryand State College in Princess Anne (which is now the University of Maryland, Eastern Shore). Many older

Blacks remembered Phoebus's attempt to overturn segregation laws for steamboats and trains during his first term in the legislature. While it was difficult to gauge the depth of his commitment to Black civil rights, on practical issues, Harry Phoebus was the best White friend that Blacks had in Somerset. In the 1940s, for example a young ambitious African American named Webster Cane joined the Phoebus bandwagon and worked hard for his election. In turn Phoebus did favors for the Cane family and Webster's sons remember the economic favors that were bestowed on them. Working for Senator Phoebus always worked out well. Honiss got a job at Maryland State College in the Student Union and Rudy got employed by the State Roads Commission. There are many stories like this in the county.

Black Republicans in response flocked to the polls to return their White tribune to the Senate. "I've been the champion of the colored people," Phoebus claimed. "I understand them and they understand me."[8] Phoebus fought for better schools for Whites and Blacks in the county and advocated increases in teacher salaries. Blacks knew that as long as Phoebus was in the legislature he would fight to advance the educational programs for Blacks at the local Maryland State College.

Also, in fighting the utility companies for fairer rates and doing battle with the oil companies over the price of gasoline and heating oil, Senator Phoebus showed how his populist philosophy transcended issues of race. In the rough and tumble of Maryland state politics only shrewd men capable of exploiting contacts and friendships survived. As one former member of the state legislature once put it, "everyone in Annapolis has got scars and everybody owes someone a favor. It's never been a pink tea around here."

Meanwhile, hard times was never history in Somerset. It was more like unending current news.

VI
These Low Grounds

Somewhere along the tide-soaked road from Princess Anne to Deal Island in Somerset there existed a fictional hell conjured by novelist Sarah E. Wright. A Black woman, raised locally on the Eastern

Shore, Wright described the lives of an impoverished Black woman and her family in a local fishing village during the Depression. *This Child's Gonna Live,* published in 1969, was considered a small masterpiece by book critics and hailed as an outstanding book of the year by the *New York Times*. Her work has often been compared to that of Zora Neale Hurston. In her time Wright was one of the few Black women writing about the experiences of Black women in the South. Today, the novel, is still highly regarded in African American literary circles but it is little known outside of them.

The book centers on the travail of Mariah Upshur, the wife of a Black oystermen living in a village called "Tangier Neck." As the story opens, Mariah is pregnant with her fifth child. She worries about whose child she is carrying, her husband Jacob's or that of the well-placed Princess Anne White physician, Dr. Albery Green, who required sexual favors for medical care for her children. She has already lost one child in infancy and is adamant that the current child she is carrying will live and escape the confines of Tangier Neck. *This Child's Gonna Live* is more than a novel. It is an anthropological snapshot of Black suffering and racial humiliation in Somerset County during the 1930s and 1940s. It focuses on conditions that Wright saw and to a great extent experienced herself before she "escaped" to Howard University and thence to New York City to become a writer and Vice President of the Harlem Writers Guild.

Despite being surrounded by an oyster fishery and the bounty of Chesapeake Bay, the people of these low grounds and marshes were always hungry. As Wright observed, you could not eat oysters and rockfish. You had to sell the good product and live on fatback and potatoes. The characters in Wright's novel knew well the tyranny of the local vegetable and fish canneries. As Aunt Saro Jane describes it:

> Jacob, eberything ain't the lord's will. Some of these things happening is these Maryland type of White people's will. I don't care how much they go to the church, they ain't living by the word of the Lord. They living by their greedy pocketbooks.[9]

Living in shacks with doors with peeling paint and wallpaper gone limp from the ever present damp, Blacks of Tangier Neck had plenty to worry about, especially the fear of contracting tuberculosis. The vast marshlands surrounding the county were full of miasmas.

Life is precarious for Mariah's struggling Black family, living down to the last slab of fatback and feeding her children molasses sandwiches and married to Jacob Upshur, a "wind-beaten, life-beaten, going-nowhere man." Mariah's suffering life takes place near an actual town called "Chance." For Mariah Upshur and her female friends, perhaps a "chance" in life will lead to true wealth – a chicken and a few rows of strawberries. Yet Mariah and her family at Tangier Neck have no control over their life. This is amply illustrated when Mariah's Aunt Cora is run down and killed by a carload of laughing White teenagers who haughtily speed away unapprehended.

In *This Child's Gonna Live* Black incest haunts Mariah's family. Her husband Jacob fathered a child by his sister. There are other sins as well. People are casually murdered out of spite; and soon Mariah gives birth to a light skinned baby girl. Her father asks "Well, what in the name of God has the Master sent us here?" Another White man contributing to Somerset's "corn-colored bastard population," folks said.

Mariah prays to God. She is willing to die for her sins if God will allow her baby girl to live. Towards the end of the story, Mariah despairs of her miserable life and attempts to drown herself in the Bay, only to be rescued by Jacob. At home the same old biscuits and potatoes in the oven await Mariah's return. Her life goes on at Tangier Neck, "a place of standing still and death."

Another Black writer from this region, Waters Turpin, once noted, to be Black, defenseless and poor in this region was to become prey.[10] Waters wrote in his novel *These Low Grounds* an account of how well-situated White families on the Eastern Shore exploited, beat down and sexually abused African Americans. Escape from these troubles was often a matter of going from the frying pan into the fire, especially when it came to Baltimore. Nearly eight decades after the Civil War, some Blacks from Somerset who traveled to Baltimore felt like fugitives crossing a border. Both Wright and Waters knew that Baltimore was hardly the promised land for Blacks eager to escape the confines of their locale. In the back rooms of many Black barber shops in Baltimore there were cheap gin joints, crap games, whore houses and loan sharks eager to fleece the innocent arrivals from down the Bay. Thus did Blacks prey on one another while the Whites preyed on them.

1. Company Store, Kings Creek Cannery

2. Handy Company Cannery Worker Housing, Crisfield

3. German Prisoners of War off to work on Princess Anne farms during World War II

Notes

1. Harold W. Hurst, *"The Canning Industry of Delmarva," Tidewater Times*, August, 2006. www. Secrets of the Easternshore.com, "The Phillips Co. Packing Strike of 1937." Stephanie Hinnershitz,"We Ask not for Mercy, but for Justice": The CannerChaptery Workers and Farm Laborers' Union and Filipino Civil Rights in the United States, 1927-1937,"*Journal of Social History*, vol. 47, Fall, 2013, 132-152.
2. U.S. Department of Labor, *Handbook of Labor Statistics*, volume 2, 1941, p.16
3. Craig Simpson, "600 Black Women Stand Strong: the 1938 Crab Pickers Strike," *Crisfield Heritage Foundation Archives*.
4. **Inspection Reports**, Camp Somerset, October 22, 1944 and April 17, 1945, Enemy P.O.W. Information Bureau National Archives; John R. Wennersten, "Behind the Wire: When the Africa Korps Came to Somerset County, *Maryland Historical Magazine*, Autumn, 1982.
5. *U.S. Census of the Population, Maryland*, Washington, 1952; Dalton, Littleton and Newport, *Somerset County Population Report*, Princess Anne,Md. 1973; John K. Garner and A. Stewart Holmes, *A Profile of Poverty in Maryland*, College Park, 1973
6. *Baltimore Sun*, November 30, 1964.
7. Interview with Mr. DeWayne Whittington, July 1977; and interview with Mr. Honiss Cane, June 1977.
8. *Baltimore Sun*, September 22,1951.
9. Sarah E, Wright, *This Child's Gonna Live*, New York, 1969, 6, 11.. A Somerset native, Wright knew well the problems of a poor Black family trying to wrest a living as fisher folk. Thus the characters of the Upshur family are in large measure a composite of her own family.
10. Waters Turpin, *These Low Grounds*, College Park, 1969.

Chapter Seven

Riots, Fire Hoses and Dogs

"It takes a lot of effort to love Black in America. You've been told all your life if you're Black you're wrong."
H. Rap Brown

National Overview

When most people think of the Civil Rights movement, they think of a politically and socially contentious time between Brown v Board of Education and the demonstrations and riots of the 1960s as Blacks aimed to eliminate the system of Jim Crow segregation and to reform some of the worst aspects of racism in American institutions and life. In the south it was a period of great social tension and conflict between Whites and Blacks over the dimensions of social change that Blacks demanded. Civil rights workers were often met with hostility, federal ambivalence, and indifference as well as mob and police violence. The "Movement" of the 1960s built upon earlier struggles against lynching and segregated schools. While most civil rights leaders followed a policy of gradualism in their approach to attacking racism in the United State, a new generation of mostly Black and White college students tackled the issue head on and battled with police, dogs, and fire hoses in defense of their right to sit in a lunch counter or have access to a hotel room. These young men and women did not believe in tapering their demands to suit their elders' notions of "propriety." White southern resistance to the civil rights movement was considerable – at times violent and murderous. The main issue before the American people in the 1960s and after was what was called "the Prize" – a redefinition of American society and a redistribution of social and economic power.

I

From the Depression onwards the NAACP and Black civil rights groups in the South campaigned in the courts and general society to win back the constitutional rights of unfettered citizenship and equality that had been granted them immediately after the Civil War. In 1954, the Supreme Court decision of *Brown v Board of Education* undermined segregated public school education and severely weakened the "separate but equal" Jim Crow laws of the South, In 1955 Black outrage over the lynching of Emmett Till, a Chicago teenager visiting in Mississippi, reinforced liberal White and African American determination to launch bus boycotts, restaurant sit-ins, and other forms of civil disobedience. Soon the most radical part of the civil rights movement would be led by Black college students and blue collar workers allied with the Student Non-Violent Coordinating Committee (SNCC) to agitate for better jobs and wages and access to segregated restaurants.

In the 1960s the civil rights movement took on a new militancy. Black communities on the Eastern Shore demanded an end to segregated schools, hotels and restaurants. Blacks were barred from the White restaurants in Princess Anne and other towns in the region. If a Black person wanted a good meal, she had to go to the takeout window, pay in advance for her food and then walk away as there was not even a picnic table outside.

In 1963 Cambridge, Maryland was a depressed working class town where Blacks and Whites cobbled together an insecure living in the cannery and local seafood companies. While they worked together side by side there was an immense psychological and physical divide between the two communities. *The Floating Opera*, a novel by John Barth, depicts a fictionalized version of Cambridge as a relatively benign town full of eccentrics and potentially suicidal oddballs.

In reality, though, Cambridge was racially one of the toughest towns in the American South. Blacks in Cambridge had no local White allies. Local White-owned businesses were uninterested in Black uplift even though an increase in Black spending power would benefit the whole community. The White churches were largely indifferent. The city council was cowardly, preferring to use police force rather than conciliation.

A former horseback-riding lane ironically called Race Street divided the town. One side was for Blacks and one for Whites, a dangerous border that neither race crossed. Blacks could not use the community swimming pool, the skating rink or other public facilities. Years after the Supreme Court's decision in *Brown v Board of Education* Cambridge maintained separate schools and local White racial attitudes seemed more characteristic of Mississippi than of Maryland.

On July 12, 1963 Black frustration in Cambridge blew up in radical protest during a summer when racial demonstrations in 186 American cities resulted in 14,733 arrests. Nationwide conditions improved for Blacks because of the civil right movement; there was an expectation that conditions should improve in Cambridge as well. As sociologist Daniel J. Meyers has observed, this made Cambridge and other southern towns ripe for "riot events."[1] While many people thought Cambridge to be a sleepy tidewater town, it was in the vortex of a changing and often violent racial climate.

VI
The Man in the Middle

As the volatile winds of social and racial change swept Maryland, its new governor, Millard Tawes (1959-1967), seemed more concerned with balancing the budget and building schools across the state. Tawes had spent his political career in the shadows of Annapolis, mostly in several terms as Maryland State Comptroller. Tawes had the personality of an unassuming genial accountant, which he had been for most of his life as part of the rich and powerful packinghouse, lumber, and banking Tawes family of Crisfield. In seeking the governorship Tawes had allied himself with Baltimore's juggernaut Democratic Party and had swept to a comfortable victory. Hardly had Tawes eased into the Governor's chair when the subject of race began to plague him. Tawes was first and foremost a good old boy from Maryland's Eastern Shore. He wasn't interested in race problems, preferring to follow whatever moderate course outlined for the state by the federal government (the National Guard was in Cambridge for most of 1963). But racists like Dr. H.C. "Curley" Byrd could not be so easily placated. Byrd and Tawes were good friends, having grown up together in Crisfield. And Dr. Byrd had for decades been President of the University of Maryland who over the years built the institution into an athletic powerhouse. Now in the 1960s and in retirement, Byrd craved either a Senate or Congressional seat. The problem for Tawes was that Byrd travelled the state espousing a "separate but equal" philosophy of education and declaring himself a "never-ender" when it came to racial segregation. "We have to keep Black schools like Morgan and Maryland State College." Byrd claimed, "If we don't Negroes will come to College Park where our girls are."[2]

Tawes ignored Byrd and his segregationist cronies. Responding to racial moderates in the legislature, Tawes used his influence to secure the passage of a public accommodations law that would end segregation in Maryland's hotels and restaurants. Although this was the first state accommodations law to be passed south of the Mason-Dixon line, Tawes was embarrassed by the fact that Eastern Shore legislators amended the bill to exempt all the counties of the Eastern Shore from its provisions.

As the local chapter of the NAACP sought to bring racial integration to Cambridge, it encountered massive resistance. The unwillingness of Dorchester County leaders to negotiate civil rights issues coupled with the endemic poverty in the Black community prompted an outburst of rioting in the summer of 1963 that could not be contained by local police authorities. Reluctantly Tawes sent in the National Guard and armed troops maintained an uneasy truce between Blacks and Whites in that town.[3] The National Guard remained in Cambridge nearly two years, the longest military occupation of an American community since the Reconstruction period after the Civil War.

While Tawes clumsily attempted to conciliate Whites and Blacks, critics, particularly in Baltimore's Black community, argued that the governor seemed to have a noticeable lack of enthusiasm for ending racial segregation in the state. Finally in 1965 Tawes found himself widely censured in the state and nationally for ordering a secret investigation of the popular civil rights advocate, Bayard Rustin. Rustin was scheduled to speak at the University of Maryland, College Park, to a large audience.[4]

VII
Gloria Richardson

In the midst of the growing discontent a firebrand would emerge in Dorchester County. Her name was Gloria Richardson. In retrospect, Richardson's involvement in the civil rights movement was unexpected inasmuch as she came from one of the wealthiest and conservative Black families in Cambridge at that time. Her grandfather, Herbert St. Clair Hayes owned numerous properties in the town's Second Ward. He was also the sole African American member of the Cambridge City Council. Her father was the town's respected Black mortician. Gloria's family had been free people of color since before the Civil War and owned extensive rental property in Cambridge. Her maternal uncle was an attorney.

Gloria Richardson attended Howard University and returned to Cambridge after World War II. Employed as a social worker Gloria had her share of difficulties with a White bureaucracy in the county with little interest in Black community problems. She was allowed to serve only Black clients in the all Black Second Ward She married a schoolteacher and concentrated on raising a family until the national civil rights organization came to Cambridge in 1961 in the form of Freedom Riders. Gloria became involved with the Student Nonviolent Coordinating Committee's efforts to desegregate public accommodations. Richardson rapidly developed a rapport with local working people. "If you could articulate the need, if you knew what the need was, if you were aware of the kind of games that White folk play that was the real thing," she said.[5] Gloria, however, refused to commit herself to non-violence as a protest tactic. As Richardson saw it "some people at SNCC saw non-violence almost as a religion, that whole Gandhi concept.... I never saw it as that. If violence was perpetuated against you, you had a right to defend yourself." When SNCC protests faltered in Cambridge in 1962, Gloria and other parents created the Cambridge Nonviolent Action Committee (CNAC), which enlarged the scope of grievances to end bad housing and employment discrimination and inadequate health care. Conservative Blacks urged Richardson to practice some restraint, but she pressed on. At first the initial protests led by Richardson involved boycotting White businesses.

But soon a number of White racists in the town began to attack the protestors. Shots were fired at Black demonstrators and police often arrested the protestors. Throughout the demonstrations no harm came to Gloria Richardson as she seemed to be protected by her upper class status. With each new Black demand White resistance increased. On the night of June 13, 1963, Richardson and other members of SNCC led a mass "freedom walk" in the town towards the courthouse. They were attacked and pelted with eggs by over 200 White townsfolk. This time armed Black men set up a defense perimeter around the demonstrators. The following night fighting broke out between two carloads of Whites and Blacks that included the exchange of gunfire. Several people were wounded and some White businesses were set on fire. When police attempted to enter the Black Second Ward of the town to make arrests, rock throwers and Black men firing shots into the air repelled them. State police used tear gas and guns to disperse the mob.

Here in Cambridge was an indigenous movement of local Blacks against Cambridge town authority as opposed to one orchestrated by national civil rights leaders. Despite her Cambridge heritage, White segregationists began to refer to Gloria Richardson as an alien radical. All of Cambridge's problems, said Dorchester School Superintendant James G. Busick, were the result of "outside agitators." It was a case, however, of local leaders trying to avoid making any progress towards peaceful integration in the town. Rather than broker White and Black concerns, Mayor Calvin Mobray retreated into his office to consult with the police.

The whole "Gandhi thing" of peaceful non-violent protest wasn't working in Cambridge, Richardson said. Black men with guns had the right to protect their families and their community. Governor Tawes sent in the National Guard to Cambridge for three weeks to defuse the situation. Tawes offered Richardson and CNAC a plan for gradual desegregation in the town which was promptly rejected. The Governor even invited Richardson to meet with him and his aides on a plush estate in Talbot County to map out a mutually agreeable course of action. Following the withdrawal of the National Guard, CNAC resumed protests.

On July 12, a mob of Whites attacked half a dozen protestors who were sitting in at a local restaurant. A brawl ensued. Later that night a mob attacked another civil rights march and armed White thugs attempted to enter Black neighborhoods, only to be repelled by gunfire. Twelve White people were wounded and another White business was set on fire. Both physically and emotionally Cambridge was hot and Tawes declared martial law and ordered the National Guard back.

President John F. Kennedy was embarrassed that so much racial trouble was happening within 90 miles of the capital. He promptly sent his brother, the Attorney General Robert Kennedy, to negotiate a truce and reach an agreement with Gloria Richardson and CNAC that would cool racial tempers and get Cambridge off the evening televised news. Kennedy brokered a settlement with CNAC and the White community that included the desegregation of public schools and construction of public housing. The Attorney General also offered a federally funded local jobs program. At this stage Richardson was garnering support from many poor blue-collar Whites who voiced their support with phone calls and messages. Poverty in Cambridge didn't necessarily follow the color line. Richardson's CNAC, however, did score some successes. By autumn of 1963 the local schools were desegregated as well as the local library and hospital. Richardson had catapulted to national fame as a civil rights leader.

Enter Cambridge's White power. The Kennedy agreement, called the Treaty of Cambridge, broke down almost immediately when the all-White Dorchester Business and Citizens Association filed referendum petitions to overturn the agreement. Richardson denounced the Association and refused to have her organization participate in the referendum. In October, 1963, the segregationists won the referendum. Meanwhile in Annapolis Eastern Shore legislators amended Tawes' public accommodations law to exempt all the counties of the Eastern Shore of Maryland from its provisions. Cambridge reverted to a kind of sullen status quo with Whites fearful of the future and Blacks awaiting the full implementation of laws guaranteeing an end to all aspects of racial segregation. Meanwhile William Wise, the head of the all White Dorchester Business and Citizens Association invited Governor Wallace to Cambridge's Firemen's Arena and on May 11, 1964, Gloria once more took to the streets of Cambridge to protest that segregationist's appearance.

The association gave Wallace a box filled with money and Wallace told them that as a presidential candidate in the upcoming election he would oppose all civil rights legislation. Black protesters were clearly agitated and the National Guard dispersed them with tear gas and mace. In June of 1964 Stokely Carmichael, a 22-year old organizer for SNCC, gave an impassioned speech attacking segregation and the Cambridge White community. Afterwards Carmichael was hit in the face with a blast of chemical mace that required him to be hospitalized.

The Cambridge protests took its toll on Gloria Richardson, leaving her exhausted after two years of continuous demonstrations and unsure of her future. In the summer of 1964 she resigned from the Cambridge Nonviolent Action Committee, married *Life Magazine* photographer, Frank Dandridge, and later settled in New York City. It was there that she met H. Rap Brown in the summer of 1967 and invited Brown to deliver the angry stump speech he was giving across the nation to the Blacks of Cambridge. Although she kept her ties with family and the local civil rights movement on the Eastern Shore, Gloria Richardson never lived in Cambridge again.

Across Maryland and in countless national living rooms, television gave currency and moral suasion to the civil rights movement. It gave liberal politicians room to maneuver on sensitive social issues like school integration while it solidified the views of segregationists who wore the "NEVER" pin on the lapel of their coats. And in the long hot summers of 1963-1967 television viewers feared for their country as they saw their cities swept by riots and demonstrations.

H. Rap Brown first visited Cambridge in the summer of 1963 during the period of Gloria Richardson's leadership of CNAC. He witnessed the first riot between Whites and Blacks and was impressed by local civil rights leaders' willingness to use armed self-defense against racial attacks. Brown was a multi-faceted man. One moment he could be mild-mannered, joking with his fellow students at Howard University and the next moment he could be leading a demonstration yelling, "I say to America, Fuck it! Freedom or Death." Little did Brown know in 1963 how much Cambridge would shape his destiny.

VIII
Dogs and Fire Hoses

While violence flared in Cambridge, Somerset County experienced its own racial crisis. During the winter of 1963-1964, John Wilson, a student leader at Maryland State College, led a protest demanding an end to segregated eating facilities in Princess Anne. Students complained for a long time that there was no place for them to have a sit-down meal in Princess Anne. Food was always a "to go" order picked up at a window in the rear of the restaurant. John Lewis, the national leader of the Student Nonviolent Coordinating Committee came to Princess Anne to assess the situation. Difficulties arose over the refusal of several White restaurant owners to serve Blacks from the college. In the summer of 1963, eight out of nine restaurants in town had finally agreed "in principle" to serve Blacks. This was because of the disturbances in Cambridge, fifty miles away. By February 1964, however, the restaurant owners had "backslided" on their agreement to lower racial barriers. This development helped to radicalize a slender Black student at Maryland State College named John Wilson who was a native of Princess Anne.

Though it was just a small historic town, Princess Anne nurtured and galvanized John Wilson. Full of mischief with an aggressive personality and infectious grin, Wilson was raised by his grandparents in Princess Anne where his solidly middle class grandfather, William Maddox, had a catering business. As a child Wilson had good clothing and opportunities that other Black families in town could not afford. Wilson entered Maryland State College in 1961 and was promptly elected president of the freshman class. He quickly became involved in local civil rights activities and helped to mobilize student protests. "My grandfather was always saying 'yassuh" whenever White folks were around," Wilson recalled. "I never did like it." The Black college student bitterly remembered a day when a White woman telephoned his grandfather and young Wilson answered. "Yes he is," said Wilson. "Don't you talk to me like that," the woman hotly responded. " You say ma'am to me, I'm White." Wilson remembered that he gave that woman "the worst cussing I ever gave anybody in my life."[6]

Under the leadership of John Wilson and the Student Appeal for Equality (SAFE), a group affiliated with the Student Nonviolent Coordinating Committee (SNCC), the students at Maryland State College were determined to organize protest marches and test the restaurants for service. These demonstrations were prompted by the failure of Somerset County to have a public accommodations law forbidding discrimination in hotels, motels and restaurants.[7]

Hoping to avoid the kind of trouble that plagued Cambridge, the Princess Anne town commissioners established a Biracial Commission composed of White and Black community leaders. The Committee chose Alexander Jones, a small town lawyer, to head the commission. The town's new racial moderator was a complex man who remained aloof from Princess Anne's booster-oriented civic life. The son of Edgar Jones, a prominent local attorney and segregationist who had been a county official during the George Armwood case, "Sandy" Jones had a good education and good connections and had enjoyed a Fulbright scholarship in England where he met his Irish wife, Cathy. Jones represented people with money in the county and among his clients was Dr. J.T. Williams, President of Maryland State College. Although Jones was indifferent towards the civil rights movement, he nonetheless was motivated by a strong sense of *noblesse oblige* towards Black people. In Princess Anne in 1963-1964, Jones had a difficult mission. As he later recalled, "I had to seek a peaceful solution to the problems of integration in a community whose racial views were more like Mississippi than the rest of Maryland."[8]

On February 21, 1964 John Wilson led forty Maryland State students into Princess Anne to test the agreement negotiated by the Biracial Commission that restaurant owners would serve Blacks. At 4:00 P.M. the students simultaneously entered the town's six White restaurants: Eddie's, the L&L Soda and Pool Parlor, Tull's Restaurant, Muir's Restaurant, Long's Confectionary, and the Washington Hotel. Blacks were courteously served in Eddie's and at the Washington Hotel by Robert Murphey. At the other restaurants, however, Blacks were either refused service or ignored. The following day when John Wilson attempted to enter Tull's restaurant, he was set upon by several Whites and beaten. Later when Black students marched up to Tull's Restaurant, there were several violent clashes and Wilson and three Black students were arrested.⁹ The situation was no better at Muir's restaurant where Herman "Red" Muir vowed that he would close his restaurant before serving Negroes. Muir chased away students with a rubber bat which he kept behind the counter. As racial tempers flared in the community, Alexander Jones worked to head off further incidents and demonstrations in the town. At the time, the town of Princess Anne had only three police officers.

On the night of February 24, 1964, the Ku Klux Klan burned a cross on the Maryland State College football practice field and the home of John Wilson's uncle was fire bombed. Jones and his fellow commissioners walked the streets urging caution and peace. The county was tense and state troopers patrolled the town and monitored traffic on the local highways. When a White threatened John Wilson with a knife, he went to Teddy Holland, the local magistrate to swear out a warrant. "Colored boy," the judge told Wilson, "I swear out warrants for colored people on Monday. Now get out of here."¹⁰

Although many students wanted to retaliate against the townspeople after the cross burning and the bombing, they heeded the advice of campus leaders who urged restraint. In a midnight speech President J.T. Williams reiterated the need for students to listen to the counsels of peace. Williams urged students to work through the NAACP and other civil rights units. The situation deteriorated, claimed Alexander Jones, because the county's officials and members of the legislature from Somerset "sat on their cans."¹¹ Jones also lashed out at students and held them responsible for the worsening situation. Jones feared that more violence would occur and asked the town commissioners to send the National Guard to Princess Anne.

On February 26 over three hundred Black marchers demonstrated again in Princess Anne. At the head of the parade that marched down Somerset Avenue was Gloria Richardson, the fiery Black civil rights leader from Cambridge. The students soon sat down in the middle of the street and blocked traffic. Fearing that they would attempt to destroy the town, many panicked Whites had weapons ready to defend their homes. Violence flared when approximately one hundred state troopers attempted to remove the demonstrators from the highway. Several troopers were hit by flying bricks, bottles and clubs and Captain Paul Randall, the police commander, yelled to his men, "there is nothing nonviolent about this operation." The troopers quickly brought in K-9 attack dogs and enlisted the local White volunteer fire department to use fire hoses to disperse the crowd. Many students were injured by the police and bitten by the dogs. One student, Warren Morgan of New York, had his jaw broken by a police billy club. The students retreated to the campus and police moved up the dogs and fire hoses on pumper trucks to confine the students near the school. Over sixty youths were treated at the college infirmary and twenty-seven were arrested, including a wet-soaked John Wilson. As darkness fell on Princess Anne, angry clusters of Whites and Blacks gathered on street corners. An emergency curfew cleared the streets by 9:15 p.m.. The next day seventy-five students marched into Princess Anne, clapping their hands and singing "We Are Soldiers in the Army," a civil rights marching song.[12] All in all, what some people called the "Battle of Princess Anne" was actually what others called a police riot against unarmed and largely peaceable college students. "Fire hoses and police dogs. It was ugly," recalled John Wilson's friend, William Dennis. "It was like something we had seen on television in Alabama."[13]

Alexander Jones was a weary and disappointed man. For a week he and the Biracial Commission tried to solve the racial impasse in Princess Anne and failed. Jones blamed the students for refusing to listen to reason and bitterly complained that he had received no support from elected officials on the county, state, and federal levels, including Governor Tawes, who was a native of Somerset. When the state police force was summoned, Jones claimed, "it no longer became a question of who's right or who's wrong, but a question of saving the town."[14] The Biracial Commission, Jones noted sadly, had been unable to keep the peace and the lawyer recommended that it be dissolved.

Shortly after the violence at Princess Anne, Maryland Secretary of State Lloyd Simpkins rushed to Somerset from Annapolis to contact local leaders and restore peace. Simpkins was another Somerset native, and his actual mission was to spare Governor Tawes further embarrassment from racial disturbances on the Eastern Shore. Tawes already had the National Guard in Cambridge. He did not want it in Princess Anne. Both Whites and Blacks dismissed Simpkins as a meddlesome "good old boy" who just wanted to smooth over the racial problem without solving it. While Senator Harry Phoebus tried to calm the Black community, Alexander Jones hotly criticized him for not taking an interest in the problem until matters had gotten completely out of control.

Shortly thereafter, Dick Gregory the celebrated comedian and civil rights activist, came to Princess Anne. Joined by John Lewis of the Student Nonviolent Coordinating Committee, Gregory urged that the Black man's goal was the desegregation of the entire Eastern Shore, not just Princess Anne. Gregory's presence guaranteed that Princess Anne would be in the national headlines.

During the first week of March, John Wilson led a group of thirty students to Annapolis to confer with Governor Tawes. After the meeting the governor pledged to use all the powers of his office to get Somerset County included in the state public accommodations law and vowed that the use of police dogs during demonstrations would be strictly controlled. Although racial tensions between Princess Anne and Maryland State College subsided with warm weather and the coming of spring, the events of February would leave a legacy of bitterness and distrust between the college and the town. Tragically for Maryland State College, the uprising in Princess Anne came at a time when the town's Chamber of Commerce had given full support to Dr. J.T. Williams and urged President W. Wilson Elkins, the President of the University of Maryland system, to develop the Eastern Shore college. After "the Battle of Princess Anne," John Wilson quit school and moved to Washington where he became Deputy National Chairman of the Student Nonviolent Coordinating Committee. Wilson sought a civil rights stage bigger than that afforded by Maryland's Eastern Shore.

Princess Anne's racial troubles also attracted fanatical members of the southern Ku Klux Klan and the National States Rights Party who travelled to Somerset to stir up racial hatreds. Before a rally of some 150 Whites outside of town, Reverend Connie Lynch a California segregationist rabble rouser told an audience, "I am going to tell you niggers out there now the best thing you can do is start making reservations for Africa ...This is White man's country." Lynch said "niggers" could leave any way they wanted. "You can leave running or you can leave in a box. Princess Anne is a White man's town."[15] A detachment of state troopers prevented a fight from breaking out between Whites and Blacks.

In August, 1966, when the National States Rights Party led by Joseph Carroll was conducting rallies throughout the south that had as their theme "death to Niggers and Jews," party organizers endeavored to hold a mass meeting on the steps of the Somerset County Court House. The Princess Anne town commissioners quickly obtained a court injunction forbidding the meetings. In handing down the injunction Maryland Circuit Court Judge E. McMaster Duer held that the First Amendment to the Constitution did not allow meetings, which are "abusing and insulting any race in a public place." The States Rights Party sued in court, claiming their right to "free speech." The case ended up in the Maryland Court of Appeals the following year and Duer's injunction held. Ultimately the case was argued all the way to the Supreme Court which unanimously upheld Carroll's right to free speech against arbitrary restraining orders by a lower court.[16] But by then, the Klansmen and States Rights racists had moved on.

Following the tragic events at Princess Anne, President J. T. Williams lamented that the "invisible walls of racism" that separated the town from the college were stronger than ever. As an example, he noted that the Baltimore Symphony came to the college to perform and less than half a dozen Whites came to the concert. Williams was particularly irked by the segregationist policies of the town movie theater that confined Blacks to the balcony while Whites sat in the orchestra. Williams asked his students to boycott the theater.[17]

IX
The Summer of Fire

Racial tension had been high in Cambridge for years as Blacks were relegated to second-class status in a White dominated political economy. Many Blacks worked in low-level jobs in the growing poultry industry but still suffered low wages and chronic unemployment. Activists had conducted protests in Cambridge since

1961; but it was not until 1963 that social conflict erupted in that tidewater town. In the summer of 1963, H. Rap Brown, a SNCC activist, visited Cambridge with Cleveland Sellers, a Howard University student and SNCC organizer to witness what Gloria Richardson's group was doing to desegregate the town. The visit came just as a riot ensued over the collapse of the "Treaty of Cambridge" accords and the announcement that city wide racial policies had to be subject to a public referendum. Brown, a native of Louisiana, was impressed by the local civil rights group's willingness to use armed self-defense against racial attacks.

After organizing SNCC's Mississippi Freedom Summer, Brown transferred from Southern University in Baton Rouge to Howard. Brown was no stranger to fiery meetings with White political leaders. In 1965 Brown and his SNCC group had a contentious meeting with President Lyndon Johnson during the Selma, Alabama crisis in 1965. Elected SNCC chairman in 1967 Brown championed Stokeley Carmichael's support for "Black Power" and rebellion in America's urban ghettos.

Meanwhile the FBI watched H. Rap Brown closely. He had already been tried for transporting a gun across state lines, a charge never proven. In a secret memo, the FBI called for "neutralizing" Brown, especially since they had information that Brown wanted to stir things up on Maryland's Eastern Shore. Brown's high profile activism got him arrested and in and out of the courts; and he was ably defended by his White civil rights attorney, William Kunstler.

When Gloria Richardson met Brown in New York, she invited him to revisit Cambridge to deliver the angry stump speech he was giving across the nation. In this speech Brown called for violent resistance to the federal government which he called "The Fourth Reich" and urged Blacks to "carry on guerilla warfare in the cities that would make the Viet Cong look like Sunday school teachers."[18]

Brown arrived in Cambridge on the night of July 24, 1967, and at 10 p.m. stood atop a car and gave a fiery speech on Black pride, a critique of U.S. White society and championed the willingness of Black people to fight for a better life. He concluded his speech with the hostile remark: "If Cambridge doesn't come around, Cambridge got to be burned down."[19] Brown stayed in town for about an hour or two. He escorted a young woman home along with several others. As Brown's group grew and proceeded towards Race Street, they were confronted by police officers and ordered to stop. Deputy Sheriff Wesley Burton fired twice with his shotgun. One shot ricocheted' off the ground and hit Brown in the head. Brown's allies quickly whisked him to safety and had his wound treated. An hour after learning that Brown had been shot, Black residents started to riot. They burned down a Black elementary school on Pine Street which was the primary social center of the town's Black community. Soon all of Pine Street was aflame and that night a total of 17 buildings were destroyed. News reporters and television camera crews swarmed the area documenting the full extent of the riot. Some Blacks tried to put the flames out with buckets of water but the inferno was too big. The all White fire department did not respond. There was no looting that night. Meanwhile the finger-pointing as to responsibility for the riot began immediately. From Washington President Lyndon Johnson said he thought the riot was the work of outsiders and foreigners. In a moment of almost classical obtuseness, Cambridge Chief of Police, Brice Kinnamon, claimed that the city had no racial problems. Brown was the sole cause of the disorder, and it was "a well-planned Communist attempt to overthrow the government."[20] Most pointed their finger at H. Rap Brown, blaming him for the riot and subsequent conflagration. The following day, newly elected Maryland Governor Spiro Agnew raced to Cambridge and said of Brown, "I hope they pick him up soon, put him away, and throw away the key." After inspecting the ruins of Pine Street, Governor Agnew said, "It shall now be the policy of the state to arrest any person inciting to riot and to not allow that person to finish his vicious speech. Two days later the FBI and local police found Brown and arrested him. Although Brown's lawyers got his trial removed from Cambridge to Bel Air, Maryland, racial tension throughout the Chesapeake region and the state was further heightened by the deaths of two SNCC activists who were killed by White supremacists who planted a bomb in their car near Bel Air on Route 1. After the trial, Brown disappeared for 18 months. His photo appeared on the Federal Bureau of Investigation's Most Wanted List. During an attempted robbery of a New York City bar, Brown was arrested and later served five years in Attica State Prison. In later years, Brown spent most of his time as a fugitive and a convict, ending up imprisoned for life in Georgia on a murder charge.

Meanwhile in Cambridge, the national Kerner Report Commission on Violence found that there was no reason to charge H. Rap Brown for the 1967 riot. Officials in blaming Brown sought to evade their own responsibility for the events that occurred.

Postscript to Summers of Fire

The men and women who fought for civil rights and human decency on Maryland's Eastern Shore in the 1960s have either passed on or are senior citizens. If you look at the pictures of people like Gloria Richardson, H. Rap Brown, John Lewis, John Wilson and Stokely Carmichael what is striking about them is their sense of urgency. These were people with a mission. They sat at lunch counters, fought on Pine Street in Cambridge and were clubbed by state troopers in Princess Anne. To a great extent they were intolerant of older civil rights leaders who wanted to do what Gloria Richardson called "that Gandhi thing" of peaceful protest and non-violence. They were not afraid of being beaten. They were not afraid of going to jail. They defined themselves not so much by their university education as by the important work they were doing to end racial segregation on Maryland's Eastern Shore and nationally. Some of them considered themselves to be shock troops on a racial battleground. Others got caught up in the movement because it either just seemed right for them or because they were profoundly angered about not being able to have dinner in a nice restaurant. SNCC lasted but 10 years; and the memories of old struggles have aged and turned sepia.

Gloria Richardson never returned to Cambridge except for quick family visits. She ultimately became employed by the New York Department of Aging. Richardson's children are both professionals – one a banker, the other an insurance analyst. To them Cambridge is a far place in their memory. Seventy-seven year-old H.Rap Brown as of 2020 was incarcerated at the United States Penitentiary in Tucson. Persecuted and harassed by the FBI for his political activities arising out of "Black Power," Stokeley Carmichael became an expatriate in Ghana and Guinea. Carmichael, now calling himself Kwame Ture, died in Conakry, Guinea at the age of 57 of prostate cancer. John Lewis went on from civil rights activity to a productive life as a 17 term Congressman from Atlanta in the U.S. House of Representatives. John Wilson, until his death in 1993 was a member of the City Council of Washington, D.C and an active advocate of the urban poor. Alexander Jones, the Princess Anne attorney, later retired from his practice and moved to Chestertown with his wife where he became an active alumnus of Washington College. Millard Tawes retired from politics to share his memories with his tidewater friends in Crisfield. In retrospect Tawes accepted responsibility for the failure to accept a peaceful racial accommodation on the Eastern Shore and identified the Cambridge uprising as the great disappointment of his administration. Spiro Agnew emerged as a vituperous critic of the civil rights movement and became Richard Nixon's Vice Presidential running mate in the election of 1968.

Somerset's gradual racial integration came after a decade of Black protest in the community. In Crisfield Mrs. Louise Whittington and others challenged local segregation policies at restaurants and movie theaters and risked confrontation with police authorities. Waging a campaign that stemmed from her own bitter experience in the Jim Crow ward of the Crisfield Hospital, Louise Whittington forced hospital authorities to integrate the wards. Further, in Crisfield Blacks directed their energies at proprietors of segregated White restaurants. Some businessmen in Somerset closed their establishments rather than integrate. The movie theater in Princess Anne was a casualty in this regard.

Racial justice is still one of the paramount issues of American life and the "Sixties," as they are called, continue to be a defining moment in our culture. The pace and trajectory of the civil rights movement in Maryland at that time helped to create a national and international awareness that Cambridge, Crisfield and Princess Anne were part of a worldwide struggle for human rights.

Riots, Fire Hoses and Dogs 181

1. John Wilson, Civil Rights leader and College Student in Princess Anne, Md.

2. Gloria Richardson confronted by National Guard troops in Cambridge, Md.

3. Destructive aftermath of Cambridge racial disturbances

Notes

1. Daniel J. Meyers, "Racial Rioting In The 1960s: An Event History of Local Conditions," *American Sociological Review*, Vol.62, February, 1997, 94-112.
2. Edward Kuebler, "The Desegregation of the University of Maryland," *Maryland Historical Magazine* 71, 1974-1975.
3. *Washington Post* February 26, 1964.
4. Wennersten, personal interviews with Governor Millard Tawes,, Crisfield, Summer ,1975; Frank White Jr., *The Governors of Maryland, 1777-1970*, Annapolis, 1970 293-299; *Baltimore Sun*, October 11, 1965
5. Vicki Crawford, et al. eds. *Women in the Civil Rights Movement, Trailblazers and Torch Bearers,* 1941-1965, Bloomington, 1993, 121-144.
6. Clippings file, John Wilson, Douglass Library, University of Maryland, Eastern Shore.
7. *Baltimore Evening Sun,* February 24, 1964
8. Interview with Alexander Jones, July 28, 1977.
9. *Salisbury Times,* February 22, 1964
10. *Salisbury Times,* February 25, 1964
11. Interview with Alexander Jones, and *Salisbury Times,* March 2, 1964
12. *Baltimore Sun,* February 27, 1964 and *New York Times* March 1, 1964
13. William Thompson, "John Wilson's Long Journey, 1960s activist, lawmaker to Tragedy," *Baltimore Sun,* May 22, 1993.
14. *Baltimore Sun,* February 27, 1964
15. Quoted in the Maryland Court of Appeals Decision of June 7, 1967. Joseph Carroll of the National States Rights Party v. Princess Anne, 230 A.2d 452. Judge Duer's father, Robert Duer had been the presiding judge in the Armwood lynching case of 1933.
16. *Salisbury Times*, August 30, 1966; Interview with Alexander Jones. United States Supreme Court, *Carroll V. Princess Anne,* 393 US 175, 1968
17. Interview with Professor Richard Thomas, June 1, 1976.
18. For background see Peter Levy, *The Great Uprising,* New York, 2018. 80-118.
19. "Maryland Town Recalls Racial Unrest in 1967," National Public Radio. July. 2007.
20. Levy, Great Insurrection, 70-89.

Chapter Eight

The Black College Down the Road

"Prior to 1970 UMES was essentially a part of the University of Maryland plantation.
It began in a subservient role. Born clearly out of segregation."
Howard "Pete" Rawlings, Maryland House of Delegates.

National Overview

Blacks have always thirsted for knowledge and a formal education. In the late nineteenth century the passage of the Second Morrill Land Grant Act created a network of federally supported land grant colleges and universities in the south to train African Americans in agriculture, industrial trades, teacher training and the liberal arts. Although the Morrill Act provided funding for the operation of these institutions, it did not provide financial endowments that matched those of predominantly White institutions. The survival of these land grant schools depended to a great extent on the political leadership of the presidents of these institutions.

Those presidents who embarked on community outreach and cultivated key leaders in their home jurisdictions and in the legislature were able to resist attempts by conservative reactionaries who set upon the idea of racial desegregation as a means of closing publically funded historically Black institutions.

In the modern era Black land grant schools or "1890 Institutions," as they were often referred to, played an important role in educating underserved populations – racial and ethnic minorities, economically disadvantaged individuals, rural-based citizens and often first generation students.

I
The Travail of John T. Williams

In addition to his problems with the town of Princess Anne, a rebellious student body increasingly confronted Dr. J.T. Williams, the president of Maryland State College. Students complained of "unnecessary" school regulations, the poor quality of food in the cafeteria and the deplorable conditions of dormitory life. Student discontent intensified as President Williams sought to recruit White students for Maryland State. Claiming that he had to satisfy the desegregation guidelines mandated by the federal government, Williams attracted 127 White students to the campus. The presence of a significant number of White students called into question Maryland State's future as a Black college, a matter that troubled both Black students and faculty.[1] The school's enrollment at the time numbered 600 and Williams was quick to point out that when he came to Princess Anne in 1947 there were only 163 students on campus and the Marbury Report to the legislature had recommended the closure of the school.

Responding to student pressure, Williams took the offensive. The only salvation for Maryland State, he decided, rested upon its incorporation into the University of Maryland system as a full-fledged campus with adequate funds to raise standards and attract students. For over eighty years, stemming from Princess Anne Academy days, the school had been the stepchild of the state. Various state commissions had recommended the closure of the school because of poor administration and "miserable" quality of instruction. The most important of these was both the Marbury Report of 1947 and Soper Report of 1950, much referred to critiques of the way the Maryland State College operated. Williams vowed that Maryland State's time for fair treatment had come at long last. In his campaign Williams was ably assisted by Maryland State Senator Vera Welcome, a sharp-tongued and pugnacious Black legislator from Baltimore who was Maryland State's self-appointed champion. In Annapolis Welcome charged that the University of Maryland Board of Regents had allowed Maryland State to "rot on the vine." The Regents, she claimed, had channeled millions of dollars to their other branches and programs at College Park and in its overseas military education divisions but had only given "crumbs" to Princess Anne. Each year the school suffered the fate of receiving less appropriations than any other state institution. After touring the campus, Senator Welcome was outraged by the "gross neglect" of the college and called for appropriations to improve campus facilities.[2] Local critics also pointed out that the Eastern Shore delegation in the Maryland House of Delegates was tone deaf to the plight of Maryland State. Williams, however, showed his strength under pressure when he succeeded in getting the US Department of Defense to establish an ROTC program for the training of Air Force officers on the campus, an important cachet for the school statewide. Enrollment in ROTC was required of all male freshmen and sophomores. Williams also recruited Coach Vernon Skip McCain in 1948 to develop the school's football team that went on to have a highly publicized twenty-five game winning streak from 1948 through 1951. Finally in 1954 Williams secured accreditation of his school programs from the Middle States Association of Colleges and Secondary Schools. New land grant funds enabled Williams to replace farm equipment, some of which was of World War I vintage. Meanwhile the legislative sniping at the college continued. Many legislators complained that Williams dwelled too much in the problems of the past and not enough in the future. Finally in 1967 the Maryland Senate passed a resolution that Maryland State College be merged with Salisbury State College located twelve miles north of Princess Anne and to become part of the University of Maryland System. The idea of merging two campuses – one Black and one White elicited considerable pushback from Salisbury's White community and in the following year the legislature relented to allow both schools to maintain separate identities.

Throughout this period the survival of Maryland State College could only be explained by the actions of one man, Dr. Harry Byrd, President of the University of Maryland. Throughout the post World War II period Byrd protected the Black college because he would not tolerate any diminishment of his higher education empire. And as a segregationist from Crisfield, Byrd wanted to keep Black students in "separate but equal" colleges to prevent "race mixing" on the College Park campus. Byrd was politically powerful, fielded successful football teams, and had many key legislators in Annapolis in his favor. His successor Dr. Wilson Elkins was no stranger to the Byzantine intrigues of higher education in Maryland and saw value in the continued existence of the Black college on the Eastern Shore. These rescues, it should be noted, came at a time when the Maryland legislature considered Black political pressure insignificant. Thus due to odd racist circumstance, Maryland State College limped into the 1970s

Ultimately pressure from the federal judiciary forced the Board of Regents to incorporate the school into the multi-campus system. Elkins, President of the university system was mindful of what the loss of federal funding could do to the University of Maryland and vowed to make the Black college an integral part of the university system. In private, Elkins referred to Maryland State College as a "nuisance."

In February, 1970, the Regents voted to accept Maryland State College as The University of Maryland Eastern Shore with a new academic thrust and a Chancellor at its helm.[3] A significant increase in state and federal funding brightened the school's future.

Before the school became a university campus, however, President J.T. Williams faced a final trauma. On April 17, 1970, 178 students were arrested after staging demonstrations on the campus to protest school conditions and to demand his resignation. At a Student Council meeting the president was verbally insulted and harassed by a yelling crowd of campus militants because he "no longer had the confidence of the students at the institution, nor any perception of the students' needs." Williams, they argued followed a "my way or the highway" brand of administration. Students argued that Williams "lacked the imagination and foresight" to lead the college.[4]

Campus discontent became a convenient vehicle for Williams' foes in Annapolis like State Senator Clarence Mitchell, Governor Marvin Mandel, and Secretary of State Blair Lee to get rid of what they called "that autocratic college president." Governor Mandel assured students that although the school had financial problems, he admitted that there was a question of leadership at the school. He assured students that President Williams would not be named chancellor of the college when it was incorporated into the new system. That August, President Williams resolved the issue by announcing his retirement after tenure of twenty-three years at Maryland State.

In retrospect, Dr. Williams had outlived his usefulness at Maryland State College. A stern and enigmatic man, President Williams had administered the college in a strict and often puritanical manner. Insightful faculty members on campus compared him to the fictional Black college president in Ralph Ellison's *Invisible Man*. A decade of civil rights agitation and the many changes in higher education in the 1960s had rendered him an anachronism. During Williams' last months the faculty had been bitterly divided on the issue of his leadership. Several faculty members disassociated themselves from Williams when it became clear that his ship was sinking. Others passionately defended him as their president.

When the college at Princess Anne became an integral part of the University of Maryland in 1970, it could trace its history over eighty years through various stages of development. Beginning as a preparatory school, the institution had evolved into an academy, junior college, four-year college and university division. In her historical analysis of the university's evolution, Ruth Ellen Wennersten chronicled the school's difficult years when the school attempted, often with great difficulty, to provide Black citizens of Maryland with training in agriculture, sciences, and liberal arts [5]

II
Troubled Times

Route 13 is a federal highway built in 1926 that runs 517 miles from Philadelphia to North Carolina and traverses the Atlantic coastal plain. In 1972 it was mostly a rural highway passing through the Delmarva Peninsula's poultry, grain, and potato farms. Dover, Delaware, and Salisbury, Maryland, brimmed with gas stations, fast food outlets and a narrow-minded civic boosterism while poverty-laced areas of Virginia's Eastern Shore were reminiscent of the Depression of the 1930s. Route 13 was always a marker for Princess Anne. "Just take 13 south if you want to find that nigger college down the road in Princess Anne," said White Eastern Shoremen.

Thus it was in 1972 that my wife and I traveled Route 13 down to Princess Anne where I had accepted a teaching position in the Department of Social Sciences at the recently reconfigured University of Maryland Eastern Shore. Little did either of us know at the time how our personal experiences would intersect with history. I had accepted this position after having taught for three years on military bases in the University of Maryland's European Division which was headquartered in Heidelberg, Germany. Accustomed to the cosmopolitan life of Europe with long weekends spent in Paris, my wife and I were startled when we arrived in Princess Anne. The town had but one blinker traffic signal and the main business district was tiny. Eight blocks long and four blocks wide, the town was a centerpiece of old homes on the National Register of Historic Places. Many had been erected between 1755 and 1855. The town had been the cultural capital of 18th century Chesapeake society and for us it seemed like Princess Anne was a time machine that catapulted us back at least a century. The town celebrated its heritage each year with "Olde Princess Anne Days," a series of open houses of plantations and manor homes that reflected a southern *"Gone With The Wind"* ethos.

After parking our car and having lunch at a converted gas station called Peaky's, we explored the town. As we walked on the sidewalk, an approaching elderly Black man stood down in the gutter, tipped his hat and allowed us to pass. My liberal native New York City wife looked at me in shock and surprise. "What have we gotten ourselves into?" she asked. In the shadow of our nation's capital we had ventured unknowingly into the deep South.

Princess Anne and the surrounding county of Somerset carried the scars and resentments of civil rights demonstrations and rioting that had taken place in the region during the 1960s. A palpable Cold War existed between Whites in the community and the Black college community that lay just across the railroad tracks. Black unrest in Princess Anne and Cambridge was not history. It was the smoldering news of the day that influenced nearly every community decision. After taking Princess Anne's measure, we eventually found a townhouse apartment in Salisbury.

Meanwhile a new sense of creative energy and urgency prevailed on the University of Maryland Eastern Shore campus. The school had a new Chancellor, Dr. Archie Lee Buffkins, recently arrived from the University of Maine where he had served as a top echelon administrator in that system. At first glance, Buffkins seemed just what the college needed: a talented Black educator with experience working in Black and White university settings. Raised in Tennessee, Buffkins had a Bachelor's degree from Jackson State, a Black college in Mississippi. and a doctorate from Columbia University. He and his wife were musicians and Carol Buffkins gave well-regarded piano concerts. Buffkins seemed determined to forge alliances with administrators in College Park and with the legislature in Annapolis to build what he called "a multi-racial" university. "The American society is without a doubt, multi-racial. Therefore, the future of higher education must become multi-racial or it will not be relevant to and for the people," Buffkins said in a number of public addresses.[6] Unfortunately Buffkins' upper class sense of entitlement and sense of academic superiority did not play well in Eastern Shore circles.

To accelerate the schools reaccreditation, Buffkins recruited a number of well-degreed White Ph.D's to the campus. Almost immediately the atmosphere on campus, however, proved problematic. Students chafed at the term "multi-racial" and thought it a dog whistle for undermining the school's Black heritage and identity. Long accustomed to having the campus as their own encapsulated Black community, Black faculty felt threatened by both the new and younger White faculty and Buffkins' insistence on building a multi-racial university with higher standards. A significant number of White Vietnam War veterans were attracted to the school, enticed by lower tuition and the fact that their GI Bill money stretched farther in a Black college than in a White one. Buffkins soon found himself facing open rebellion from students, faculty and some Black clergymen. In April, 1972, a campus protest attracted 100 students and was widely carried in the news wire services. "The issue is the direction of this institution under my leadership," Buffkins told reporters from the Associated Press. Tempers cooled, however, when the new Chancellor secured large amounts of federal money to increase student aid and further support an education curriculum that had a Black heritage focus. The latter was part of a larger program involving 13 predominantly Black colleges in the South. Buffkins recruited international students from Nigeria and Ethiopia. He also forged loose alliances with experienced Black faculty members like Mary Fair Burks, a professor in the English Department and Richard Thomas in the Industrial Technology Department. Burks had impeccable civil rights credentials from her work in Alabama and was a close friend of Coretta Scott King , the widow of civil rights leader Martin Luther King and Thomas, a native of Uniontown, Pennsylvnia, was one of the few Black faculty with contacts in the greater White community. Opposition to Buffkins, however, continued to simmer beneath the surface. A faculty group led by science professor Dr. William Lynk visited Buffkins at his home frequently in the evening to voice their concerns about the school's direction.

Meanwhile, new program directors like John Groutt, a former Catholic priest, created bonds with the greater Black and White community through the Head Start Program for school children. Also intiated was a new student guidance program to retain students and help them gain admittance to graduate and law schools. Buffkins began tours of the campus for visitors and legislators as he touted his multi-racial vision. Most White faculty had come to UMES from distant places and universities and were relatively ignorant of the dispute raging behind the scenes. Professors concentrated on their courses and found their students to be mostly polite and academically ambitions. They were, as was often said, "anxious to have their academic ticket punched in order to get the hell out of Princess Anne."

Events came to a critical point late in March, 1975, when Cleveland Harris, the Director of Student Recruitment got into a heated argument over what kind of students to recruit and Harris's financial management of recruitment funds. After an exchange of harsh words, Harris savagely assaulted Buffkins who had to be taken to a hospital in Salisbury where his wounds required surgery. Although the campus was largely scandalized by the Buffkins beating, some faculty murmured that the Chancellor had it coming. Harris was arrested and fired from his position. That summer Buffkins resigned as Chancellor and ultimately embarked on a long term career as a senior arts and music executive at the John F. Kennedy Center in Washington, D.C.

Dr. William P. Hytche, a professor from UMES math department became chancellor. The school's public image had been tarnished by the student campus protests and the Buffkins assault and Chancellor Hytche immediately moved to cultivate better relations in both the Black and White communities. Previously Dean of Students and Chairman of the Mathematics and Computer Science Department, Hytche was open, friendly, and spoke with the twang of his native Oklahoma. People in the Somerset community knew him because he also owned a restaurant on the north side of town, called "the Hawk's Nest." He attended numerous civic events and spent so much time in Annapolis cultivating legislators that some faculty members began to joke that he had a second home there. Dr. Hyche had an uncanny ability to do favors for people and to call upon them when he needed a favor himself. "One hand washes the other," was his operative phrase.

III
The School that Would Not Die

In 1975 Dr. Hytche had scarcely gotten a chance to lead the University when he was confronted by a serious problem. The legislature again wanted to close the university. Enrollments at UMES had flattened out at about 875 full time equivalent students while the student population at Salisbury State College was skyrocketing. Legislators in Annapolis saw little value in financially pumping up UMES when a school of greater value in terms of enrollment and programs existed just a few miles north on Route 13.

At that time the state was looking for property on which to build a state prison and the UMES campus seemed an ideal candidate. The agricultural component of the campus could be turned into a prison chicken farm. The students could enroll at Salisbury State. It wasn't as simple as it seemed, however.

First, UMES was part of the 1890 Land Grant University system in the South and administrators at these schools knew that an attempt to close UMES might be the first salvo of an attack on all the Black land grant schools by White legislatures. The schools all had lines of communication open to the Congressional Black Caucus in Washington and other civil rights organizations.

In 1970 the NAACP Legal Defense Fund sued the Department of Health, Education and Welfare (HEW) stating that HEW had been derelict in its duty to enforce the Civil Rights Act regarding the nation's historically Black public institutions of higher education. In *Adams v Richardson* (1970), the District Federal Court in Washington ruled that public historically Black colleges could not be unilaterally eliminated, dismantled or merged. In subsequent law suits waged by the NAACP, the courts ruled that the process of desegregation must not place a greater burden on Black schools and that a school like the University of Maryland Eastern Shore should be allowed to realize its institutional objectives. In retrospect, then, court decisions on behalf of Black public colleges virtually guaranteed that UMES could not be dismantled without a lengthy and bitter fight in federal court. However, Dr. Hytche and his team worried that by the time the court made its decision, UMES would have suffered damaging wounds to its existence. Fortunately The Maryland Commission of Higher Education adhered to federal guidelines that the process of desegregation must not place a burden on Black institutions or Black students ability to receive a quality public higher education. In *Adams v Califano* (1974) the courts ruled that schools should be allowed to reach their institutional objectives and stated that "each historically Black public college should develop its own specialty areas or programs within the state system." UMES needed to be given funds to publicize its programs and recruit students, especially from other races. By 1974 Hytche had gotten his school into the mainstream of funding within the University of Maryland system.

Meanwhile, the Maryland Higher Education Commission's university policy conundrum was morphing into an intense political and emotional issue. The Commission turned to John W.T. (Jack) Webb, a wealthy and politically well-connected native Eastern Shore lawyer. Webb's influence was extensive both in Salisbury and across the Bay. He was a banker and lawyer, founder of the Greater Salisbury Committee, and served on hospital boards. Despite his aristocratic manner, people knew Webb as a civic-minded attorney and an eminently fair man. When Jack Webb talked, people listened.

During racial disturbances in Salisbury in the 1960's Webb entered the fray, chaired the Salisbury-Wicomico County Biracial Committee and negotiated a public accommodations agreement acceptable to both Whites and Blacks in the town. In 1962 his committee won a Sidney Hollander Foundation Award for progress in race relations.

IV
The Webb Task Force

In 1976 Webb chaired a special Task Force on the fate of UMES and the future evolution of higher education on Maryland's Eastern Shore. In a series of four hearings, the Task Force heard from a number of businessmen and civic leaders who championed Dr. Hytche's work and saw the school as a valuable educational and business asset in Somerset. UMES was the county's largest employer. Tony Bruce, a Princess Anne attorney active in political circles, also rallied a large group of citizens from the lower Eastern Shore to join Dr. Hytche's Chancellor's Advisory Committee to speak on behalf of the struggling Black school. This all had been part of Chancellor Hytche's action to move quickly with a plan of regional political resistance against any merger with Salisbury State College or possible dissolution of the school. Hytche said, "we can no longer continue under a situation where the odds are clearly against us and we feel that this can only be remedied by action at the state level." Hytche reiterated that in its history the school had had several different names: Centenary Biblical Institute, Princess Anne Academy (1886-1935), Princess Anne Branch of Morgan College of Baltimore, Princess Anne College (1936-1948), Maryland State College (1948-1970), University of Maryland Eastern Shore (1970). At all times the school was confronted with the hostility of the White community and state legislatures and battled against closure.

As Jack Webb and his Task Force quickly found, the main problem that bothered the legislature was the program duplication and lack of academic cooperation between the two schools. In regard to the latter, Dr. Sheldon Knorr, Commissioner of the Maryland State Board for Higher Education, grew irritated by the actions of President Norman C. Crawford of Salisbury State. Crawford talked a lot about cooperation, but never did much, Knorr said. "He wanted everything for SSC and nothing for UMES. He was a real operator." Crawford's actions may have stemmed from the fact that when he arrived at Salisbury State Teachers College in 1969, the state legislature was taking steps to recommend the closing of the school and the reconfiguration of Salisbury State as a two year community college. But Crawford reacted quickly to build programs and enrollment which began to skyrocket in the 1970s. The Associated Press identified Salisbury State, now a University, as the nation's fastest growing state college or university. Crawford seemed to hold all the trump cards in the game of academic futures.

As Jack Webb quickly ascertained, there were enough actors on this academic stage to constitute a Shakespearean drama. Some of the actors had powerful parts. Commissioner Sheldon Knorr had been impressed by Hytche's vitality and integrity in getting new programs launched. And Princess Anne attorney Tony Bruce awakened much of Princess Anne from its segregationist era slumber with his litany of more jobs and taxes for economic development of the county. John Toll, the new chancellor of the University of Maryland System, liked Hytche and felt confidant about his leadership at the UMES Campus. One angry actor in the wings, however, was the Department of Agriculture, at College Park which fiercely resisted President Toll's suggestion of its being transferred to the UMES campus. Students, faculty, and community leaders had their walk-on parts. Finally, the state legislature was the bemused audience where even liberals had a chance to impress their conservative colleagues by criticizing UMES as an academic waste of money.

V
The Webb Task Force Report

The Webb Task Force conducted four open hearings that resulted in 900 pages of testimony and 200 position statements. Webb and his group met fourteen times over a six month period and reviewed detailed educational, fiscal, and enrollment data at both institutions. Jack Webb interrogated, lectured, and teased them all about the weighty future of higher education in the lower Chesapeake. The Task Force also relied upon the history of the University of Maryland Eastern Shore. This work constituted the only long range historical analysis at the time of the evolution of a Black land grant college in the state.⁷

Webb and the Task Force saw a chance to bring about significant improvements in the way higher education could be implemented in Maryland. Webb talked about universities in California that had been reconfigured around specific programs or industries like California viticulture. First, could UMES excel in marine science, Webb asked Toll and Hytche? Second, Webb found that Black students did not want to attend Salisbury State where they would probably have a second rate status. Thirdly, UMES only had a few short years to restructure and rebuild itself. Blacks on the Eastern Shore were still aggravated by the fact that when Salisbury State got a new swimming pool, they asked for one to be constructed on the Black campus. Replied one Annapolis legislator, "if Negro students at that college want to swim, they can swim in the Manokin River." For those who cared to look beyond the provincial pages of the local *Salisbury Times*, the issues in terms of civil rights, integration, and Black institutional survival were of great import.

The Task Force reached a unanimous conclusion. Webb stated that "we believe that our recommendations, if implemented in good faith, will remove the uncertainties surrounding the future of both institutions and will provide educational opportunity for all citizens, not only of the region, but also of the state." In summary the Webb Task Force Report claimed that "we believe the educational needs of the lower Eastern Shore at this stage of the areas's history require two separate institutions, but with separate roles and missions clearly defined to prevent duplication of resources and to maximize choice based on the quality of programs."

Addressing the future of both schools the Task Force recommended that Salisbury State should offer the traditional liberal arts curriculum and UMES should be a science-oriented institution with graduate and undergraduate programs in the marine, estuarine, and environmental sciences and in agriculture. Further the Task Force recommended that there be no enrollment limitation on out of state enrollment at UMES. The task force concluded its report by urging the Princess Anne-Somerset County community to improve its relationship with UMES.⁸

The Webb Report was a major breakthrough. The survival of Dr. Hytche's university campus was no longer in doubt. With stability and new programs, enrollments would grow.

The UMES crisis of 1976-1977 left President Hytche physically exhausted, however. A short while later he suffered a mild heart attack. At Salisbury State University President Norman Crawford began to experience difficulties over the financial management of his school. After three years of problems, Crawford was fired by his Board of Trustees.

During the decade of the 1980s each campus squabbled with the other over programs and enrollments. Occasionally President John Toll of the University System and the State Commission of Higher Education intervened. Aside from a university bus service program to give students access to both campuses, relations between the two universities remained cool.

VI
The Prospectus

By 1978 it was apparent to Bill Hytche and John Toll that the school would face a better future if it fully became part of the University rather than be a problematic appendage. As President Toll said to UMES faculty and administrators, to strengthen the entire university, one had to build up its weakest link. Both Toll and Hytche went on the offensive and working with staffs at both College Park and Princess Anne, they came up with a long range Prospectus for institutional advancement. As a first step, Chancellor Hytche went on a massive recruiting effort to lure professors with Ph.D. degrees to the campus that would enable him to launch new programs. Hytche had grown tired of playing defense in his stewardship of the school. As he told his staff, "any team whose defense is on the field all the time very seldom wins. You've got to have an offense." As part of the "offense" Chancellor Hytche and President Toll identified five new programs in graduate and undergraduate education at the school, the capstone of which was a "stand alone" Master's Degree program in Counseling and Guidance. This was quickly followed up with program designs for academic degrees in Hotel and Restaurant Management, Construction Technology, Airway Science, Engineering, and Poultry Management. Throughout this time Hytche encountered resistance from faculty who feared that he was trying to turn the campus into a trade school. With the support of College Park, Hytche scored a notable coup in recruiting Raymond Blakely, one of the few Ph.D Black professors in the field to head a new Department of Physical Therapy. Hytche recruited Abraham Spinak, a former administrator of the Wallops Island Space Program, to establish an Airway Science program for the training of minority pilots and air traffic controllers, a burgeoning employment field.

Meanwhile, students grumbled, and old line faculty went up the back stairs to the Chancellor to complain about the changing identity of the school. Chancellor Hytche was undeterred. The Prospectus and the programs that sprang from it were highly popular with business and civic leaders in the region and remained true to the recommendations of the Webb Report some three years earlier.

With new budget lines for faculty, building construction, and programmatic initiatives as part of the school's land grant mission, Chancellor Hytche and his university faulty and staff demonstrated that if given a chance a Black university with equal resources could successfully compete in the world of American higher education.

Over time the sequence of semesters and the quotidian rhythms of the college reflected a busy student and faculty life. Professors chased research grants and taught their classes. Stokeley Carmichael, tailed by a White FBI agent, came to the campus and gave a hell-raising speech to an excited audience. An overflow of students took residence in newly constructed apartment buildings in Princess Anne. Seniors prepared their applications for graduate and law schools The Black community turned out for the annual Ebony Fashion Fair. And life at UMES moved on.

1. Chancellor William P. Hytche of the University of Maryland, Eastern Shore in the 1970s. Courtesy of the University of Maryland Easten Shore Archives.

2. Dr. John Taylor Williams.

Notes

1 *Washington Post,* March 11, 1969
2 *Baltimore Afro-American,* March 16, 1968
3 *Salisbury Times*, February 18, 1970.
4 "Demands and recommendations from the Maryland State College Student Body," typescript, April 19,1970, Vertical File, University of Maryland, Eastern Shore, Douglass Library.
5 Ruth Ellen Wennersten, "From Negro Academy to Black Land Grant College: The Maryland Experience 1886-1910," *Agriculture and Human Values,* vol 9, 1992, 15-21.
6 "Archie L. Buffkins" University of Maryland, Eastern Shore Archives. Home, 125.
7 Ruth Ellen Wennersten, "The Historical Evolution of a Black Land Grant College: The University of Maryland, Eastern Shore, Unpublished Master's Thesis, University of Maryland, College Park, 1976.
8 For this analysis I relied upon my notes and recollections of the "crisis of 1976." Also, I testified before the Webb Task Force in defense of Dr. Hytche's programs. The full and complete analysis of the Webb Task Force including interviews and oral testimony as well as the Final Webb Report in its entirety is contained in Carl S. Person, "Realization of the Historically Black College: A Maryland Eastern Shore Case," Unpublished Ph.D. dissertation, Virginia Polytechnic Institute and State University, 1988. Person relied extensively on Wennersten's earlier study.

Chapter Nine

Semper Eadem

"The Past does not lie down quietly."
Archbishop Desmond Tutu

National Overview

Today the United States has a thriving, if somewhat tenuous, Black middle class. It is a creation largely of federal government policy, coupled with Black litigation and social militancy that has been multi-racial in nature. There has been an astonishing change since the 1960s when the one thing that Black people owned was the "equality of poverty and systematic intimidation." Today African Americans have begun to test the limits of the American polity by seeking a greater share of political power and holding state and federal government agencies accountable for a greater share of money for Blacks in public and higher education.

Currently affluent African Americans seem to have greater mistrust of White society than poorer members of the race. It is working class Blacks' continued faith in the American Creed of democracy and social mobility, however, that lends stability to American racial encounters We may-be at a tipping point where Whites feel that Blacks deserve the success they have achieved and Black aspiration is part of the American dream for all.

I
"Coming up Black"

A member of the last segregated high school graduating class in Somerset County, Kirkland Hall, Class of 1969, recalls that there were no overnight miraculous integration transitions in a resentful community of Whites and Blacks. A generation of Black school children would remember segregation even as they prepared themselves for better-integrated schools, better school texts and laboratory equipment and perhaps better treatment in the public sector. Hall remembers an end to the rickety unheated old school buses that carried Blacks to their schools. He also recalls that there was a sense of change in the air.

Things seemed better than when as a boy he used to pick strawberries on a large White farm before school to earn some extra money. A White supervisor kicked over one of his baskets to see if he was padding the basket with green berries. Hall's temper flared but his mother who was also picking, told him to keep his mouth shut. The family needed the money.

Change is a double-edged sword. Schools as learning environments showed improvement. With integration, however, came certain unwelcome changes: Black principals in segregated schools became Vice Principals in charge of teacher oversight and school discipline. White teachers thought of them as "integration cops." Black coaches and Black guidance counselors were demoted back into the class rooms as teachers as a new, mostly White administration emerged to lead the county school system. Newly trained Black teachers formerly could count on employment in segregated schools. Now they had to compete for jobs. Some White teachers quit or retired, claiming that they did not want to teach Black kids that they viewed as disruptive and unhygienic.

Kirkland Hall was determined to leave all that old segregation stuff behind when he enrolled as a student at the newly configured University of Maryland Eastern Shore. Encouraged by his schoolteacher mother and lumberyard worker father, Hall stuck to his studies in physical education and coaching basketball. After graduation, Kirkland Hall went to graduate school at Ohio State University. "The school opened up a whole new world for me, one far different from Maryland's Eastern Shore. I excelled in a better social and educational climate," he said. He went to football games not held in some bleacher field, but in an awe-inspiring Ohio State stadium with 100,000 seats that were constantly sold out. Hall returned to the University of Maryland Eastern Shore and coached winning basketball teams. Hall's personal crisis came in 1978. In that year the two colleges, UMES and Salisbury State, agreed to have a basketball contest at the gym of Salisbury State. At that time there were very few Black students at Salisbury State and the school was popular with White families who wanted to keep their offspring closer to home. Salisbury would field a White team; Hall would field a Black one. Early in the game, Hall began to protest the calls of the two White referees against his players. During one temperamental exchange, recalls Hall, "a White referee used the N-word and I pulled my team off the floor and went home." The incident was embarrassing to both schools. Hall received a severe "tongue lashing" for bad conduct from President Hytche. "The only reason I was able to keep my job," Hall remembers, "is that a White sportscaster sitting next to the Salisbury bench at WBOC TV heard the referee say the hated word." The sportscaster testified in Hall's behalf. Later Hall gave up coaching and concentrated on being a professor of Physical Education.

In 1986 Kirkland Hall became involved with the local unit of the NAACP and began to ponder the true significance of the county motto, *Semper Eadem*, (Always the Same). For Hall that motto came to mean stagnation for Blacks in the county. The old segregation stuff kept catching up with him and Hall was soon agitating in concert with the American Civil Liberties Union lawyer to have Blacks as paid members and volunteers of the previously all White police and fire departments. The local volunteers of the county's fire facilities pushed back hard. They did not want Blacks. The fire department for volunteers was more than a fire-fighting agency. It was a "good old boys" social club whereby they could celebrate events and parties "down at the firehouse" with their wives and families. The court sided with the NAACP's suit and that was that.

But a disturbing message came from within the Black community itself. As Hall and his NAACP allies discovered, there was a disturbing amount of Black pessimism in Somerset County that enabled White candidates to win even in Black majority county districts. "What's the use of voting," Blacks told Hall. "Things won't change." It was during this time that the demography of White voters in the county shifted from the Democratic Party to the Republican. And with the shift came, what Hall and others believed, a chance for the NAACP to field Black Democratic candidates for office. After all, Somerset County was 40 percent Black. But as soon as the NAACP fielded a candidate, Whites encouraged a second Black candidate to run against him, insisting that he was more qualified than the first man. The end result was that the two Blacks canceled themselves out in the voting and the White candidate won. The voting situation may have changed a bit from the days when Whites bought Black votes with $2 and a whiskey miniature, but it was still egregious.

Hall ran for House of Delegates in a district that encompassed Somerset and Worcester Counties. "I was popular in Worcester with both Blacks and Whites and went to a lot of homes and political dinners," he said. "But I lost because my fellow Blacks in Somerset did not turn out to vote as I would have liked. They let me down." Afterwards, some Blacks in Princess Anne noted that his defeat was not "a Black thing." It was "a Hall thing." He just got hot under the collar too often to suit them.

II
The Hegemonic Power of the Racial State

In slavery days White men could legally marry White women and at the same time force their sexual desires on Black women. In the colonial period a White woman who attempted to marry a slave, became herself a slave. Perhaps the most famous Maryland case of interracial sex at this time is that of Nell Butler or "Irish Nell, a White servant girl. Living in 1681, Irish Nell fell in love and decided to marry a Black slave known as "Negro Charles." When Nell went to her master, Lord Baltimore, and told him of her plans, he warned her that she was condemning herself and her children to a life in slavery. Defying her master's wishes Nell replied that she would rather marry Charles than Lord Baltimore himself. She spent the rest of her life enslaved.

Lord Baltimore was wrong, however, about her descendants. In the 18th century a Maryland Court held that neither Nell nor her children were slaves. Later, slave owners complained of runaway mulatto slaves who insisted that they were the "descendants of the famous Nell Butler."[1] During the unsettled years of the American Revolution several thousand slaves went over to the British side in search of freedom. Slave masters employed White women whose sole job was to castrate rebellious Black males.² This says something about American patriots of the time and the women they employed. Black sexuality came to be associated with rebellion and war against Whites.

Without historical perspective, one cannot understand the complicated and traumatic history of interracial relationships in the American South. Historian Nell Painter has characterized the kind of physical and psychological sexualized violence towards Blacks as contributing to what she calls the "soul murder" of African Americans. Further, sexualized violence directed by White men against Black men with White females has often happened when there have been affectionate bonds between a White woman and a Black man.³

Historically in the Chesapeake Bay Country consensual conjugal relationships between Black men and White women were viewed as particularly dangerous to the maintenance of White supremacy. This explains, in a perverse way, why Whites in Somerset and elsewhere in the South attempted to maintain their power by citing the alleged rape of White women by Black men as a justification for lynching. It also explains why violence against Black sexuality both physically and psychologically characterized much of Chesapeake culture throughout the nineteenth and twentieth centuries. Brutal punishment of Blacks who had sex with White women was a way of maintaining the "hegemonic power of the racial state."⁴ As the 1955 Mississippi murder of a teenage Black student named Emmitt Till for supposedly whistling at a White girl exemplified, any kind of interracial sexual congress, real or imagined, could result in a Black man's death. In 1974 there were still plenty of people in Somerset County who remembered that George Armwood's lynching had the sexual overtones of a Black man assaulting a White woman.

There has always been a historical taboo against a Black man having sex with a White woman in Somerset County. And on the night of April 3, 1974, history came calling at Jimmie Mosley's trailer.

III
The Murder of Jimmie Mosley

On April 4, 1974 the body of Jimmie Mosley, Chairman of the Fine Arts Department at the University of Maryland Eastern Shore was found near his trailer home on Peggy Neck Road just south of Princess Anne. Neighbors later testified that they heard approximately eight shots fired around 11:30 p.m. the night of April 3. Two .357 slugs and two .22 slugs were recovered from bullet wounds in Mosley's head and back. His face was nearly obliterated by the power of the .357 bullets.

It was at this time that Jimmie Mosley was acquiring regional fame for his watercolors, which fetched commanding prices on the art market. Some critics thought him to be potentially "the Black Thomas Hart Benton" for his regional depictions of Black migration and country scenes. A taciturn man, Mosley joined the faculty in 1951. The National Council of Artists recognized his work in shows throughout the country including Arkansas, Delaware, Missouri, New York, and Pennsylvania. As Mosley summed it up, "I am an artist; I have something to say. I hope I have said it well." Recently divorced, Mosley's ex-wife and several children lived in nearby Wicomico County.

Mosley taught an evening course in studio art at the University that had an adult following from Salisbury. Among his students was Ann Wentworth, a married White housewife and daughter of a prominent Salisbury veterinarian. Mrs. Wentworth was an eager student and Mosley was impressed by her work. A student-teacher relationship evolved into a kind of social intimacy.

Ann's husband, David Wentworth, began to harbor suspicions that something more was going on in his wife's art course. David Wentworth had a history of uncontrollable fits of anger and volcanic jealousy. Three years prior, Wentworth attacked Ann's father after a drinking bout laced with drugs and came close to killing him. He looked like he was in a trance, his wife later recalled. This was part of a history of family violence that was part of Ann Wentworth's life. In her testimony, Ann Wentworth said she learned to respond to violent situations "by laying low and doing what you are told and not to aggravate the angry beast." An enraged Wentworth resolved to settle the matter by confronting Mosley at his home. Before he left Salisbury with his apprehensive and tearful wife, he put a .357 revolver in his belt.

The Wentworths came to the trailer at approximately 9:30 p.m.[5] at the time Mosley was entertaining his girl friend, Dr. Delores Taylor, the Assistant Dean at Salisbury State College. Initially the visit was convivial. Mosley served the Wentworths drinks. Anne had two drinks and her husband had four. About forty-five minutes later the conversation turned nasty when David Wentworth accused Mosley of having sexual relations with his wife. The sudden change of mood caught Mosley and Taylor both by surprise. Mosley denied Wentworth's accusation. At that point Wentworth in drunken temper pulled out his revolver and ordered Mosley to lie on the floor with his hands behind his head. Pointing his gun Wentworth asked Mosley if he had sex with his wife. A terrified Mosley said "yes." Wentworth learned in the interrogation that Mosley owned a .22 caliber pistol and sent his wife to get it. She later went back into the bedroom and got bullets for the revolver. Again, Wentworth demanded to know if he would own up to having sex with his wife. Mosley finally replied. "Yes, if it means saving my life, I'll say yes."

Meanwhile Ann Wentworth searched the bedroom for money and narcotics and guns. She took money from Dolores Taylor's purse. Then she proceeded to wipe fingerprints from surfaces she had touched in the kitchen dining area. Surveying the scene, Wentworth announced that he was going to take them for a ride in Mosley's car, handcuff them to a tree and then return to thoroughly search the trailer for valuables. While the Wentworths focused on Mosley, Dolores Taylor seized the moment, bolted out of the trailer and fled into the night. Running across a field in desperation, Taylor banged on a neighbor's door for help. They called the police and both returned to the trailer and found no one there.

Ann Wentworth later testified that her husband was " very paranoiac and was in another fit of rage." Once her husband pulled out his gun she feared for Mosley's and her life. She was forced to drive the car while her husband held his gun on Mosley. "I felt that I would be killed at any minute and that Mr. Mosley would be killed at any minute," she said.

Mosley's bullet ridden body was found the following morning on the shoulder of the road. The FBI put out an all points bulletin for the murderers. Meanwhile the Wentworths fled the Eastern Shore and a week later their car was recovered in Georgia. Renting another car, the couple got as far as Idaho where police arrested them on May 5, 1974. Mosley's credit cards were in Wentworth's pocket. The police also recovered a .375 magnum revolver whose bullets were a ballistic match of those found in Mosley's body.

The couple returned to Maryland for trial for murder and manslaughter. On February 30, 1975, they entered guilty pleas to four counts of murder, kidnapping and armed robbery. David Wentworth was sentenced to 70 years in prison on three consecutive counts of murder, kidnapping and armed robbery. His wife, Ann, also received a prison sentence as her husband's accessory. She later successfully appealed her sentence claiming that she had acted under extreme psychological and physical duress.

No longer would it be possible for a White man to kill a Black man over an interracial sexual encounter on the Eastern Shore without consequence. The Mosley family got justice of a sort but it paid a terrible price. As Sherri Lynn Ifill, Director of the NAACP legal defense fund said, "The assumption of most Whites is that history is dead, unimportant, and irrelevant to the modern reality of life on the Eastern Shore. But in fact a town's reputation as a racially violent one often lives on in the lore shared among Blacks."[6]

IV
The Elephant In The Room

In February 2009 the Black community in Somerset thought it was about to make history. A county commissioner seat had opened up and the County Democratic Central Committee sought applicants to make recommendations to Governor Martin O'Malley for appointment to the seat. Two Black men, Clarence Bell, the Director of Pubic Safety at the University of Maryland Eastern Shore and Kenneth Ballard, local branch president of the NAACP advanced their candidacy. To their disappointment, a White commissioner was selected. How could it be, members of the NAACP asked, that a county whose population was 42 percent African American could not get one Black person on the Somerset County Board of Commissioners? In 2009 no Black person in the history of Somerset County had ever held elective or appointive political office – from State's Attorney, Sheriff, County Commissioner, State Delegate, or Fire Marshall or any other appointment. As Dr. Bess McCallister, a local pastor, claimed, the racial divide was " like the elephant in the room in Somerset County and it's in every room, church, office, school, business, private club and public meeting."[7] Shortly thereafter a group of ACLU officials and members of the NAACP assembled a task force to document "the yawning racial gulf that has always existed in Somerset County and that remains virtually unchanged in the 21st century." They pointed to the career of DeWayne Whittington as illustrative of the corrosive racism in the county.

    To many on the Eastern Shore Dr. DeWayne Whittington symbolized the struggle against racism that remained even after the smoke of civil rights battles in the region had long cleared. Whittington's life story was an upward ascent of a well-mannered man of intelligence and sensibility who triumphed over the racial restrictions of his region. Raised by grandparents in Crisfield, Whittington graduated from Crisfield Colored High School in 1948. After getting his Bachelor's Degree at Morgan State College in 1952 he was inducted into the military where he rose to the rank of Captain. Afterwards he took a teaching job as a physical education teacher and coach in Somerset's segregated school system . When Somerset schools integrated Whittington rose rapidly in the system, holding a variety of important administrative positions dealing with human relations and instruction. In 1988, Whittington, a much loved teacher and educator with a Master's Degree from Penn State and a PhD from Nova University, became the first Black superintendent of Somerset County Schools, the first Black to hold such a position in any school system outside of Baltimore. After nearly four decades in the Somerset School System, Whittington enjoyed wide popularity with everyone but the White members of the school board. As the time approached for the renewal of Whittington's appointment in 1992, the school board voted 3 to 2 not to renew his four-year contract. "I just had that gut feeling that racism was to blame, " he later said. "When no one has complained about your performance, that's the first thing that pops into your mind."[8] In 1994, aided by the American Civil Liberties Union, Whittington sued the county in federal court in Baltimore. A two-week trial followed in 1996. School board members denied that they were motivated by race, citing differences over management style, discipline and the overall performance of the school system.

Whittington's witnesses stressed his professionalism. In what was perhaps the most dramatic moment in the trial, a local freelance writer testified that during the 1988 election for school board, the future board president had said, "the last thing we need is a nigger running the school system." The board member denied having made the remark.

The jury found unanimously in Whittington's favor and awarded him compensation and penalties that amounted to over $930,000. The jury also concluded "monetary compensation alone is not a sufficient punishment for an act of racism." Jurors recommended naming a county school for him. The county assented and named a primary school in Crisfield the H. DeWayne Whittington Primary School. The Governor of Maryland later appointed Dr. Whittington to the Somerset County School Board. Shortly after the Whittington verdict in 1996, Betty J.Miles became the first African American elected to the school board. She replaced the Board President.[9]

In gathering data for its 2009 report on continuing racial disparities in Somerset County, the local NAACP and the American Civil Liberties Union revealed a disturbing body of facts showing an astonishing lack of progress for the Black community as it entered the 21st century of American life. The study revealed that no African American in history had been elected or appointed to a top job in county government and that the county in 2007 spent "in excess of $5,715,000 on the salaries of White employees while only spending about $750,000 on the salaries of African Americans. At that time no Blacks worked in a professional capacity in Somerset County other than teaching. In the school system where Blacks have had a history of employment dating from segregated schools, in 2009 there were 188 White teachers and only 46 Black teachers in a county that was over 40 percent Black. A study of hiring trends in the county showed "no evidence to address the lack of diversity among the employees of the county or its school system."[10] The report ended with the hope that county leaders and residents would open a dialogue about race and make a commitment to keep talking and listening.

In 2010 a dramatic breakthrough occurred. For the first time in Somerset's 344-year history, a Black man was elected to office in the county. Craig Mathies a local pastor and former car dealer was elected to the Board of Commissioners from District One. For decades the Black majority district had been represented by James Ring, a White politician skilled in office keeping by playing Black candidates off one another. Mathies did not campaign hard for the position. He later said, "If God meant this to happen, it would happen. It did." After his election Mathies told newscasters that it was now "up to him to speak in behalf of those who may not have the courage or may not have enough knowhow or may not be bold enough."

Shortly after his election, Whites who lived outside Princess Anne but could vote in municipal elections were incensed by a lawsuit filed by Rev. Mathies and the ACLU to keep people who lived outside of Princess Anne and owned property in town from voting in town elections. A handful of White landowners were so angry that they put forth a referendum that would have dissolved the town of Princess Anne altogether. The controversy ended when the town looked at the financial implications of town closure and the lengthy lawsuits it and the White landowners would face.

To Kirkland Hall, President of Somerset's NAACP Chapter, Mathies' election to the County Board of Commissioner was a joyful event. "Finally our children can say to themselves 'There's hope for me. I can get a job in the government. I can be a County Commissioner.' I feel like a weight has been lifted from my shoulders." But change, both racial and economic, still comes slowly in Somerset County. From perhaps a politically cosmetic viewpoint, the county has grown more conscious of such matters. But that is it. People don't apply for jobs because information is tightly restricted. In the past Whites that were in charge passed jobs along to the people they knew. Said Commissioner Mathies, "That's the biggest thing. There are lot of qualified African Americans here. They just don't know about the government jobs." This should be seen against the last census analysis that put Somerset County in the bottom of all 24 counties with per capita income of $16,471.[11]

In the county there are important community events and not everyone is invited. The last class of 1969 of Washington High School before it opened its doors to Blacks was having its reunion in the fall of 2004. A ballroom was decorated like an old senior prom and there were paintings of the school and an old soda fountain. Organizers called it a Grand Homecoming for graduates of the 1940s, 1950s, and 1960s to share memories of sock hops and football games. A poster was circulated in the community advertising the event that read "Travel Back to the Old Times."

Some Black leaders like Kirkland Hall found the all-White reunion to be a sad and painful reminder that decades after the Supreme Court outlawed school segregation, things had not changed that much in their community. "It's just as divided as it's ever been," noted a former Black resident, Leon Johnson. "The old folks did a good job of teaching the young ones, of teaching them the old system." For Kirkland Hall and the NAACP, it might have been better if Blacks and Whites combined their respective reunions as an event of racial understanding. Mickey Wigglesworth, a retired Somerset banker and other reunion organizers retorted that there was no attempt to exclude Blacks on their part. The event would have had no appeal to Blacks, said the White organizer.[12]

For Somerset County and many communities in the South, the course of racial and ethnic politics over the next few decades will depend upon the dynamics within the African American community. Just up the road from Princess Anne lies Wicomico County, a polity that was carved out of Somerset and Worcester counties after the Civil War. Largely due to an influx of government programs spearheaded by Shore-Up, a federally funded organization, the county has a thriving though somewhat tenuous Black middle class. Blacks have left Somerset to live in Salisbury, the Wicomico County seat. Wicomico offers Blacks a better chance at material success but with an exceedingly complex social and cultural arena to navigate. Success does not alleviate Black mistrust of White authority especially when it comes to local police activities. A recent Brookings Institute Study has found that nationally by the 1980s "Blacks with low status were perceiving less White hostility than were their higher-status counterparts."[13]

Since 2013, according to a Gallup Poll, even after the election of a two-term African American president, Black Americans' overall positive perceptions on racial change have cooled. "This period of decline has witnessed high-profile police shooting incidents involving Black citizens," the poll reports. Although race relations have improved both in the Chesapeake and the South since 2000, most Blacks (53%) say relations between Blacks and Whites will always be a problem.[14] According to a recent Pew Research Report, most Americans say it has become common for people to express racist or racially insensitive views since the election in 2016 of Donald Trump.[15]

For Black people in Somerset County, and in the nation generally, the struggle continues. The death rate for Blacks compared to Whites is still much higher in the region and Black infant mortality in the period 2004-2008 was 2.6 times higher than that of Whites. Asthma and HIV continue to scourge the Black community. That Blacks have less access to affordable medical care in Somerset and elsewhere on the Eastern Shore continues to reflect the region's problematic racial heritage.

1. Professor Jimmie Mosely at the height of his artistic career

Notes

1. Martha Hode, *White Women, Black Men: Illicit Sex in the Nineteenth Century South*, 1997, 19-38.
2. Diane Miller Somerville, "Rape, Race and Castration in the Colonial and Early South," in Catherine Clifton, ed., *The Devil's Lane, Sex and Race in the Early South*, New York, 1997
3. Nell Irvin Painter, "Soul Murder and Slavery: Toward a Fully Loaded Cost Accounting," in Linda Kerber ed. *U.S. History as Women's History*, Chapel Hill, 1995, 125-146.
4. Peggy Pascoe, *What Comes Naturally: Miscegenation Law and the Making of Race in the United States*, New York, https://youtube/QpQXMetEbT42009, 310.
5. What follows is largely an account summary of *Wentworth v State of Maryland*, Court of Special Appeals 29 Md. App110 (1975), Ann Louise Wentworth v. State of Maryland, Decided November 28, 1975
6. Sherrilyn A. Ifill, *On the Courthouse Lawn: Confronting the Legacy of Lynching in the Twenty-First Century*, New York, 2007, 21.
7. *Semper Eadem, "Always the Same"?, A Report by the ACLU of Maryland and the Somerset County NAACP On Continuing Racial Disparities in Somerset County Government*, 2009.
8. Quoted in *Washington Post* obituary, December 2, 2012.
9. *Semper Edem Report*. P.6
10. Ibid. 14.
11. Maryland Counties Ranked By Per Capita Income, US Census Data, *Census of 2010 and the 2010-2014 American Community Five Year Estimates*.
12. "The Grand Homecoming." *Associated Press Newswire*, September 22, 2004.
13. Jennifer Hochschild, "American Racial and Ethnic Politics in the 21st Century: A Cautious Look Ahead" *Brookings Institution*, March 1, 1998.
14. *Gallup Poll Social Series*, February 21, 2019
15. Pew Research Center, *Social and Demographic Trends*, "Race in America," April 2019.

Afterword

I

Endings

There is not a corner of our country that has been untouched by slavery and racism. Unfortunately, to a large extent we misremember it. There is a kind of amnesia that touches us all and oppressors in the South have been exceptionally skilled in constructing a mantle of victimhood about the "lost cause" and various aspects of southern valor A 2015 study by the Equal Justice Society, *Lynching in America,* documented 4,084 lynchings of Black people in twelve southern states from 1870 to 1950. It is a fearsome chapter in our national story.[1] In her recent book, **Caste**, Isabel Wilkerson writes that "Lynchings were part carnival, part torture chamber and attracted thousands of onlookers who collectively became accomplices to public sadism." She adds that photographers made picture postcards of the lyinchings "for people to send to their loved ones."[2]

Somerset County sits 135 miles and a world away from the fast-paced metropolitan life of Washington, D.C. Yet Somerset's history and culture are at the heart of the American story. It is part of the Atlantic seaboard where the history of our country begins in the seventeenth century. The low grounds, marshes, and dark rivers serve as counterpoint to the grain farms and chicken houses that dot the landscape. The land stretches out towards the white horizon of Chesapeake Bay in summer and watermen prepare their boats for yet another crabbing season. Winter seasons are mild and flocks of geese and ducks attract hunters. Spring is wet and turns the normally brown marsh to green with muskrats busily rebuilding their nests. Tourists marvel at the scenery and see the county as a bucolic paradise. We are just beginning to see markers along the highways of the county that say slavery once thrived here and commemorates those like Frederick Douglass who fought against it.

As this book is being written, a disturbing ethno-nationalism is beginning to gather strength in the United States. It traces its roots back to the founding of the country when historians like George Bancroft could praise his New England forebears for there steadfast "Anglo-Saxon leadership" in the development of the country. Later rich and very influential southern planters and writers like Edward Lloyd of Wye House could extol the virtues of Anglo-hierarchy from the vantage point of a 12,000-acre Wye House plantation with 500 slaves in the Chesapeake's Talbot County.

The Civil War demonstrated how our country could come perilously to the brink of destruction. The southern states lost their bid for sovereignty; but their ethno-nationalism of "the Lost Cause" reinforced an American story of a triumphant White Anglo-Saxon nation-state. For a brief period from the 1960's to the 1990's a liberal civic nationalism eclipsed Anglo-Saxon doctrines and became the received narrative of our Union. Racism and inequality were perceived to be on the wane. Equal opportunity was on the rise.

Now, we are distracted from the truths about ourselves most of the time. Things don't quite make sense and it is not possible to put all the pieces together to form a perfect whole, a perfect truth.

What history in Somerset reveals is that the White sons and daughters of Somerset have always held the old ways close; and there are always secrets and truths most people would rather not know about, especially when it comes to race. It is easier to change a law than to change people's thinking. Until the advent of this new century, the region was mostly quaint, relaxed and suspicious of outsiders. The White community of Somerset has historically been arrayed against Black people; but it has not prevented Blacks from moving towards a better outcome.

What will be the new social narrative of the Chesapeake's Eastern Shore as Somerset and the other counties move forward in the 21st century? The Eastern Shore has long produced the strange fruit of racial subjugation, violence, and death. The question for the future depends on whether cooperation and altruism will counter apathy and hostility and hopefully overcome intolerance.

II
The Issue of Race

Using a microhistorical approach, in this book I have written a story by gazing through the window of a number of ordinary lives. It is essentially the story of local racism and the African American experience of freedom for well over a century since emancipation. The African American experience in the Chesapeake generally and in Somerset particularly was an experience that took place within the boundaries of a claustrophobic world of closed doors. In the Chesapeake as in the South generally, the region unified around the issue of race. Although we cannot comprehend slavery and its racial aftermath the way a survivor could, it is a possible for us to recognize their world and the duty that we have towards these people to explicate as best as possible various facets of their experience. Anti-Blackness still runs deep in America but in our modern age it does respond positively at times to humanist appeals for justice and human rights. We have to view the history of the Chesapeake region, however, through the framework of racialized thought.

Until recently, America was profoundly influenced by the south's racial orthodoxy. In the period between 1877 and 1932, Congress passed 15,232 laws that codified segregation and prohibited much federal intervention in southern matters. Often Whites defended White supremacy at all costs when legislators voted against their own economic interests on matters of interstate commerce and federal spending on internal improvements. In addition, the first few decades of the twentieth century saw more Congressional votes giving locals control of federal programs like those of Roosevelt's New Deal.[3]

Since the 1960s racial conditions have improved on the Eastern Shore. The Civil Rights movement witnessed its share of battles in Somerset, Dorchester, and other counties in the Chesapeake. Racial segregation in public places is no more. Today Blacks on the Eastern Shore are gaining elective office in the legislature, county and local governments. Recently Blacks in Princess Anne succeeded in electing a majority Black town council. Blacks serve in the local police forces. While Black middle class attainment in the region is now much better than a distant possibility, there remains a yawning gap between White and Black occupational incomes.

As this is being written a national uprising against police violence towards Blacks and racial discrimination generally is taking place. It remains to be seen whether it constitutes a turning point in the way we think about and act against systemic racism. Given the terrible burden of Chesapeake's history, it is a question that is yet to be answered. As social and environmental activist Naomi Klein has written: "There can be no reconciliation when the crime is still in progress."

Notes

1 Equal Justice Initiative, *Lynching in America: Confronting the Legacy of Racial Terror*, New York, 2015
2 Isabel Wilkerson, *Caste, The Origin of our Discontents*, New York, 2020. 93.
3 For a complete historical overview see Ira Katznelson and John S. Lapinski, *Southern Nation: Congress and White Supremacy After Reconstruction*, Princeton, 2018.

Index

Adams V. Califano (1974), 194
American Colonization Society, 18
Apprenticeship system of Blacks, 72
Armwood, George, lynching 116, 119-121
Armwood's Somerset lynchers, 129

Baltimore, Lord, 2
Baltimore Sun denounces lynchers, 126
Birney William, Colonel, 53
Blacks Churches and Education, 88
 Demonstrations in Cambridge, Md. 1963, 165
 desertion of Eastern Shore plantations, 54
 Hunting and Guns, 82
 Methodists, 88-90
 oystermen, 85-86
 Politics in Reconstruction, Maryland,79
 colored troops on Eastern Shore, 52, 53
Brown, H. Rap, 170, 177
Brown, John, Raid at Harper's Ferry, 27
Buffkins, Archie L., Chancellor of University of Maryland, Eastern Shore, 190-192
Byrd, H.C. "Curly", 165

Cambridge Non-Violent Action Committee, 169
Cambridge Riot and Burning in 1967, 177
Canneries, 146
Carmichael, Stokeley in Cabridge, 170
Carroll, Anna Ella 15
Claibourne,William, 2
Colored Regiment, 9th of Maryland, 51
Constitution of 1864 and Public Schools, 89
Crab Pickers Strike in Crisfield, 1938, 148
Crawford, Norman, President of Salisbury State College, 196, 198
Crisfield, John W., 15,46,48,50,54,60,61,84,86
Crisfield Packing Company 146
Crisfield, town, of 87

Delaware Conference of Methodists, 100
Dennis, George, 84
Dennis, James U.,33, 62-63
Driggus family, 5
Douglass, Frederick A. 27
Dunmore, Lord, 8

Eastern Shore Railroad, 84
Emancipation of Slaves in Maryland, 51
Euel Lee Case, public execution, 119

"Farming Without Negroes," 88
Free Blacks, 4, 13
"Free Negroism," 31-34
Freedmen and Civil Rights, 74
Freedmen's Bureau in Maryland, 73

Gregory, Dick, and Princess Anne demonstrations, 175
Groutt, John, Upward Bound, 192

Hall, Kirkland, 203, 206
Handy, Alexander, secessionist, 46
Hicks, Thomas H., Governor of Maryland, 48
Howard, General O.O. and Freedmen's Bureau, 73

Jones, Alexander, and Princess Anne Riot, 172, 174
Jones, Isaac, Attorney General of Maryland, 63
Johnson, Anthony, 4

Holiday, Billie and *Strange Fruit*, 11
Hurricane of 1933, 115
Hytche, William P. Dr., President of University of Maryland, Eastern Shore, 190-198

Ku Klux Klan, 175

Lane, Preston, Attorney General of Maryland, 130
Liberia, 18
Lynchings, public denunciation of, 124
In the South and nationally, 117

Maryland Constitutional Convention of 1864, 18

Meeropol, Abel, author of poem *Strange Fruit*, 137
Mencken, H.L., of *Baltimore Sun*, 118
Methodism and Slavery, 7
Metropolitan Methodist Church, 88
Mitchell, Broadus, 117
Mitchell, Clarence, *Baltimore Afro-American*, 123-124
Morrill Land Grant Act of 1890, 190
Mosley, Jimmie, murder of, 208-210

National Guard in Cambridge, 169
National States Rights Party, 176

Phillips, Albanus, 146
Phillips Cannery Strike of 1937, 147
Phoebus, James, 62
Phoebus, Harry T., Senator, Md. Legislature, 153-154
Plessy v Ferguson, 104
Princess Anne Academy, 99-104
Princess Anne, student uprising, 1963-1964, 171
Pro-Slavery Politics on Eastern Shore, 34

Race Issues on Eastern Shore, 104-108, 221
Revell, Randall, 3
Richardson, Gloria, 167, 179
Ritchie, Albert C., Governor of Maryland, 114, 125, 128, 131, 133,

Secessionists on Eastern Shore, 48
Slavery, 19-22
Slave Resistance and Flight, 27

Somerset Prisoner of War Camp, 1944, 149-151
Somerset White gentry, 14,15
Steamboats, 98
Stockbridge, Henry, Maryland Freedmen's Bureau, 73

Tawes, Millard, Governor of Maryland, 165. 166
Townsend, George Alfred, author of *The Entailed Hat*, 22
Turpin, Waters, author of *These Low Grounds*, 156
Tubman, Harriet, 29

Underground Railroad, 28

Webb Task Force Report, 195-196
Whittington, De Wayne, Dr., 211,212
Whittington, Stephenson, Rev,, 65
Williams, Matt, lynching of, 1931, 117
Williams, John Taylor, Dr. President of Maryland State College, 186-189
Wilson, John and Princess Anne Academy, 171-173
Wilstach, Paul, author of *Tidewater Maryland*, 99
Wright, Sarah, author of *This Child's Gonna Live*, 155-156

www.ingramcontent.com/pod-product-compliance
Lightning Source LLC
Chambersburg PA
CBHW051046160426
43193CB00010B/1085